THE LOGIC OF

Alice

THE LOGIC OF

Alice

CLEAR THINKING IN WONDERLAND

Bernard M. Patten

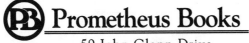 **Prometheus Books**
59 John Glenn Drive
Amherst, New York 14228-2119

Published 2009 by Prometheus Books

Inquiries should be addressed to
Prometheus Books
59 John Glenn Drive
Amherst, New York 14228–2119
VOICE: 716–691–0133, ext. 210
FAX: 716–691–0137
WWW.PROMETHEUSBOOKS.COM

13 12 11 10 09   5 4 3 2 1

Library of Congress Cataloging-in-Publication Data

Patten, Bernard M.
    The logic of Alice : clear thinking in Wonderland : chapter by chapter discussions of some principles and contemporary applications of logic and clear thinking demonstrated by Lewis Carroll in his book Alice's Adventures in Wonderland / by Bernard M. Patten.
        p. cm.
    Includes bibliographical references and index.
    ISBN 978 1–59102–675–4 (pbk. : acid-free paper)
    1. Carroll, Lewis, 1832–1898. Alice's Adventures in Wonderland. 2. Logic in literature. 3. Fantasy fiction, English—History and criticism. 4. Children's stories, English—History and criticism. I. Title.

PR4611.A73P38 2008
823'.8—dc22

2008030716

Printed in the United States on acid-free paper

To Her

Sine te nihil
Nulli secundus
Ego Ipse Habeo Facto

Contents

Introduction

Charles Lutwidge Dodgson, better known as Lewis Carroll, the author of the Alice books, was, according to legend, a shy, eccentric bachelor who taught mathematics at Christ Church, Oxford. He was said to have had a great fondness for playing with photography, mathematics, logic, and words, for writing nonsense, and for the company of little girls, particularly a little girl named Alice Pleasance Liddell (rhymes with fiddle), the daughter of Henry George Liddell, dean of Christ Church, Oxford.

Much of the Lewis Carroll legend, we now know by informed scholarship, is not true. But what is true is that Carroll, the cleric, a deacon of the Anglican Church, hence Reverend Dodgson, practiced what he preached: the Gospel of Amusement. And in that gospel, Dodgson's passions fused into two great masterpieces of English literature, the Alice books, immortal fantasies whose fame surpasses that of all of Carroll's colleagues at Oxford put together, then, now, and probably for all time.

What else?

If the Alice books had any "porpoise" besides entertaining little girls, it is to send you, dear reader, to the pleasures of logic and clear thinking and, as Carroll says in the introduction to *Learners* (1897), "to give a chance of adding a very large item to your stock of mental delights."

What?

Alice's Adventure in Wonderland is about logic and clear thinking? I thought it was a book for kids. You're kidding, right?

Nope.

Are you sure?

You bet!

Carroll's special genius lies in his ability to disguise charmingly and to charmingly disguise the gravity of his concerns by making the most playful quality of his work at the same time its didactic crux. Thus, in the case of Alice, we are dealing with a curious, complicated kind of knowledge disguised as nonsense—nonsense that combines playfulness with instructive exercises to explore the use and abuse of language, the rules of clear and crooked thinking, the nature of childhood, and the making and breaking of arguments.

Really?

Yes.

And, furthermore, it is my belief that a long-neglected and yet important aspect of Carroll's immortal narrative, the story of Alice's adventures in Wonderland, also raises venerable philosophical concerns about the relation of mind and body, free will, the uncertainty of knowledge, and the very nature of existence (particularly [our] human existence). The tale deals as well with the more contemporary para-noia(s) about the abuse of power, autocracy, and the futility of inces-sant moralizing.

Why think that?

Item 1. These concerns populated Lewis Carroll's private life as displayed in his diary and in his letters to friends, foes, and newspapers. We know this because of the amplitude and quality of the paper trail he left. Remember, this is a guy who indexed his own diary, who for thirty years kept a record of every letter that he sent or received. (His letter register alone runs over twenty-four volumes.)

Item 2. This is a man who, for over forty years, taught mathematics and logic at Oxford. That was his job. That was his mission. And as a matter of fact, age stopped neither his momentum nor his sense of "calling." Growing older made him more intense: Toward the end of his life, Lewis Carroll became obsessed with the idea of truth as a virtue in its own right. I suspect he even thought truth was THE VIRTUE. His lifelong gift of clear thinking and logic then crystallized into the con-trolling idea that his mission lay in teaching clear thinking to everyone, not just to Oxford students—not just to the girls' high school where he volunteered to teach, but to everyone, then, now, and in the future. *Symbolic Logic*, his last book, was, he told his sister, his "work for God."

O.K. That's what I believe the Alice book is about. Let's talk about what the Alice book is not about. Got your seat belts fastened? Are your tray tables stowed? Your seats in the upright position? Carry-on baggage properly tucked under the seat in front of you? It needs to be. Some of you are in for a rough landing when you find out what Alice is not about.

WHAT *ALICE'S ADVENTURES IN WONDERLAND* IS NOT ABOUT

The Alice narrative is not about the zoo of interpretations that critics have contrived for it and for Carroll. It is not about (and I am not making this up; these things have been seriously argued) the proposition that Alice equals phallus. Alice's tears do not represent amniotic fluid or the secret history of the Oxford Movement. "Pig and Pepper" is not about toilet training. Carroll is not a latent homosexual, an atheist, or even a faithful Anglican Christian. The narrative is not about a lot of things. In fact, the class of things that it is not about is much larger than what it is about—much, much larger. Just as (and here I am quoting the man himself) the classes of nonexistent things far exceed the classes of things that do exist.

Whoa!

Can that be right?

If the classes of nonexistent things don't exist, how can they be larger or more numerous than those classes of things that do exist? How can nothing exceed something? See the puzzle? See the puzzle that often gets us caught up in a logical argument, especially when the argument is literally about nothing? Get the fun? Get the paradox? Get the answer?

A mental class exists in our minds even if it contains nothing. The class is about nothing, but it is itself something and because it is something it is not nothing. This may sound like a paradox, but if you sit there and stare into space for a while you will see that it is not a paradox. It is a truth.

About nothing—we shall talk about (and think about) more later. Meanwhile, what about the book, what about the book that does exist?

THE OFFICIAL HISTORY OF THE ALICE STORY

The original Alice story was told ad hoc on a rowboat on the river Thames, commissioned by the three little Liddell sisters. At their request, Carroll's story contained the things of interest to them (and by extrapolation to other Victorian children and to all children everywhere):

Animals
Conversations
Adventure
Eating and Drinking
A Child as Hero and Main Character
Games—especially their favorite game

It is no accident that the featured game was the Liddells', and particularly Alice Pleasance Liddell's, favorite outdoor game. By extrapolation and by deep sympathetic identification, it was also Lewis Carroll's favorite game.

Test Question 1. Name that game.

Answer 1. Croquet, of course.

MORE HISTORY

The original Alice manuscript, handwritten and illustrated by Carroll for Alice (at her request), was given to her as a Christmas present in 1863. At the time, the title was "Alice's Adventures Underground." That was Alice's version. It was not the book to be published.

The tome that Carroll intended to publish, the immortal book that we and the rest of humanity were destined to get, had been already rewritten, expanded, edited, and professionally illustrated by Sir John Tenniel. Carroll changed the title from "Alice's Adventures Underground" to "Alice's Adventures in Wonderland." But before publication, Carroll dropped that title and inserted a new one—"Alice's Hour in Elfland."

Probably on the advice of Tenniel, Carroll switched the title back to *Alice's Adventures in Wonderland.*

Yes, thank God! One wonders how many people would be reading *Alice's Adventures in Wonderland* (AAW) under the Elfland rubric. Not many. Certainly not me.

Where would you rather be: Wonderland or Elfland? And what would you rather have: an adventure in Wonderland or an hour with the elves in Elfland?

To keep control of his masterpiece, Carroll self-published, bringing out AAW in 1865. The pictures were poorly printed, the ink running through some pages and marring the opposite sides. Many images were burred. Tenniel asked that all the copies of this press run be recalled and destroyed. Carroll obeyed and paid to have another, better printing done. Thus, like the Cheshire Cat, AAW appeared, disappeared, and then reappeared.

In her adult years, Alice Pleasance Liddell Hargreaves sold the handwritten manuscript probably for fifteen thousand British pounds. After a long and devious passage, which I don't care to recall, the original manuscript ended up in the British Museum. There it remains today.

DOCTOR PATTEN'S PURPOSES IN WRITING
A BOOK ABOUT LOGIC AND ALICE

Porpoise 1. Although *Alice's Adventures in Wonderland* (AAW) is based on a profound knowledge of the rules of clear thinking, informal and formal logic, symbolic logic and human nature, I could find no chapter-by-chapter skeleton key to this great work addressed to laymen and pseudoscholars (like myself) that specifically explores those areas of information and instruction. I have, therefore, tried to produce such a skeleton key. Along the way, I have used AAW for what every Irishman loves—good talking points to illustrate some interesting philosophic topics. My hope is that this book will show that *Alice's Adventures in Wonderland* is more complex and much more interesting than it may seem. It is a book for children all right, but it is also a book for scholars and logicians.

Porpoise 2. For better or worse, I believe that clear thinking will help you. I want to show how modern rational empiricism uses its toolkit for such thinking. The toolkit is particularly well suited for science but also applies to a wide variety of other everyday enterprises, as illustrated in Carroll's depiction of the activities and thoughts of Alice and her friends. What I want to emerge from our reflections is that, while there is no one tool that works best, experience by itself begets chaos in the absence of pattern recognition, memory, association, and reason. Reason by itself is pretty sterile without a database that is testable and has been tested. So the magic, as Lewis Carroll understood so well, is in the mix of reason and experience, with not too much of one or the other. That approach gives human beings the best chance of logical certainty. Logical certainty helps us understand reality, predicts what will happen, and, maybe, enables us to alter events to suit our needs. As far as we know, the first person to use this method to do some serious thinking about the nature of discovering truth was Thales of Miletus. His method (observation + thought) is still used today. Those of you who are interested in money will delight in learning how Thales predicted a bumper crop of olives, then cornered the olive press market, made a fortune, and retired early. Thales did this on a dare as a demonstration of the practical utility of clear thinking. Depending on how I feel, later on in this book I might tell you more about Thales's market corner, the first recorded monopoly. What worked for him might work for you.

O.K. Those are my "porpoises." But as I have not been entirely true to my "porpoises," I should like to tell you why:

Some passages of AAW are so charming (seductive, you might say) and amusing that I could not forbear to let them enliven and color my own pages. Furthermore, I had to select and again reselect and sometimes then deselect from each chapter only a few items among the many that reside there—twisted with curiously melding nuances of implication, deep to deep.

Such selection and reselection reflects my interests and none other. My choices are organized using Carroll's chapter titles as my chapter titles. This is much like the arrangement of that great classic by Martin Gardner, *The Annotated Alice*, a redaction without equal, but Gardner doesn't cover much of the principles of logic embedded in Carroll's entertaining story.

Wherever possible I have quoted Carroll directly. And then I have shamelessly and solipsistically discussed in extenso his heavily freighted text, its implications, and the logical and philosophical "messages" as they appeared to me.

Except for my wife, Ethel, who reminds me of this point daily, and sometimes several times daily, no one is more conscious than I of the ineptness and truncated nature of my numberless decisions on what to leave out and what to emphasize in this, my humble book-like-object.

The book you now have in your hand could have easily numbered over six hundred pages. Due to pruning and selection, it is less, much less. Nevertheless, enough is here, despite failures and omissions, to demonstrate the majestic logic of Alice and to prove, as well, its humor and its fun.

ABOUT THE FUN

Most of the fun relates to Carroll's aperçus and his jokes, which, we will soon see are inversions or distortions of the rules of logic, plays on words, or demonstrations of the ambiguities of language. We learn that words (for many reasons soon to be exposed) are more devious and slippery than we had ever imagined.

Here we shall find regions crowded with the problems and paraphernalia of metaphysics and philosophy, with theories of knowledge and ethics. Here are superbly imaginative treatments of logical principles, the meanings of words, the functions of names, the perplexities connected with time and space, the problems of personal identity, the status of substance in relation to its qualities, the mind-body problem, shambolic childrearing, anti-Tractarianism, and famously—the ubiquitous "null set," the set of nothing and nonexistent things. Here, thank goodness, always and forever, with Carroll reason operates in the service of imagination, not vice versa, and not without providing cool enjoyment, entertainment, and pleasure.

ABOUT THOSE ODD-BALL CHARACTERS

Part of the fun of AAW relates to those odd-ball characters. What about them? Who are they? Where did they come from? What do we make of them? What does Alice make of them?

I like to think that some of the characters that Alice meets are Oxford dons (thinly disguised and disguised thinly). They are probably men and women whom the real Alice Pleasance Liddell, Carroll's child friend and the person for whom the book was originally made, knew and knew well. The men certainly sound like Oxford dons with their fine mastery of Socratic logic, their crushing repartee, and the disconcerting and totally unselfconscious eccentricity of their conduct. Having spent over forty years in academic life, I can assure you, dear reader, that the scholastic environment breeds, nourishes, and in most cases overnourishes gigantic egos. Prick your average professor and he will deflate by 90 percent, as most of them are mostly hot air.

From long experience Lewis Carroll knew that fact. For over forty years, he was on the academic scene at Christ Church, Oxford, where he taught mathematics and logic. Thus, we shouldn't think it at all in any way remarkable that the adults in AAW (the Dons in disguise), despite the intellectual sophistication they represent, behave like children, indeed they often behave like naughty children.

Other characters exist for the "porpoise" of examining abuses of power, irrational thinking, and silly actions. Carroll is particularly concerned with silly actions and silly rules formulated by adults and those in control (of government and everything else who should know better).

Certain characters are there for contrast. In his article "Alice on the Stage" Lewis Carroll wrote:

> And the White Rabbit, what of *him*? Was *he* framed on the "Alice" lines, or meant as a contrast? As a contrast, distinctly. For *her* [Alice's] "youth," "audacity," "vigour," and "swift direction of purpose," read his (the White Rabbit's) "elderly," "timid," "feeble," and "nervously shilly-shallying," and you will get *something* of what I meant him to be. I *think* the White Rabbit should wear spectacles. I am sure his voice should quaver, and his knees quiver, and his whole air suggest a total inability to say "Bo" [*sic*] to a goose!" (Note: The italics are Carroll's. Why these five words are in italics, no one seems to know. Me neither.)

WHY IS THE WHITE RABBIT WHITE?

Who knows? But here's a hint: According to Bryan Talbot, Alice's father, the dean, grew up in a rectory at Boldon, about a mile from the city center. Sir Hedworth Williamson owned all the land between the bridge in the city center and Whitburn, and lived in Whitburn Hall, close to Carroll's cousins. Carroll visited the hall at least once for a croquet game. It was Williamson who introduced white rabbits to his estate— because they made an easier target to shoot at as his eyesight failed!♥

WHITE RABBIT AND ANTHROPOMORPHISM

The White Rabbit also introduces the literary element of anthropomorphism. The rabbit's human characteristics (vest, watch, verbally skittish nature) prepare the reader for the other anthropomorphized characters that appear later and indicate that the book is really about humans and not about animals.

Last but not least, a word about Alice. Don't confuse the real Alice with the character. They are two different things. (I almost wrote two different persons.)

Considerable evidence adduced by Karoline Leach (author of *In the Shadow of the Dreamchild*) and Colin Gordon (author of *Beyond the Looking-Glass*) shows that Lewis Carroll lost interest in the real Alice, even coming to express dislike for her in his diaries. No one seems to know what the real Alice felt for "Mr. Dodgson" as a child, although some have filled the gap in the spirit of sentimental Alice-olatry, because they confuse "Alice" with Alice and they want and hope that the real girl loved him.

LIKE MOST CLASSICS AAW
CAN BE REREAD WITH PROFIT

My prediction: The more you read AAW, the more you will like it. And the more you like it, the more you will read it. The more you read and like it, the more you will think about it; the more you will think about

♥ *Lewis Carroll Review* 36 (October 2007): 5

it, the more treasure you will find submerged in it. The more you find submerged in it, the more you will know that you will find on further reading. In fact, even laying aside the Freudian field days that we could have spent our time discussing—for instance, the deep dark significance of deep dark presumably round and moist rabbit holes and the tiny keys that open the slitlike locks of small doors that admit to beautiful fragrant gardens, and so forth—you will reach the conclusion, as I have, that AAW is a story so deep as to yield results in exegesis almost beyond belief. A really great piece of literature is like that—bottomless and topless.

AAW WAS WRITTEN AS ENTERTAINMENT FOR YOUNG VICTORIANS

Not unnaturally, I prefer to emphasize that Carroll sent Alice down the rabbit hole for the immediate pleasure of children, beginning with three small Victorians, rather than for the future benefit of a generation of Freudian or other commentators, myself included. A subsequent interest, namely, making money from this book, is clearly shown in Carroll's diaries. Then as now, entertainment and the money motive, for better or worse, for weal or woe, often together go.

A (DISMISSIVE) WORD ABOUT FREUD AND FREUDIANS

When Carroll gaily improvised the opening chapters of AAW, sitting in the boat with his friends, the soon-to-be Canon Duckworth and the three little Liddells, Carroll did not know, poor fellow, that falling down a rabbit hole would be called a symbol of coitus, or that a little door with a curtain in front of it might be construed as a female child with a skirt. If Canon Duckworth, the Oxford fellow, had been able to enlighten him, Carroll doubtless would have collapsed in horror into the bottom of the boat. There probably would have been a grand mal seizure, and we should have had no Alice and no *Alice's Adventures in Wonderland*.

Freudians take note: The myth of Lewis Carroll as a pederast, sexual deviant, or pervert is just that—a myth. Relevant and adequate evidence from the diaries, the letters, and from historical fact proves that Carroll had a normal adult social life (cf. Karoline Leach).

Still overwhelming evidence shows Dodgson, although he was a church official, marched to a different drummer: He defied a High Church dictum and went to the theater. He fell in love with what he found there. We know this because surviving diary commentaries point to theater as a vital and passionate part of his life. He also enjoyed other "tabu" things of the time including novel reading, alcohol consumption, and the company of children, both male and female. In fact, many of the activities that he considered fun were looked down on by the Anglican Church to which he belonged.

In the winter of his days, he enjoyed the company of adult women, with many of whom he had close and intense personal relationships, many of which liaisons were dogged by scandals, probably for good reason. The history of his relationships with actress Isa Bowman, Constance Burch, Ellen Terry, and others shows Carroll's instincts were toward loving the opposite sex, in the full meaning and sense of the term, and that love of the opposite sex was a powerful motivating force in his adult life. Of all of that, I have no doubt. It is possible to love both adult women and children. Why not? There are as many types of love as there are hearts. And he once remarked famously, "I love all children, except boys." He said this for effect. The facts show he liked boys as well as girls and entertained and photographed both in his apartments at Oxford.

Final note to Doctor Freud:

No Sirs! The Kingdom of Nowhere is much larger than pert little Freudian minds might think. And that kingdom will not die so long as the language of Shakespeare continues to be spoken. So mark that day,

July 4, 1862, annalist—mark that day, the day of the boat trip. Mark it not on the pad of the Freudian analyst, but as the ancient Romans would with a white stone.♦ July 4—a day in the history of literature as important as it is in the history of statecraft—for it was the day of the founding of the United States of America and the day of the beginning of the story of AAW.

ALICE'S ADVENTURES IN WONDERLAND STARTS WITH A POEM

All in a golden afternoon
   Full leisurely we glide;
For both our oars, with little skill,
   By little arms are plied,
While little hands make vain pretence
   Our wanderings to guide.

Call that day *dies mirabilis* (Latin: the miracle day) and note the three "littles" in the poem (lines 3, 4, and 5), representing the three little Liddells (in real life, Lorina Liddell, age thirteen, as prima, Alice Pleasance Liddell, age eleven, as secunda, and Edith Liddell, age eight, as tertia), playing their parts thusly:

Imperious Prima flashes forth
   Her edict "to begin it":
In gentler tones Secunda hopes
   "There will be nonsense in it!"
While Tertia interrupts the tale
   Not more than once a minute.

♦ The Romans marked a good day by putting a white stone in front of their homes. Lewis Carroll marked a good day by writing in his diary, "I mark this day with a white stone." Carroll started his diary in 1855 and continued it until his death in 1898.

READ *ALICE'S ADVENTURES IN WONDERLAND* YOURSELF

There exists, of course, no substitute for the rewarding experience of exploring AAW yourself. So please go ahead: Plunge headlong into its unexplored depths. Retrieve some treasure from the bathos of the abyss. Get a previously hidden measure of meaning for yourself. Read all of AAW. And then, when you have finished, reread it. And then, when you have finished, read certain books in addition to this one. Read books on clear thinking, logic, neuropsychology, and philosophy. And then, if you consider yourself a real scholar, tackle Carroll's major work, *The Game of Logic*, solving all the problems. If you can, if you can.

This *Game of Logic* text, although Lewis Carroll meant it for children, is certainly not suitable for a modern child. Carroll's approach assumed much more patience than the child of today expects to be asked for. "Mark the correct answer" is all he or she expects, where *The Game of Logic* begins with five pages of closely, if nicely, printed prose. The explanations of the Propositions that "Some new Cakes are nice" (the Categorical Particular Affirmative), "No new Cakes are nice" (the Categorical Universal Negative), and "All new Cakes are nice" (the Categorical Universal Affirmative) are best savored by an adult as the children are usually saying at this point, "Can't we cut all this out and get on with the game?"

On page ten, when Carroll asks whether the Proposition "The Cake you have given me is nice" was Particular or Universal (believe it or not it is Universal as all the cake is referenced, not a particular part of it) a modern eleven-year-old couldn't and wouldn't see it mattered anyway. Was this a game or wasn't it?

By page thirteen there is no more pretending that this is a game for children—well, perhaps Carroll could go on pretending, but the children cannot—Carroll starts talking in algebraic symbols. And not only are these totally devoid of interest for children, they are **TOO DIFFICULT** even for most modern adults. Thus Carroll's book *The Game of Logic* swims out of the ken of all but the chosen few. If you want your ego shrunk further, take a look at Lewis Carroll's *Pillow Talk*, which contains seventy-two problems that Carroll solved in his head and which he proposes as good questions for "ordinary mathematicians" to develop their powers of mental calculation! Whew! Those problems are not for the fainthearted.

Rather, I think—or rather, I hope—that the seventy-five pages of *The Game of Logic* and the seventy-two questions of *Pillow Talk* were meant for postgraduate university students or those who will have first read my other book *Truth, Knowledge, or Just Plain Bull: How to Tell the Difference*, a beginner's text on practical thinking and informal logic.♦ Having worked all the problems in the game of logic myself (and the only three of *Pillow Talk* that I could do), I have reluctantly reached the conclusion that those books are meant in part to show up the abysmal illogic that passes for thinking in normal life. My experience also exposes the unnerving fact, mentioned, but not highlighted by Carroll, that logicians do not themselves agree on what is logical. As we shall learn at the end of chapter 12, it turns out that most products of human mental activity in this wide world, logic included, exist by fiat. All of them depend on which system you choose to believe in, which system you wish to emulate or propagate. This is sad, I know, but it also happens to be the truth, the truth that professional logicians don't like. Sorry, pals, sometimes—nay—often, the truth hurts.

Carroll has no desire to enter into controversy with logicians who operate according to their own quite separate arrangements; that is their prerogative, no matter how little he (or we) approve, no matter what the consequences. "Let us not quarrel with them, dear Reader!" said Carroll. If Carroll wouldn't quarrel with them, if he won't enter the lists, should we?

There is room enough in this wide world for everyone. Let us quietly take our broader system. Here I quote Carroll directly: "If those idiots choose to shut their eyes ... we can but stand aside, and let them rush upon their fate!" (By the way, note the prejudicial and biased term that Carroll uses: idiots.)

After you have finished *The Game of Logic* or (which is more likely)

♦ *Truth, Knowledge, or Just Plain Bull: How to Tell the Difference* (Amherst, NY: Prometheus Books, 2004).

after *The Game of Logic* has finished with you, reread AAW again. Your pleasure (and genuine appreciation) will multiply a thousandfold.

No kidding!

While we are on the subject of reading, I can't resist giving you one more piece of advice that you may find strange and surprising:

Read AAW at your leisure while sober. Read it again at your leisure while drunk. Sober and drunk, read it so that both the left and the right hemispheres of your brain (each of which as we have learned have different interests and different cognitive styles) can fully participate in the fun. Along the way, try to capture some of the full wit and wisdom of Lewis Carroll as I try to capture some of those splendid essences in the chapters that follow.

WHAT'S WITH THIS TALKING WHITE RABBIT?

Herman Ebbinghaus and, after him, a century of brilliant neuropsychologists have taught us that the human brain is specialized to focus its attention on whatever departs from the routine. It's peekaboo all over again, but now in words. It is the unusual that catches our attention and keeps it. Fair seas and calm weather—blah! Who cares! It's the trouble that interests us. The sinking of *Titanic* has occupied more pages of text than all the discussions of easy cruising and safe crossing ever concocted.

Yes, a story usually begins (after an interval of warm-up and descriptive scene setting) with some breach in the expected state of things, the *peripeteia* (according to Aristotle), the complication and conflict that gets the story going: Something goes awry, must go awry; otherwise there isn't much to tell or talk about. And after the disturbance (to use my granddaughter Callie's term for peripeteia—two pages into the story and Callie wants to know what's the disturbance?), the tale considers how the characters come to terms with the problems and try to restore their homeostatic equilibrium and original status.

AS IN REAL LIFE,
AAW USUALLY OPERATES ON TWO LEVELS

Usually, the story operates dually (just the way we operate in real life). We are simultaneously or alternatively in the heads of the characters and outside the heads of the characters in the real world in which they are (supposedly) functioning.

Kant holds that there are two realities: The subjective reality in our mind and the objective reality in the external world. Both are important, he says, but the external world's reality is more important (according to him) because it exists independently of what we think of it. Admittedly, I am not in a position to pick an argument with Kant, but he is assuming that the external world exists without our thinking about it. The external world probably does exist without our thinking about it, but strictly speaking that is not proven. So what? Well, even assuming that is true, does that make the external world more important? Furthermore, Kant assumes that the internal mental world that we have cannot exist without the external world. The internal world probably needs the external physical world for existence, but strictly speaking that is not proven. Many people (neurologists like myself for instance) would argue the opposite. So what? Even assuming that is true, that the mental world does need the external world, does that in and of itself make our mental world less important? And if it is less important, to whom is it less important? And when and under what circumstances is it less important?

Lewis Carroll, from what I know of his character, would question Kant's assumptions, demanding relevant and adequate evidence in support of the Kantian assertions. As for me, I think the external world is more important sometimes and I think our internal (mental) world is more important other times. If I want an Irish whiskey and none is available, then the external world, the reality prevents me from having a drink. If I don't want an Irish whiskey and some is available, the internal reality prevents me from having a drink. Dig?

In the movie *Hustle & Flow* we get the same Kantian message that you have probably heard before: "There are two types of people. Those who talk the talk and those who walk the walk. Those who walk the walk can talk the talk, but usually they are too busy walking the walk to talk the talk." Dig?

For exercise you might try breaking down the *Hustle & Flow* overgeneralization the same way I broke down the Kantian overgeneralization: Question assumptions. Demand evidence. Give counterexamples. Destroy the overgeneralization by finding the exception.

The walk is real and important, but the talk is real and important. The talk is a work of the imagination that enables us to read the world, turning facts into literary symbols, tropes that point to the complex patterns embedded in the real and that help us deal with the real realistically. The magic is in the mix of reason and experience. That's the ticket.

By masterful manipulation we see in Alice both views of reality: a personal view of what's happening and what's happening itself. The magic is in the mix.

THE DISTURBANCE THAT STARTS AAW

And so we have Alice who leaves her routine (boring) riverside life to enter the extraordinary world of Wonderland. The appearance of the White Rabbit is the disturbance that changes Alice's normal existence into something special. It channels her attention onto the plane of the unusual, the weird, the bizarre.

Shall we go with her? Shall we go see how she handles all the sudden reversals and alterations of circumstances that are thrown her way?

What do you say?

Yes?

No?

Maybe?

Don't care?

What?

O.K.?

Really, O.K.?
Do you really want to continue?
Great!
Let's do it!
Let's go down the rabbit hole!

Ready?
Set?
Go!

1

Down the Rabbit Hole

The phrase "down the rabbit hole" has become the symbol for adventure into the unknown. That is why Neo in the movie *The Matrix* is told to follow the White Rabbit, which he soon sees is a tattoo on a woman's arm.

Neo's curiosity, like that of Alice, leads him to follow the signaling woman (her arm has a White Rabbit tattoo) to the disco. From thence he goes on to meet Trinity. Thus begins Neo's journey of enlightenment and adventure.

Which pill would you choose, the red or the blue? Is ignorance bliss? Or is the truth worth knowing, no matter what? The blue pill contains nothing and will not change Neo's situation. The red pill has neurotrophins and lysins that will liberate Neo from the pink goop in the pink pod. The red pill will take Neo out of the (pleasant) unreal world of the Matrix and release him into the (harsh) real world of the non-Matrix.

Those of you who saw the movie may recall that Neo took the red pill. His reason: he wanted to "see how far down the rabbit hole goes."

What? What are we talking about here? What have a rabbit hole and *The Matrix* to do with anything?

On the anagorical level—well, I'll leave that to you to work out. Mystical interpretations are not my forte. And Carroll repeatedly denied that any exist in AAW. He wrote to Edith Rix, "I have a deep dread of argument on religious topics. My vew [*sic*] of life is, that it's next to impossible to convince anybody of anything because one of the hardest things in the world is to convey a meaning accurately from one mind to another."

CURIOSITY DRIVES ALICE
AND THE ALICE NARRATIVE

O.K. Alice followed the rabbit down the hole for the same reason that Neo followed the rabbit tattoo, for the same reason that you are probably reading this book—(no special reason at all) just **CURIOSITY** and a certain bursting youthful spirit avid for mischief, adventure, and new knowledge. Recall how Alice plunged right in: "never once considering how in the world she was to get out again."

Humans are by nature a curious lot. Our expansive sense of time and space stimulates us to ponder our place in the scheme of things. That's what we do.

But what is curiosity? Who has it? And why? And what good is it?

The fact that you are reading this book is evidence that you are curious. In general, our species remains curious about anything and everything. Aristotle held that certain basic drives were part of human nature, among these he reckoned drives toward food, drink, sex, and knowledge. Yes, knowledge. "All men," said Aristotle, "desire to know." Aristotle was therefore asserting that all men are curious; they want to experience and understand. They want to know.

That's good. I like the idea. And wouldn't it be nice if it were true?

In a sense, curiosity is the seeking of the truth and knowledge. Truth seeking is good and normal. Most of us are curious. Most of us normally seek the truth. That's what Aristotle implied when he said in book I of *The Metaphysics*: "All men by nature seek to know."

But was he right?

ARISTOTLE WAS WRONG

Strictly speaking, Aristotle was wrong. He was wrong because the all-inclusive word "all" makes his claim overly general, simple and simplistic, and easily refuted by finding just one counterexample.

If just one man does not seek to have knowledge, then the statement "All men by nature seek to know" cannot be true. If the statement cannot be true, then it is false.

The reason that the statement would be false is that the word *all* means all. In the parlance of logic school and logicians, the statement "All men seek the truth" is a statement in the Universal Categorical Affirmative form (what the medieval scholastics called mood A) that entails several subaltern claims including multiple particular claims like "some men seek to know," "many men seek to know," "this man currently drinking his can of Bud seeks to know," and so on, as well as the bigger and more general claim "No man seeks not to know."

Here's the nub and the rub: If we find one man who doesn't seek to know, then Aristotle's statement is proven false.

Personally I know quite a few men who don't want to know (much about anything) and prove it every day. Whether or not *most* men seek to know is also debatable. If that were true, then how come most men don't know the names of the bushes, flowers, and trees in their front yard? How come most men don't have the foggiest idea of how their TV works or what mathematical algorithms let their computer fetch the e-mail?

Neo and Alice are different. They are not like all men. They are not like most men. They are like us, you and me. They are curious. They are curious in both senses of the word. They are curious (inquisitive and prying) to explore, learn, find out, and know. And they are curious (strange, unusual, and odd—set off from the group and the ordinary), arousing our attention and interest.

It so happens that "curious" is also the favorite word of Mr. Spock, an emotionless Vulcan, an almost purely intellectual personality on the television series *Star Trek*. Spock is never excited, amazed, or dreadfully afraid. He is detached, sometimes amused, and (like Alice) always curious (interested in finding out stuff) and also he is always curious (strange and unusual), especially with those long ears (or are those ears just pointy, simply appearing long?). But unlike Alice, characters like Spock and the others in *Star Trek* are as unbelievable as the rest of television.

What I did just then by using a word like "curious" in a single context while implying different meanings is an equivocation, something Carroll is fond of demonstrating and that is of course a classic error in thinking. For in a given context the meaning of a word must remain constant else we are likely to reach an erroneous conclusion. Here's the classic example of this error:

> All men are rational.
>> Women are not men.
>> Therefore, women are not rational.

Women not rational? That can't be true. So where is the error?

The error is in the equivocation or double meaning of the word "men." In the first sentence (the major premise) "men" means all humans. In the second sentence (the minor premise) "men" means the male sex. Hence, the meaning of the word "men" has changed. Therefore the conclusion cannot follow. This error was known to our ancient ancestors as the error of the fourth term because the argument contained four terms (men*1*, men*2*, women, rational) and not three. Cool!

SOMETIMES EQUIVOCATION IS ON PURPOSE

One famous example concerns the oracle at Delphi, the supreme court of the ancient world to which important political and military questions were often referred: "Croesus, king of Lydia and other countries, believing that these are the only real oracles in all the world, has sent you such presents as your discoveries deserved, and now inquires of you whether he shall go to war with the Persians, and if so, whether he shall strengthen himself by the forces of a confederate."

Both the oracle at Delphi and the oracle at the shrine of Amphiaraus agreed in the tenor of their reply, which was, in each case, a prophecy that if Croesus attacked the Persians, he would destroy a mighty empire. There was also a recommendation to look and see who were the most powerful of the Greeks and to make alliance with them.

At the receipt of these oracular replies, Croesus was overjoyed. Feeling sure now that he would destroy the empire of the Persians, he attacked, leading his forces into Cappadocia, fully expecting to defeat Cyrus and destroy the empire of the Persians. In so doing, the ancients believed he had interpreted the oracles in the wrong sense. An empire was in fact destroyed. However, it was not the Persian Empire. It was his, his own empire.♣

The Delphic oracle was great at equivocation. Take for instance the prediction given to expectant parents. The question was, "Will it be a boy or a girl?" The answer was, "Boy not girl."

This statement equivocates because "Boy, not girl" means a boy is predicted and "Boy not, girl" means a girl. Irate parents who complained that the prediction was wrong were told, next time around, to listen more carefully.

NEO AND ALICE ARE CURIOUS AND CURIOUS

When Neo and Alice don't know something, they want to know or at least they want to try to find out. In fact, Neo and Alice both made an existential choice to find the truth. That they were able to make that choice indicated that free will exists: that choice, their choice, was an exercise of their free will.

Neo chose the red pill, proving he could choose what to take. Neo chose not to choose the blue pill, thereby proving he was free not to choose the blue. If he was free to choose and if he was free not to choose, he was free because "free to choose or free not to choose" is logically equivalent to "free."♥ In the same way, if I tell you never speculate if you don't have money and never speculate if you do have money,

---

♣Herodotus, *The Persian Wars*, bk. I, chs. 53–54, 71.
♥Two statements are logically equivalent, if and only if they have the same truth value under all possible circumstances.

I am actually saying never speculate, as that is the logical equivalence of what I said. And, by the way, it's good advice.

CARROLL PROVED BY TRUTH TABLE
THAT FREE WILL EXISTS

f = false

t = true

Let F = free, C = choose, then $(F\&C)V(F\&\sim C) \equiv F$ where "$\equiv$" means "is logically equivalent" and "V" equals the logical operator "or." This "or" is the inclusive "or" meaning either one or the other or both.

	F	C	~C	(F&C)	(F&~C)	[(F&C)V(F&~C)]
1.	t	t	f	t	f	t
2.	t	f	t	f	t	t
3.	f	t	f	f	f	f
4.	f	f	t	f	f	f

Note that in every case the truth values of F are the same as for $(F\&C)V(F\&\sim C)$, which in symbols says free to choose or not choose, proving that the complex expression is logically equivalent to "free."

By the same token and the same reasoning and demonstration, it can be proved that Alice was free. She was free to choose to make a daisy-chain and free to choose not to make a daisy-chain:

> So she was considering, in her own mind (as well as she could, for the hot day made her feel very sleepy and stupid), whether the pleasure of making a daisy-chain would be worth the trouble of getting up and picking the daisies.

And Alice is free to choose not to follow or to choose to follow the rabbit down the rabbit hole.

FREE WILL EXISTS

Epicurus (341–279 BCE) thought that if every event is caused by other events, there can be no free will. That idea is obviously nutty. So he postulated that the atoms (following Democritus, he believed that these small units constituted the material universe) randomly "swerve" as they move through space. The random swerve, according to him, knocks out complete determinism and permits a degree of indeterminism that in turn permits free will.

The problem with indeterminism so conceived is that it seems to undermine the notion of causal responsibility. Think about this: "Alice chose to go down the rabbit hole" compared to "Alice happened to go down the rabbit hole." The second version clearly does not involve a causal claim about choice and seems to make going down the rabbit hole more a matter of happenstance, if not chance. Well, which is it? Did she choose or did she not choose to go down the hole? Read the AAW text for the answer or read on and I will give you the answer.

Modern physics backs up Epicurus with evidence that certain events—like radioactive decay—are purely random. The concept is important because if there were no free will, there would be no responsibility for action because nothing humans do would be up to them.

This faith in human freedom despite our deterministic sciences is the first postulate of moral experience and is a key point in AAW where Alice makes so many choices. Her first choice is not to make a daisy chain and her second choice is to follow the White Rabbit down the hole. Yes, that is the answer to the aforementioned question: Alice actually *chose* to go down the rabbit hole.

By the by, the demonstration of Alice's freedom also curries favor with children. If Alice is free, then the children reading AAW might also be free. If Alice has enough freedom to make choices, the kids who are reading the book, and the kids who are having the book read to them, might also have the freedom to make choices. If Alice can sit on the riverbank and "consider, in her own mind (as well as she could, for the hot day made her feel very sleepy and stupid), whether the pleasure of making a daisy-chain would be worth the trouble of getting up and picking the daisies," so can the kids reading the book consider what they might or might not want to do.

We adults, too.

This stuff might apply to us. We might be free. If we are free to choose or free not to choose, we *are* free.

EVERYDAY EVIDENCE PROVES WE ARE, AT LEAST IN PART, FREE

But of course we all know that we don't need atomic physics to prove that we have free will. We prove that we have free will every goddamn day by making the multiple choices that we make. Just the way Alice proves her freedom by making the multiple choices that she makes.

It's true, of course, that we are not entirely free to do entirely what we want, which is to say that our choices are limited—often severely limited—by constraining reality: I can't flap my arms and fly to the moon. To go to the moon, I need a rocket ship. There have been many days that I would have liked it to rain Irish whiskey. But alas, there was a disappointment ahead. To get a good stiff drink, I would have to go to a package store or a bar. The reality is that I would stand outside with my tongue out forever and it would never rain whiskey, neither Irish whiskey nor any other type of whiskey. Water is just about all that I can reasonably expect from rain, no more and no less.

Thus my will is not entirely free. My will is constrained by the external realities of this wide world. Immanuel Kant (1724–1804), the philosopher of the 1700s who ranks with Aristotle and Plato of ancient times (the guy we took down a peg above), said the things of the world are real, but it is the job of the human mind to form and shape those realities and to give meaning to the relationships between them. And then (and this is the kicker) in so doing to alter them as much as possible for human benefit.

So . . .

We have free will all right: Not a whole lot of it. Not that much. Just enough—just enough of it to make life interesting. And just enough for us to change the world or get it into trouble.

Once a choice is made, it becomes a thing of the past, a past that is closed and fixed, indestructible really. Yes, the past is beyond change and fixed and indestructible such that we can't change it. We can't change what's happened, as this quote from Omar the tent maker says:

LI (verse 51)
> The Moving Finger writes; and, having writ,
> Moves on: Nor all thy Piety nor Wit
> Shall lure it back to cancel half a Line,
> Nor all thy Tears wash out a Word of it.

Rubàiyàt of Omar Khayyàm (1048–1022)
—trans. Edward FitzGerald

THE PAST IS CLOSED AND FIXED; THE FUTURE IS OPEN AND FLUID

Once Neo takes the red pill, he can't go back into the Matrix. Once Neo takes the red pill, he must emerge from that pink goop in that pink pod, never to return again. Once Alice heads down that rabbit hole, she can't return again until her adventure is over.

So please remember this: The past is closed. You can't change it. But because of free will, the future is open. The future can unfold in multiple ways. Some of those ways depend on your choices—the good, the bad, and the ugly.

Wow!

Free will allows us to direct the future. In a sense, make the future. Think about that! Making the future is a big deal—a major responsibility. Isn't that fantastic? Are you up to it?

About free will and (no excuses) existential philosophy, more later. Meanwhile, let's consider that Alice's opting for adventure is human enough. It has advantages and disadvantages.

ADVANTAGES OF CURIOSITY
AND THE QUEST FOR ADVENTURE

The quest for adventure led humans out of Africa to inhabit (eventually) most regions of this planet. The quest for knowledge, especially new knowledge, led to our fictive downfall in the Adam and Eve story, wherein that primal couple suffered exile from the Garden of Eden for eating (I am not making this up, as fantastical as it may sound) some kind of fruit (an apple) from the tree of knowledge. Weird, right?

Lots of stories in the Bible are weird. But they have a message behind them. Take for instance the tale of Adam and Eve. They ate the fruit of the forbidden tree, learned in the process the difference between good and evil, and suffered a big penalty. Weird, right?

But that's the story. In a sense, the original sin is the sin of curiosity born of the desire to know things. Why did God not want humans to be fully informed about the nature of good and evil? Why God did not want humans to know things is an interesting question for which we have no intelligent answer. Yet in the very first interaction between mortals and their deity, Yahweh, female curiosity was branded as a great sin, a sin that led to the downfall of the whole human race, not just Adam and Eve, but all their children. Weird, right?

The Pandora curse (from the religion of ancient Greece and Rome) is similar: Zeus gave Pandora as a wife to the slow-witted Titan Epimetheus, and then entrusted him with a box containing the ills of the world. Disobeying her husband's orders to leave the box untouched, Pandora opened the lid and released a collection of evil spirits, which, from that day forward, wreaked havoc on the world. In punishment for her disobedience, Zeus sentenced Pandora and all her daughters to experience difficult childbirth. If this sounds familiar, it is because it is: the first book of the Bible, Genesis, says something similar.

Pandora disobeyed the order not to open the box because she was curious. Pandora disobeyed just as Eve disobeyed. Pandora's crime and punishment mirror Eve's with one exception: The only thing to remain in the box was hope—*Spes, solum donum deorum bonum*—Hope, the only good gift of the gods. Apparently, nothing good came from the Eve thing.

CURIOSITY LEADS TO GOOD AND BAD RESULTS

The quest for knowledge, our basic curiosity, not only led to our damnation, it also led to Neil A. Armstrong's moon walk, July 20, 1969. Where else will curiosity lead humanity? I wish I could live a thousand years to find out. But alas that doesn't appear possible under the present constraining biological realities.

Real investigation of the unknown powered by real curiosity—real research, not fake beliefs in UFOs, psychokinesia, extrasensory perception, crystal power, intelligent design, and so forth, has led to real science. Real science had led to real control over the real world and humanity's emergence from its self-imposed nonage. These benefits follow directly from humanity's alleged original sin, proving that sin can result in progress. And, by the by, sin can be fun. That's the reason many of us involve ourselves in it. That's the reason so many of us do it—actually sin.

CURIOSITY CAN BE DANGEROUS

But sometimes going out into the unknown is dangerous. Sometimes you make a killing. Sometimes you get killed. That's the rub. And that's part of the excitement. Magellan never made it around the world because he got into a rather negative situation at Mactan in the Philippines and the natives ate him for dinner. Eating a human isn't nice. Captain Cook ditto, only he was eaten by the Hawaiians.

What's another, nonexistential, meaning of the rabbit hole?

It's a literary device—a trick to get us into narrative time.

In plays, the house lights dim. In fairy tales, we get the immortal words "Once upon a time." In AAW, we head down a big dark hole and enter Wonderland.

Although Carroll skips "Once upon a time," he does, as in most forms of children's literature, begin the actual narrative by mentioning the name of the protagonist. In the case of AAW, he starts in the classic mode with the name destined to become immortal wherever English is spoken—Alice:

> *Alice was beginning to get very tired of sitting by her sister on the bank, and of having nothing to do: once or twice she had peeped into the book her sister was reading, but it had no pictures or conversations in it, "and what is the use of a book," thought Alice, "without pictures or conversations?"*

LITERARY POINTS

Is Carroll puffing his own book?

Times haven't changed. Authors puff their books. If they did not, who would? From long experience, I have found that if you don't blow your own horn, it is unlikely to get blown. Let's work through the syllogism:

Authors puff their books.

Lewis Carroll is an author.

Therefore, Lewis Carroll puffs his book.

Is that bad?

The appeal to children to dislike a book with no pictures or conversations and by inference to like a book, such as the one in hand, the AAW book itself, this masterpiece of children's literature that has (not coincidentally) lots of pictures and conversations, is a blatant advertisement, transparent in its self-serving self-interest. Ought it to be dismissed out of hand? Ah, but all serious literature has to explain itself, justify its existence so to speak. That's one of the principles of narrative and a very big topic that I don't care to discuss.

In a sense the puff is the means by which Carroll asserts the value of his technique in creating an interesting story for children. He is suggesting that a book for children is good if, and only if, it has conversations or pictures or both.

The assertion proves that Carroll knows how to tailor his story and the expectations of his audience to further his own ends. This strategy is human enough and usually starts at an early age beginning with those sly twists that shift the blame for the spilt milk to a younger sibling, then advancing to more-sophisticated deceptions, such as, "He hit first."

Keeping in mind that AAW was written and published specifically at the request of Carroll's little friend, Alice Pleasance Liddell, we can, by the evidence of the nature of the book, assume that Alice wanted the following:

1. The narrative to start with her name
2. Lots of nonsense
3. Pictures and conversations
4. Animals, especially cats, of which she had four
5. A child as the main character
6. A child who triumphs over adults
7. Fun
8. Eating and drinking
9. Games, particularly Alice's favorite outdoor game—did you remember?—the game of croquet

WHAT IS THE DEEP MEANING
(OR A POSSIBLE DEEP MEANING) ATTACHED TO
THE RABBIT HOLE AND WONDERLAND ITSELF?

In her real world, Alice finds herself in an environment that is not fully understood by her or by us. Alice can't appreciate why she is bored while her grown sister is engrossed in reading a book, especially when that book seems to have no pictures and no conversations. Later we will see her puzzled even more by other even weirder adults, by adult behavior, and by bizarre situations and conversations that come up in Wonderland.

Thus, Alice is a child a little lost in two worlds—the objectively real world and the subjectively real world of her dreaming mind, both of which are worlds that she does not fully understand. Her situation reflects in the microcosm what we (adults and children) experience, more or less, in our everyday lives. We have to deal with the objectively real world and we have to deal with the subjectively real world that exists inside our heads, neither of which we fully understand. That concept is one of Carroll's main points. But his point aside, let's look at Alice's thinking because in this opening statement Carroll is showing us the baseline standard of Alice's thinking from which we will measure her progress or lack of progress. At the same time, Carroll is showing us more points in logic and clear thinking than Liz Taylor and Zsa Zsa Gabor have husbands combined.

REFLECTING THE WAY CLEAR THINKING
WAS TAUGHT THEN AND IS TAUGHT NOW

The classic way to demonstrate clear thinking in Victorian times and the classic way to teach clear thinking at present is by the demonstration of fuzzy thinking. The teacher shows what is wrong and, by that demonstration, implies what might be right.

In that classic mode, in the very first paragraph of AAW (quoted above), Carroll demonstrates elements of clear thinking by illustrating Alice's defective version.

TYPES OF DEFECTIVE THINKING
ILLUSTRATED IN THE OPENING PARAGRAPH OF
ALICE'S ADVENTURES IN WONDERLAND

1. Begging the question
2. Unwarranted or unsupported assumption
3. Overgeneralization
4. Partial selection of evidence
5. Neglect of opposing or contradictory evidence
6. Argument contrary to fact
7. Simple and simplistic thinking
8. Vague definition or idiosyncratic definition
9. Weak sense thinking as opposed to strong sense thinking
10. Circular argument
11. Conclusion not justified because the premise is wrong or questionable
12. Imprecision due to fatigue and boredom

Whew!

That's a lot of freight for just one opening paragraph. But we can handle it. We can handle it the Cartesian way,♠ by breaking the problem down into small parts by reducing it to manageable size. This process is called unpacking, or reductionism.♦

♦ Cartesian way—René Descartes (1596–1650) arrived at the conclusion that the universe has a mathematically logical structure and that a single method of reasoning could apply to all natural sciences providing a unified body of knowledge. He believed he had discovered such a method by breaking a problem down into parts and solving the problem by solving the parts. Cf. *Discourse on Method* (1637).

♦ Reductionism—the practice of reducing a phenomenon to apparently more basic elements. It is supposed that reduction both explains and also simplifies. Reductionism is therefore often used in some quarters (Dover School System, Pennsylvania, for instance, in its assessment of Darwinian and creationism theories) as a term of abuse.

This opening paragraph is there because the eminently logical Carroll put it there. He put it there, I believe, for two reasons:

1. To illustrate Alice's defective thinking
2. To establish the set-point from which Alice's thinking improves as her character arc advances with the advancing story

To explore these two matters, let's follow the (very unsound) advice of the King of Hearts in chapter 12 of AAW: "'Begin at the beginning,' the King said, very gravely, 'and go on till you come to the end: then stop.'"♣

BEGGING THE QUESTION

When we assume the point in dispute and take for granted the truth of something that requires proof, we are begging the question. Alice assumes a book without pictures is bad. Thus Alice begs the question. Assumptions (including those begged) not supported by evidence are irrelevant. Therefore, a conclusion based on them is likely to be wrong. In this case, the fact is that Alice is wrong, books without pictures or conversations can be useful.

UNSUPPORTED ASSUMPTION(S) AND OVERGENERALIZATION

In her assumption, Alice overgeneralizes when she takes for granted that because she doesn't like books without pictures, other people would not like such books either.

♣ The King of Hearts is mistaken. The great stories start not at the beginning but in the middle (in *media res*) and a good many of them don't end at the end. Take, for example, Homer's *Iliad*: the story starts not with the start of the Trojan War but with the rage of Achilles. The story ends not with the sack of Troy but with the burial of Hector, breaker of horses.

By the way, egocentric views of the world are not confined or restricted to little girls, as we all know. An egocentric view (one might say cat-centric view) of the universe is characteristic of my cat, P. J. Patten, and of all five of my grandchildren. But why are such egocentric views wrong?

They are wrong because egocentric views of the world tend to distort our understanding of the real situation out there in the real world. To the extent that our egos interfere with correct perception of reality, we may be led away from the truth and toward error.

HOW TO PROVE A GENERALIZATION WRONG

To prove Alice's general statement about books wrong, we need find only one exception. This, in logic, is the principle of refutation by counterexample. We need find only one book that has no conversations or pictures but is still useful. If we can find such a book, Alice has overgeneralized.

Since there are literally hundreds of thousands of books without conversations and pictures, it would be highly unlikely that at least one of them wouldn't be useful to someone. Therefore, Alice is wrong. But, of course, the demonstration is even more closely at hand, supplied by Carroll himself: Alice's sister is deeply engrossed in the book. Therefore, the book is interesting to Alice's sister. As Alice's sister is interested in the book, the book is probably useful to her, else the sister wouldn't be reading the book so intently. Thus Carroll shows us a major defect in reasoning: Neglect of evidence. Alice neglects evidence right in front of her nose.

PARTIAL SELECTION OF EVIDENCE
AS AN ERROR IN THINKING

By singling out two of the many criteria that can be used to judge a book, Alice partially selects evidence (trivial evidence at that), constructs a straw man for defeat, and reaches a conclusion that is not justified by the data: She has not read her sister's book. Therefore, she is in no position to make an intelligent judgment about its usefulness or uselessness.

Here's a recent example of partial selection. Read it and see if you can pick up why it's a partial selection: "Man was not an accident and reflects an image and likeness unique in the created order. Those aspects of evolutionary theory compatible with this truth are a welcome addition to human knowledge. Aspects of these theories that undermine this truth, however, should be firmly rejected as an atheistic theology posing as science" (Sam Brownback, senator from Kansas, op-ed in the *New York Times*, May 31, 2007).

Sam's thinking involves partial selections of evidence. He agrees with evidence that supports his view, but disagrees with evidence that goes against his view. Therefore, he uses evidence not to find the truth of the matter, but to merely boost his argument. This attitude is unscientific and will not improve the good senator's understanding of the nature of life on this planet. It will only confirm him in his ignorance as he chooses to neglect evidence that he does not like and partially select the evidence that he does like. With senators like Sam no wonder the good old US of A is so fucked up.

One more example: If I tell you only about my assets, you will reach the erroneous conclusion that I am rich. If I tell you only about my debts, you will reach the erroneous conclusion that I am poor. What you need is a complete statement of assets and liabilities so that you can get the complete and correct picture of my personal financial situation from analysis of all the relevant information.

NEGLECT OF EVIDENCE IS WRONG

Alice is overlooking factual evidence: Her sister is interested in the book, even though the book the sister is reading doesn't appear to have any conversations or pictures in it.

CONCLUSIONS CONTRARY TO FACT
ARE ALWAYS WRONG

In fact, Alice's big sister is deeply engrossed in reading her book. Therefore the book is, as mentioned above, already of some use to someone—her sister. So Alice is actually denying the factual evidence at hand. Denying or ignoring available relevant evidence is an error in thinking. It has to be! Denying or ignoring contrary evidence goes against the principles of correct reasoning because it leads us away from truth and toward error. In "Pig and Pepper" (chapter 6) Alice seems to verge on ignoring evidence she has just seen with her own eyes by telling the Duchess:

> "I didn't know that Cheshire-Cats always grinned; in fact, I didn't know that cats could grin."
>> "They all can," said the Duchess; "and most of 'em do."
>> "I didn't know of any that do," Alice said very politely, feeling quite pleased to have got into a conversation.
>> "You don't know much," said the Duchess; "and that's a fact."

And the moral of that is: If you see a cat grinning, it is safe to conclude that at least one cat can and does grin. And that's a fact.

By the by, "Grin like a Cheshire cat" was a common phrase in Carroll's day. Its origin is not known. Charles Lamb answered the question "Why do cats grin in Cheshire?" with the quip: "Because it was once a country palatine and the cats cannot help laughing whenever they think of it, though I see no great joke in it."

Not knowing what the word "palatine" meant, I had no idea what this quip meant. According to the *Oxford English Dictionary*, *palatine*: of the character or befitting a palace, palatial. By this definition, Lamb must be saying that the cats enjoy contemplating the steep decline of Cheshire (Carroll's boyhood shire) from previous palatial to present poverty.

That of course explains the grin. But what about the vanishing? It must relate to the moon as it slowly turns into a fingernail crescent, resembling a grin, before finally disappearing. No wonder the Chershire Cat is a **luna**-tic!

Only kidding of course, and in the process of trying to show how easy it is to construct stupid arguments about AAW—arguments that are weak and probably wrong. Chersire Cat is not a lunatic. He (she? it?) is a master logician as we will soon see.

WRONG ARGUMENTS ARE ALWAYS
WEAK ARGUMENTS

Alice's conclusion is contrary to fact. All arguments that are contrary to fact are weak arguments because by definition a weak argument is an argument that is not likely to be true. Alice's argument appears to be an inductively weak argument because an inductive argument is weak, if and only if, it is not probable that it is true.

As her sister is reading and interested in the book under discussion, it is probable that it is not probable that the book is useless. The fact is that the book has interested Alice's sister whether the book has pictures and conversations or not. Therefore, Alice's generalization is wrong. Her inductive argument is weak as it is not probable that it is true.

DEFINITION OF STRONG AND WEAK INDUCTIVE ARGUMENTS

An inductive argument is strong, if and only if, it is probable that it is true. And conversely, an inductive argument is weak, if and only if, it is not probable that it is true. That is, an inductive argument is weak, if and only if, it is not strong. This is a recursive definition, I know, but reasonable, and more important, true. From which it follows, and you probably guessed, that an inductive argument is strong, if and only if, it is not weak.

AVOID BEING SIMPLE AND SIMPLISTIC

Alice is being simple and simplistic. A book is often a complex thing. Writers work long and hard trying to get their book right, fashioning out of chaos, in the torment of their souls, something intricate, intelligent, interesting, and occasionally beautiful. A critic of books should exercise the same due diligence in evaluating books as was exercised in creating them. Without a complex analysis, a reasonable conclusion can not be reached about a book's usefulness. Anything less is simple and simplistic. Anything less is less than the truth. Anything less than the truth, the whole truth, and nothing but the truth is unsatisfactory.

CAUTION ABOUT THE WHOLE TRUTH

When an entire set of particulars is known, it is possible to know the entire truth about that set. So if I tell you that all the members of my immediate family are doctors, that is the whole truth as all four members of my immediate family are doctors. However, when the entire set of particulars is not known, it is not possible to know the entire truth about that set. Hence, people who swear in a court of law that they will tell the whole truth might actually be swearing to an impossible standard. In fact, some philosophers might claim that, since nothing is the whole truth, every statement to that effect must be unsatisfactory if anything less than the whole truth is unsatisfactory. Don't get it? Think about it for a while. If need be, reread the above paragraph.

VAGUE DEFINITION IS OFTEN
A SOURCE OF CONFUSION

By way of introduction to this important aspect of clear thinking, in a certain sense, there is, in this opening paragraph of AAW, a semantic problem, a linguistic confusion in Alice's conclusion. The confusion arises because she is using the word "useful" idiosyncratically.

Vague definitions preclude correct conclusions. Until we know what Alice means by "a useful book," we can only guess at her definition. I sense that by "useful" she means entertaining and easy to look at and easy to read. Others, myself included, might consider such a book pretty much useless. Regardless, all vagueness must be clarified before the conclusion can be understood, much less justified.

WEAK SENSE THINKING OFTEN LEADS TO ERROR

Poor Alice! She is using "weak sense" thinking. Weak sense thinking is the type of thinking in which persons have already decided something using an emotional or other irrational basis (as with Senator Sam from Kansas) and then construct arguments to justify their position. This error puts the cart before the horse. We will see this mistake time and time again especially in the early parts of Alice's journey in Wonderland. Later, as Alice matures, her thinking will mature as well. But here in this opening paragraph, Alice's reasoning is weak, mighty weak because the reasons she uses are weak, mighty weak.

The reasons derived from weak sense reasoning are not reasons at all. They are rationalizations. They are excuses proffered as truths. Alice often uses weak sense arguments to justify her decision. We will see that shortly when she decides to try DRINK ME.

Advice: Always argue from the data (evidence) to a conclusion and not vice versa from the conclusion to the data. Never ever argue regardless or in disregard of the data. Conclusions should be as strong as the data indicate, no more and no less. Justification of the conclusion by data is what happens in strong sense thinking and is the basis on which the superlative achievements of Western science rest.

STRONG SENSE THINKING IS BEST

Strong sense thinking is just the opposite of weak sense thinking. Strong sense thinking examines evidence for relevance and adequacy and then reaches a conclusion about the reality situation, regardless of whether that assessment of reality matches our needs, desires, fantasies, or wishes. For this reason, strong sense thinking more often matches up with and corresponds to reality.

In strong sense thinking, we quest toward truth. In weak sense thinking, we quest after justification of a previously acquired position. As Alice travels through Wonderland, her use of strong sense thinking increases in frequency and intensity until it reaches a crescendo in the trial scene at the end. Conversely, as Alice travels through Wonderland, her use of weak sense thinking decreases in frequency and intensity until it reaches a nadir in the trial scene at the end.

It therefore follows that Alice should be using strong sense thinking to evaluate all evidence, claims, and beliefs, including her own biased opinions about what constitutes a useful book.

IS ALICE ENTITLED TO HER OPINION?

Understand that if Alice had said she doesn't like books that have no conversations and no pictures, then there could be no argument. We would have to accept that statement at face value as her preference, her personal taste in books. *De gustibus non disputandem*—about taste there is no dispute.

But when Alice gives reasons (no pictures or conversations equals useless) for her opinion, then those reasons are subject to inquiry and refutation. Her reasons are subject to refutation if they are not supported by relevant evidence that is adequate in amount, kind, and weight. And that is the main point in logic that Carroll makes in the opening scene of AAW: **A conclusion must be justified by evidence. If the evidence is relevant and adequate, then the conclusion is justified. If the evidence is not relevant and adequate, the conclusion is not justified.**

In symbolic logic this might look like:

Let R = relevant

Let A = adequate

Then a conclusion is justified, if and only if, R is true and A is true. If R is false or A is false or both R and A are false, R&A is false, and the conclusion is not justified.

Symbolic logic was important to Lewis Carroll, so important that he devoted the last years of his life to the subject, apologizing for declining multiple social invitations to make time for this pursuit. In fact, in 1891, he wrote to his cousin Fanny Wilcox, "If only I could manage, without annoyance to my family, to get imprisoned for 10 years, 'without hard labour,' and with the use of books and writing materials, it would be simply delightful."

His desire was to teach people how to think clearly and he saw *Symbolic Logic* as his most important work, intended to make accessible to others the tools for living well by thinking well. The first volume on the subject appeared in 1896; the final volumes in 1977. Especially important (according to me) are his visual methods of solving syllogisms using red and black circles to mark off and clearly define category classes. Using his methods, the exact logical structure of any syllogism can be quickly and clearly understood.

Symbolic logic, by the way, in the modern sense, is defined as an instrument of exact thought, both analytic and constructive (that is, creative); its mission is not only to validate scientific and logical methods, but also to clarify the ubiquitous semantic confusions and the mental muddles that beset the human mind. Semantics, as the Alice books demonstrate, is in dire need of responsible analysis and skillful handling. Carroll thought symbolic logic one of the most effective preparations for a frontal attack on the everyday muddles engendered by language. Symbolic logic blasts natural misconceptions, not by debunking and jokes, but by purposeful and lucid interpretation of ideas.

Carroll especially hated sloppy thinking, weak logic in argument, viewing analogy as identity, and reiteration as proof.♥ "Avoid having a FAT MIND," Carroll urged in a lecture in 1884: "I wonder if there is such a thing in nature as a FAT MIND? I really think I have met with one or two: minds which could not keep up with the slowest trot in conversation; could not jump over a logical fence, to save their lives; always got stuck fast in a narrow argument; and, in short, were fit for nothing but to waddle helplessly through the world."

WHEN IS ALICE ENTITLED TO HER OPINION?

Alice is entitled to her opinion when she is talking about her personal taste. We must assume that she is the final arbiter of what she likes and what she dislikes. But if she gives a reason for her likes or dislikes, then that reason or those reasons can be subjected to examination to see if they are relevant and adequate. For example, if Alice said that she likes vanilla ice cream because it is always colored green, then we must question her statement as vanilla ice cream is usually white or off yellow.

♥Reiteration is not proof. I wish my mother-in-law would stop using it as if it were.

Work out on this quotation from Tom DeLay, erstwhile representative from the 22nd Congressional district in Texas and, at this writing, under several indictments: "High school students should not apply to Texas A&M or to Baylor University because they don't teach creationism and they have sex in the dorms."

Compare your answer to mine, keeping in mind that there are many possible responses that would be correct and that mine is just one of those many: DeLay is not entitled to his opinion if the reasons he gives for that opinion are wrong. Columbia, Harvard, Yale, Princeton, Oxford, and Cambridge don't teach creationism, so by the DeLay criterion, are those schools not worth going to? (Notice my use of the counterexample to refute DeLay's poor thinking.)

Where does Mr. DeLay want them to have sex? If they can't have sex in the dorm, where can they have sex? Out on the lawn? In the library? In chem lab? How about on the football field?

The dark side doesn't like humor. My use of absurd humor counters the stupidity of DeLay's statement. In a certain sense, I have unfairly selected the place of having sex as the focus of my argument. I also have assumed (probably correctly based on my own college experiences) that the students will have sex. If the students will have sex, the only reasonable points for discussion would relate to the usual crucial questions about where, when, how, why, with whom, and in what positions.

Now criticize Mr. DeLay's response to the reporter who asked him about his opinion of A&M and Baylor: "The guy who recorded my speech was a former member of the ACLU (the American Civil Liberties Union)."

Watch out for politicians. Like DeLay, they often bypass intelligent discussion of issues by making irrelevant statements. Whether the guy who recorded DeLay's speech is a former member of the American Civil Liberties Union, a present member of the ACLU, a future member of the ACLU, or never was and never will be a member of the ACLU is irrelevant to whether or not the congressman's statement is the truth. Mr. DeLay is diverting attention from having to defend his reasons and his statement by resorting to a personal attack on the

reporter. DeLay's response is an ad hominem argument of no merit.♠
DeLay's answer is at the level of third grade or lower. From adults we
expect more rigor.

Here's the refutation of DeLay that I might use if I were in my
more analytic (what my wife calls the insufferable) mode:

Selection of a proper college is not simple. Rather it is a complex
multifaceted task that should include more reasons than the two mentioned by Mr. DeLay. To say Baylor University is bad simply for two
partially selected small pieces of evidence is to disregard a massive
amount of evidence that Baylor is good. Such partial selection of evidence is an error in thinking. Any conclusion based on partial selection
is, to extent of the selection, wrong.

Further, Mr. DeLay implies that because there is sex in the dorms
and no creationism, Baylor is bad for all students. Some students might
thrive in such an environment as in *The Harrad Experiment*, a book by
Robert H. Rimmer, where, in a nice cozy isolated New England college,
co-ed roommates are computer-assigned to each other on the basis of
sexual compatibility. Would that I could get dormed with someone like
Sheila, a sexy character from the novel.

So, DeLay's statement is overly general. He is assuming that every
student is the same and that therefore the prescription for their education should be the same. As each student is different in some way, this
generalization about supposed educational needs cannot be true for all.

Overgeneralization is an error. Any conclusion based on an overgeneralization is, to the extent of the overgeneralization, wrong.
Besides, if educational institutions were to be judged by the two criteria
mentioned, then Harvard, Columbia, Princeton, Yale, Stanford, Rice,
Oxford, Cambridge, the Sorbonne, and most of the other great univer-
sities of the world would be excluded.

Above and beyond those considerations, it's hard to consider the
teaching of creationism a standard for a positive evaluation of educational institutions. Quite the opposite is true: Creationism disregards

---

♠ Ad hominem argument—an error in argument wherein the person and not his or her argument
is attacked.

thousands of scientific studies and a fossil record that goes back millions of years. A discipline that disregards massive amounts of carefully gathered scientific evidence is not worthy of serious attention.

If I were really in my insufferable mode, I would ask DeLay to prove his conjecture. My usual question would be: How do you know for sure that they have sex in the dorms? Have you actually seen it? Who is they? What's the evidence? What kind of sex was it? Etc. Etc. Chances are that his evidence for sex in the dorm is nonexistent or hearsay. I would not attack the conjecture that Baylor doesn't teach creationism as that is probably true. Instead I would make a value argument that it is good that creationism is not taught because it is a silly, unscientific, stupid idea of no merit that has no place in any system of education, much less in the curriculum of a university. I would also ask Mr. DeLay to clarify what he means by creationism. Chances are his definition would be wrong at least in part. So I would attack that also. In the event that, to DeLay, creationism means God created everything at once, I would reply that there is no evidence for or against that idea, but scientifically it doesn't add up. If DeLay cites the usual dictionary definition of creationism, the theory that God immediately creates a new soul for every human being born (as opposed to traducianism, wherein the soul comes from the parents), I would lead him down the garden path about the justification for punishing a new born for Original Sin when his or her new soul had nothing to do with the actual sin of Adam and Eve itself.

The advantage to arguing with people like DeLay is that those guys quite literally don't know what they are talking about. Usually a little research will uncover facts that easily rebut their statements. Baylor is the oldest and largest Baptist university in Texas. It would be unlikely that its administration would officially condone sex in the dorm except between married couples. The board of directors has repeatedly affirmed that Baylor is a Christian institution and that being a Christian is expected of every faculty member.

Will DeLay's thinking improve? Who knows? The future is contingent, not yet determined. Hope springs eternal. But, you know, you can lead a politician to water, but you can't make him think.

OPINIONS CONTRARY TO FACT
ARE NEVER JUSTIFIED

Alice is not entitled to an opinion if that opinion is wrong. Nor is anyone entitled to an opinion if that opinion is wrong. If someone says that two plus two equals six, he or she must be wrong. Two plus two is four, now and forever. That's a fact. Don't forget it. Because it is a fact, there is no need to consider compromise on the issue. If someone says that two plus two is six and you know it is four, do not compromise at five.

Winston Smith, the main character in George Orwell's novel *1984*, wrote in his diary that all freedom follows from the freedom to state that two plus two makes four. At the end of the novel, government officials torture Winston in a vain attempt to get him to say two and two makes five. They finally succeed, of course, but only after they extinguish Winston's individual personality. Never ever, out of courtesy or for any other reason, grant something that you know is not true. There is too much bullshit out there already. Don't add to it. Never compromise about such truths. Let your response be in this wise:

He: "You say two plus two is four. I say six. Let's compromise at five."

You: "Two plus two is four. In your fantasy world and occasionally in the world of religion, politics, and philosophy, people might, for a short while, be able to pretend that it is something else, but to build a car, or a gun, or a computer that works, or a bridge, or an airplane, two plus two must equal four. If you think differently, you are wrong and likely to get into trouble sooner than you think."

ALL CIRCULAR ARGUMENTS LEAD NOWHERE

Remember, too, that all circular arguments are irrelevant. In standard form Alice's reasoning looks circular:

1. Any book without pictures or conversation is not useful. (major premise)

2. My sister's book has no pictures or conversations. (minor premise)

Therefore, my sister's book is not useful.

Pretty circular, right?

Not only circular, but also unsound. Let me explain:

Although the argument is formally valid, the conclusion is wrong because at least one premise is false. Any argument with a false premise, though valid, has to be unsound:

The major premise (premise one), for us to accept it, would need to be proved. In fact, premise one is false. There are books that have no pictures or conversations that are useful. All I need to prove that point is one counterexample.

The minor premise (premise two) might be true. We don't know for sure. Neither does Alice. Alice has not looked at her sister's book in its entirety. She has only "peeped into" the book "once or twice." If the book is the usual run-of-the-mill English book, Alice might have seen only four pages of what is probably a two-hundred-page volume. Therefore, she has sampled only 4/200 or 2 percent of the actual pages of the book. Therefore, there is a reasonable chance that one or more of those pages (that she has not seen) might have a conversation or a picture. Thus, even premise two might be false. We simply don't have enough evidence to say one way or the other. Never accept as true a statement that is not supported by relevant and adequate evidence. In this case, Alice may have reached a conclusion about her sister's book on the basis of inadequate, incomplete, and possibly misleading evidence.

Whether premise two is true or false hardly matters because premise one is false. Any conclusion based on a false premise has to be unsound, meaning not justified—just plain wrong.

DON'T DO SERIOUS THINKING
WHILE YOU ARE TIRED OR BORED

This opening paragraph of AAW also illustrates an important principle of neuroscience:

Thinking done while you are bored or tired is likely to be defective thinking. Though this basic principle of human thought probably goes back a long, long way, its quantification is attributed to a nineteenth-century scholar of human memory, Herman Ebbinghaus (1850–1909), who tested himself by memorizing nonsense syllables (WUX, CAZ, ZOL, BAZ) and trying to recall them twenty-four hours later. In testing his own memory for these nonsense syllables, Ebbinghaus quantified the rules of the neuropsychology of learning:

1. The more time you spend learning, the more you learn. (You get what you pay for.)
2. The more you review and the more you repeat, the more you learn. (Study helps.)
3. Maximum efficient learning occurs when the time spent in exposure to new material equals review and study time.
4. Learning occurs best when the tasks are varied because the human mind is easily bored.
5. Learning occurs best when tasks are distributed over time. A little study on multiple days is more effective than a lot of study on one day even if the total time spent is the same. (Don't cram.)
6. Associations facilitate learning, memory, and recall. The associations that work best are those that are vivid, visual, in motion, unusual, violent, over- or undersized, and in color. (Carroll knew this too and packed his book with such-like to make it memorable.)
7. When one is sick, tired, or bored, mental efficiency seriously degrades.

Of course, serious thinking goes far back to before the times of Ebbinghaus. Thales of Miletus (fl. 585 BCE), as mentioned, was probably the first to do really serious thinking. His method was observation and thought about the observation. According to Herodotus, when Thales was hired by the pharaoh of Egypt to measure the height of a pyramid, Thales waited until the shadow of a stick vertically placed in the ground was the same length as the stick and then he measured the length of the pyramid's shadow. Cool!

Talking about Thales reminds me to mention how he made all that money.

SIDEBAR ABOUT THALES AND MAKING MONEY

Thales charged parents a fee for him to educate boys. Some parents came to Thales seeking a practical justification of the fee. Specifically, they wanted Thales to prove that logical thinking could make money. So Thales told them that by that time the next year he would have accumulated enough money to live comfortably for the rest of his life. Then, according to Herodotus, Thales used his observations of the weather to predict an abundant olive harvest. Herodotus says Thales may have learned how to predict weather from the astronomy studies that he did during the four years he stayed in Babylon. Before harvest time, Thales cornered the market on olive presses by buying every press he could and contracting to rent the others. When the abundant olive crop came in, anyone that wanted to make olive oil had to pay Thales for the use of the presses. Thus Thales became rich. Remember observation alone is O.K. and thought alone is O.K., but the real power behind scientific rational empiricism is in the combination of observation and thought. The magic is in the mix. Thales made a correct observation about weather that enabled the correct prediction of an abundant olive harvest. But that was not enough. He also had to think of a way to capitalize on his observation and prediction. Most of us would have bought up olive trees. Instead, he bought presses. Thinking things through provided a surefire way of profiting from the situation. Brilliant!

BACK TO ALICE AND THE
PROCESS OF POLICY DECISION

Danger alert!

Alice is bored. Because she is bored, her boredom is likely to interfere with her judgment and color her observations. That mood likely colored Alice's judgment about her sister's book. Indeed, Alice was so bored that she was considering in her own mind (as well as she could, for the hot day made her feel very sleepy and stupid) whether the pleasure of making a daisy-chain would be worth the trouble of getting up and picking daisies.

Whether to make a daisy-chain is, of course, a policy decision, that is, a decision about what to do. Alice is correct in appraising the cost-benefit analysis before undertaking the task.

ARISTOTLE ON POLICY DECISIONS

Long ago Aristotle talked about the usual places in the human mind that should be considered when making a policy decision about what to do in the future. These usual places are called *topoi*. The topoi for policy decisions, for instance, are four in number: 1. Problem. 2. Cause of the problem. 3. Solution of the problem. and 4. Cost of the solution.

Here the problem is that Alice wants the pleasure of making a daisy-chain. The cause of the problem is that she doesn't have a daisy-chain and would need to get up to gather daisies. The solution is to gather daisies and make the chain. But the cost appears too much for her as she is too much into her lethargic mode. The daisy-chain policy issue is thus mooted by Alice falling asleep.

BECAUSE ALICE IS BORED SHE FALLS ASLEEP, WHICH IS REASONABLE AND EXPECTED, ESPECIALLY WHEN SOMEONE IS BORED

What's doing with your life? Are you bored?

A recent survey found that the average American adult spends about one-third of his waking hours bored. The cause appears to be an overall lack of interest in and discontent with life itself, a condition that results in the unpleasant mental and physical state of boredom. In general, there are two types of boredom: 1. Situational boredom, the most common type, which is due to (guess what?) a specific, identifiable situation such as visiting uninteresting people, watching too much television, or going to a bad movie. And 2. Chronic boredom in which everything is boring. Symptoms of chronic boredom include endless telephone conversations with friends or even strangers, fantasizing activities such as daydreaming, and generalized ennui. Because of the deactivation of the brainstem's reticular activating system, the most common symptom of chronic boredom is drowsiness.

WHY DOES THE HUMAN MIND LOSE EFFICIENCY WHEN IT IS BORED?

Numerous neuropsychological studies subsequent to those of Herman Ebbinghaus have confirmed that the human mind does not function at peak efficiency at all times. Efficiency significantly degrades when the brain is bored or tired. Therefore, it is unreasonable to expect great thinking from Alice while her brain is functioning below par. Why this happens is not known. What is known is that it does happen.

CONCLUSION

Instead of clear thinking, such a brain state usually leads to sleep, which, not incidentally, in Alice's case, it did. Sleep usually entails dreaming, which in this case, not incidentally, it did.

And so, Alice falls asleep.

To sleep. And in that sleep, perchance to dream. And in that dream, perchance to see a white rabbit.

Let's follow the trail blazed by that formally dressed, officious White Rabbit. Let's fall down the rabbit hole with him. Let's be like Neo. Let's be like Alice. Let's see how far down the rabbit hole goes.

* * *

"Well," thought Alice to herself. "After such a fall as this, I shall think nothing of tumbling downstairs! How brave they'll all think me at home! Why I wouldn't say anything about it, even if I fell off the top of the house*!"*

Ha! Ha! Ha!

She wouldn't say anything about it—that's very likely because if she fell off the top of her house, she would have likely broken her neck or, worse, be rendered dead. If Alice were dead she would, therefore, be unable to say anything about her fall or, for that matter, say anything about anything at all, for the dead do not speak. Not only do the dead not speak, they also (and this is a subaltern claim that follows from the fact that the dead cannot speak)—they cannot speak about anything.

Thus, we have a double entendre—something at the core of Carroll's humor. The double meaning is based on the double meaning of the word *say*, which means both talk about and talk. If you think about it "talk about" and "talk" are two different things. The difference turns on the broadly Kantian distinction between things as they exist in themselves and things as they are thought to exist or are experienced.

As mentioned, according to Kant, the real world counts more than the unreal world because the real world's existence is independent of what we think of it. The unreal world (that is, our thoughts about the real world) has a weaker ontological status than the real world (according to Kant) because the unreal world depends for its existence on things in the real world. Thus the ability to talk and the act of talking are more important than what is talked about. I won't go into this further. It might bore you. It certainly would bore me. And I am trying to write an interesting book, not an obscure philosophical treatise.

So, let's get back to the double entendre because in AAW there are lots of them.

Mae West was famous for her double entendres: "Come up and see me some time. I won't tell." Meaning in this context the word "see" has more implications than usually meet the eye. If "see" didn't mean more than see, then why would she have to assure the man she just invited to visit (who incidentally was Cary Grant playing a missionary) that she wouldn't tell?

"When I am good, I am very very good. When I am bad I am better." Meaning that what Mae is good at is what is considered by others bad behavior, especially for a woman.

"Pull the blinds. I'm going to make this place a heaven because I'm no angel." Meaning—well, you get it.

So Carroll is making fun with the double meanings of the word "say." But that isn't his main point in this section about the fall. Carroll's main point during Alice's fall is a denial of the real. Teachers of logic like Carroll are keen about the importance of dealing with reality realistically. Hence, denial of the real is an error in clear thinking, an error that may have dire consequences.

DENIAL OF THE REAL IS DANGEROUS

This kind of denial is a mental mechanism, well known to psychiatrists, whereby the danger of a situation is concealed from conscious awareness. Alice is not recognizing her danger. She is in fact denying its existence. Alice does that often. And when she is not denying danger's existence, Alice is minimizing it.

Alice, alas, alack, is off the track. Her thinking is focused on the wrong issues. During her long fall, she should be worried about if, when, how, and how hard she will land and how much it will hurt. Instead, she has focused her thoughts on the irrelevant issues of how brave people will think she is at home after she falls off the roof and says nothing about it.

EXTERNAL REALITY IS NOT CHANGED
BY WHAT PEOPLE THINK

Furthermore, Alice's focus is off because she is concerned about what other people think. What others think is often irrelevant to the consideration of the reality of a situation. There was a time in which most people thought the world was flat. That was not true. What most people believed did not correspond to the actual material situation. The implications are nowhere as obvious as in the discovery of Copernicus that the sun does not revolve around the earth, as it appears to do. The earth goes around the sun, contrary to appearance. Human vanity once even placed our little blue planet (as seen from space we're blue) at the center of the universe. That also is baloney. And so on: What others think about a situation is often irrelevant. It is always irrelevant when what others think does not jibe with the facts.

REALITY IS OUT THERE:
DEAL WITH IT REALISTICALLY

South of my home there is a rather large body of water. It is called the Gulf of Mexico, but in the past it was called the Gulf of Florida, and in a bygone era it was called the Gulf of Texas. Its existence does not depend on its name. It was there before humans looked upon it and named it. It will be there when humans go on to pollute some other planet. If the president or the US Congress or the Supreme Court declared that that body of water doesn't exist, it would still be there lapping the shore with its usual petite waves. The fish would continue to frolic and the pelicans would continue to eat those fish.

If I get in my Lincoln automobile and head south, depending on traffic and how fast I travel, I will reach this body of water. Because of the reality of the situation, my further progress south in the Lincoln will be impossible as the Lincoln does not float. To go farther south, I must swim or boat or submarine or use some other means of transport that effectively deals with the reality of the gulf. See what I mean? Either you deal with reality or you don't. If you don't deal with reality realistically, it might deal with you. Sometimes it might deal with you rather harshly.

MAKING A JOKE OF DANGER
IS A MENTAL MECHANISM THAT REDUCES ANXIETY
BUT MAY ALSO DECREASE ABILITY
TO DEAL EFFECTIVELY WITH REALITY

In a sense, by this sort of irrelevant thinking, Alice is falling (pun intended) into the all too human trap of minimizing the danger of death by joking about it. This, the first death joke in AAW, is evidence of a type of dark humor that appears throughout. Many more death jokes follow. Jokes about death are not an altogether bad thing. Diversionary humor helps get us through. It is bad when it prevents us from doing something constructive about improving the dangerous situation that we have entered. Meanwhile, we all must function under an ineluctable and probably inexplicable sentence of death. So why not learn to live with it? My father started each morning by toasting with his orange juice, "Another day and another step closer to the grave." Besides being a demonstration of the usual Irish fatalism, it is a warning to make the best use of time. It is an attempt to face the reality and deal with it, rather than deny the reality (of death) and not deal with it.

Herodotus tells of the ancient Egyptians who in social gatherings among the rich, when the banquet was ending, had a servant carry around to the guests a coffin, in which there was a wooden image of a corpse, carved and painted to resemble nature as closely as possible, about a cubit or two cubits in length. As he shows it to each guest in turn, the servant says, "Gaze here, and drink and be merry; for when you die, such will be."◆

REMINDERS OF DEATH REMIND US OF WHAT WE WOULD RATHER FORGET

Death, suffering, and meaninglessness are obvious examples of numerous phenomena that we would prefer to deny. Most people have difficulty accepting these aspects of reality. They prefer to comfort themselves by not thinking about them, just like Alice. This mental mechanism of denial is the emotional basis for people accepting comforting ideas without much evidence. Ancient scholars considered denial an error in thinking.

Take a look at some examples taken from the *American Scholar.*

A poll of Americans showed that:

82% believe in the reality of heaven.
63% believe they are headed to heaven.
51% believe in ghosts.
72% believe animals and plants did not evolve.
77% believe Jesus was born to a virgin.
80% believe Jesus rose from the dead.♣

The promise of transcendental purpose and cosmic redress of perceived inequities has immense appeal to the downtrodden. Wouldn't it be nice if some of the things in the above list were true? The fact that

---

◆ *Persian Wars*, bk. 2, ch. 78.
♣ *American Scholar* 73, no. 2 (Spring 2004).

some of these ideas are not true has caused lots of trouble. In an interview in the *New York Times Magazine*, psychiatrist Peter Watson, author of the book *Ideas: A History of Thought and Invention, from Fire to Freud*, was asked, "What do you think is the single worst idea in history?" Doctor Watson replied, "Without question, ethical monotheism. The idea of one true god. The idea that our life and ethical conduct on earth determines how we will go in the next world. This has been responsible for most of the wars and bigotry in history."♥

NOT ONLY ALICE, BUT POLITICIANS ARE NOTORIOUS FOR USING HUMOR TO DIVERT SERIOUS THINKING

Q: "Mr. Perot, it seems to me that if you were elected president, the Congress with which you would have to work would not be very cooperative."

A: "Well, if I were elected, about half of the members of Congress would drop dead of heart attacks. Half of my problem would be solved."

H. Ross Perot doesn't address the reporter's question. Instead, by using humor, he diverts consideration from a real issue. Such diversions are called red herrings after the famous trick used in fox hunting. The partially baked red-brown herring was rubbed over the fox's tail so the dogs would have a good scent to follow. People who disliked fox hunting could divert those dogs by using their own red herring, placing it under bridges or other out-of-the-way places where the fox is not.

In 1984, during the presidential campaign, President Reagan's age was an issue of concern to some people. I remember the TV debate where the issue was raised (again) as the president was running against Walter Mondale, a much younger man.

♥*New York Times Magazine*, Sunday, December 11, 2005, p. 31.

Reporter: "Mr. President, might you be too old to handle a nuclear war?"

Reagan: "Not at all. And I am not going to exploit my opponent's youth and inexperience."

Reagan did not address the issue (except with a general denial unsupported by evidence), but diverted attention from the issue with humor. The president cleverly pointed out that using age as a sole criterion to appraise the president's ability in handing nuclear war could work both ways. Reagan flipped the argument, a classical rhetorical tool of persuasion called turning the tables.

Sometimes politicians use irrelevant evidence that is not humorous, just stupid—as we learned when we examined Tom DeLay's answer to the reporter who asked if he (DeLay) did actually make that statement about Texas A&M and Baylor being unsuitable for students. DeLay's response was (as you may recall): "The person who recorded my speech is a former member of the ACLU [American Civil Liberties Union]." Whether the speech is recorded by a former member of the ACLU, a present member, or a future member, does not relate directly to the issue, which DeLay evidently doesn't wish to discuss. Like Alice, DeLay is trying to focus attention away from the real issue.

THE EXAMPLE OF ALICE'S DENIAL OF DANGER AND IN GENERAL THE DENIAL OF THE REAL DEMONSTRATES A COMMON HUMAN FAILING: DIVERTING ATTENTION FROM THE REAL PROBLEM AND FOCUSING ATTENTION ON WHAT IS NOT IMPORTANT

Existentialists assert that this feeling of the denial of the real is pervasive because most people (like Alice during her fall) do not want to know the hard truths of existence. People, instead, prefer to comfort themselves with a vast array of lies about life. These lies range in significance from major metaphysical fibs to the tiny tales we tell ourselves about ourselves. Tales we want to hear. Most people, for example, would rather flee the facts and remain in a "dream world" of their own or someone else's design than face up to the fact of death.

Come to think on it, to think about death too much, would be too much to think about. Even for us realists, we who are reading this book. So instead of having a roundtable discussion of this important topic, let's move on to thinking about something more pleasant—some literary points.

LITERARY POINTS

Alice's fall is one of the famous plunges in literary history. Indeed, the morphology of human history (when you think about it) seems excessively concerned with falls: There's Lucifer's fall and Adam's fall, the fall of Rome, a Wall Street crash, thimblerigged no doubt, but still a fall. There's Humpty Dumpty's fabulous fall and the famous fall of Newton's apple, Napoleon's fall at Waterloo, Hitler's downfall, and every man's, frequently daily, falls from grace.

And all these various fallings should remind Alice and us of our final fall, the finished nadir of our frequent falls, a nadir fixed fast by (what else?) death—another fall and the last.

Which is to say: Life can be dangerous. So many of our plays, movies, and books make this point that it must touch humans at their deep heart's core. One of the lessons about this unexpected deep dark hole through which Alice falls is that sometimes the unexpected and unexpectable just happen. We must deal with these all too common problems as best we can. How not to deal with them is demonstrated by Alice's fuzzy thinking about her fall as she falls.

As we have seen, Carroll shows clear thinking by illustrating Alice's defective thinking. What's the defective thinking here? Let's consider some points and then discuss them one by one:

1. Continuum arguments are not reasonable.
2. False analogy leads to false conclusions.
3. Fantasy thinking is wrong.
4. The absence of evidence hardly ever justifies any conclusion except that there is not enough evidence to reach a conclusion.
5. Diversionary humor is irrelevant to real issues.

CONTINUUM ARGUMENTS

The future is contingent. The reality is that the future can't be predicted. Not entirely. To assume that the future can be predicted is a false assumption that I call the error of future fact. The error of future fact treats a prediction about the future as if it were sure to happen. This way of thinking is wrong and was known to be wrong over two thousand years ago:

Defeat is impossible.
Defeat is unthinkable.
We have always been the favorites of fate.
Fortune has cupped us in her golden palms.
It has only been a matter of choosing our desire.
Which fruit to pick from the nodding tree.

The playwright is Aeschylus. The year is 479 BCE. The speakers are Persian. The place is Susa, capital of Persia. The enemy is Greece. The play is *The Persians*, the earliest surviving play in Western literature. The message is clear: The future is not secure. People who think it is had better watch out. Hubris leads to nemesis. The message was a warning to Greek audiences who knew that the Persians subsequently lost that war. History, that tired old jade, fooled the Persians. Despite overwhelming power, wealth, numbers of soldiers, weapons, and so on, the Persians lost the war. The united Greeks, by clear and careful planning, clear thinking about winds and tides, and a major understanding of the psychology of the Persians, outwitted their enemy and won. See Herodotus for the details.

MOST ASSUMPTIONS ABOUT THE FUTURE ARE IFFY

In the case of Alice, she is assuming that she will land alive and unhurt. She is assuming that she will live on to eventually fall off a roof and say nothing about it. As the future is not yet here and is undetermined, Alice's assumptions are not justified.

So far Alice's free fall has not resulted in any injury.

So what?

Can we really reach any intelligent conclusions from that fact?

No way, José.

Because Alice is O.K. so far doesn't guarantee that the situation will continue that way. In fact, everyone or almost everyone who is falling from a great height is relatively O.K. until he or she hits ground. Because something in the past or the present has continued to be as it is does not mean that it will continue that way into the future. If a gambler has a lucky streak, it does not mean that he will continue to win. By the same token, if he has had an unlucky streak, it does not mean that he will continue to lose. Nor does either circumstance mean his luck will change. The gambling statements:

"Boy, am I hot tonight. I am going to make a killing."
"Boy, my luck has been lousy tonight. It has got to change."
"Boy, am I hot tonight. I am going to drop out before I start losing."
"Boy, my luck has been lousy tonight. I had better drop out because it won't change."

These are four fallacious statements because they are based on wishful thinking and not on the grim reality of what happens when one gambles.

More examples, some from prime time:

That the space shuttle *Columbia* had survived six times with significant damage to the leading carbon-carbon alloy in the left wing did not mean that on time number seven the *Columbia* would return safely to Earth. (In fact, that time it blew up. All aboard died.)

If someone is shooting at you and has missed five times in a row, it does not mean you are out of danger. It doesn't mean that you should welcome shot number six. Shot six might connect and might be the killer.

That Alice in free fall has suffered no damage doesn't mean she won't get hurt when she hits ground. Her safe landing certainly doesn't mean (as she seems to assume) that she is immune from the future consequences of all falls. The past, present, and future are often not continuous. To claim that they always are continuous is to make the error of the continuum argument.

FALSE ANALOGY LEADS TO FALSE CONCLUSIONS

Another way of looking at this situation is through the magnifying glass of false analogy:

The false analogy here is that since one fall has not (so far) seemed to hurt her, all subsequent falls will not hurt her either, not even a tumble down stairs, not even a fall off the roof of the house. Such arguments base themselves in the idea that, because things continue, the past is analogous to the future.

Thus we have a false analogy based on a (false) continuum argument. There is no rule that two false arguments can't coexist at the same time and in the same place. Bad arguments can wear several hats. They often do.

All continuum arguments tend to be false analogies based on the false idea that the present and the past and the future are identical. Unless supported by relevant and adequate evidence, such arguments should be dismissed because the present and past, though similar in many respects, can become radically different in many other respects.

In fact, the future probably will be similar to the past and also different. You can bet on that:

> Yesterday is swept away the windy shore.
>   No tomorrow by the sea
>   is like the day before.
>
> —D. Morgan

Heraclitus, who flourished about 500 BCE, was chiefly famous in antiquity for observing that everything is in a state of flux, a doctrine succinctly expressed by his statement "No one enters the same river twice."

Conclusion: Past, present, and future, though they share some elements, are not the same. To consider them the same is to neglect a rather large body of evidence, and therefore to err. Any and all mathematical programs based on past performance of the stock market, for instance, are doomed to failure simply because of the fact that the future is contingent. If you are invested in a hedge fund that tells you differently, watch out.

Work on this analogy. Explain why it is false:

> Fish oil is made from fish.
> Corn oil is made from corn.
> Peanut oil is made from peanuts.
> Coconut oil is made from coconuts.
> Therefore, baby oil is made from babies.

FANTASY THINKING AND WISHFUL THINKING ARE WRONG

Alice's fantasy thinking is wrong. Instead of concentrating on the point at issue (the key question), which is whether she will get hurt when she lands or not get hurt, Alice is concerned about what she will tell others after similar falls in the future that might or might not happen. She is not concerned about being hurt but about what others will think about her when she doesn't say much about her falls: "How brave they will think me at home."

What Alice says about the falls or what others say about them is not particularly relevant to the main problem of falls in general and this fall in particular, which is how much damage will occur on impact. Her fantasy that people will think well of her might give her a false consolation for the moment. In the long run such thinking will impair her ability to perceive reality and deal with that reality realistically.

ANY CONCLUSION BASED ON ABSENT EVIDENCE IS LIKELY WRONG

Yes, Alice is in free fall. She should be worried about the consequences of hitting the ground. She should not be thinking about how nice future falls will be if they turn out the way this one seems to be turning out. Because the future is not determined yet, neither Alice nor anyone else has a right to predict it assuming accuracy. Hence, Alice is committing the error of future fact. The future doesn't exist. Therefore, the evidence on which Alice has based her conclusion is not any evidence at all because the future outcome on which Alice bases her conclusion doesn't exist. It might exist at some time in the future, but it doesn't exist in the present. Conclusions based on nonexistent evidence are inadequately supported, often mere fantasies and often wrong. The reason for this is that contingent events in the future can go either way. Remember that fact. Always try to flip the argument to see what the opposite side might be. For example, if you are thinking of buying a hundred shares of Microsoft, consider what might happen if the stock price crumbles as well as what might happen if it soars. As the future is contingent, the price could go either way, though with Microsoft, soar is more probable than crumble.

If the stock market has gone down last year, it does not follow that it will go up this year. If the stock market has been down two years in a row, it does not follow that it will go up this year. Whether the stock market goes up or down depends not on what happened last year or the year before but on a complex mix of Federal Reserve action, tax policy, energy cost, confidence in the integrity of the American corporation, random walk, and so forth.♦ The stock market will not go up because we want it to go up. The stock market doesn't even know we exist, much less that we own stock.

DIVERSIONARY HUMOR IS IRRELEVANT TO THE REAL ISSUE

Though funny, diversionary humor or other attempts to redirect attention from real issues by the ostrich approach are irrelevant because they lead away from the truth to a false idea of reality. Here Alice is focusing away from the real concern about her continued fall, which is or which should be: "Will I get hurt."

* * *

She took down a jar from one of the shelves as she passed: it was labeled "ORANGE MARMALADE" but to her great disappointment it was empty . . .

Holy cow! This is one of the most important discoveries a human can make: Things may not be what they are said to be. Language can deceive us. Statements can be false. Even statements made by great authorities like the label makers of a marmalade jar. And, yes, Virginia, sometimes even the statements made by great authorities like the president of the United States can be false or misleading or both.

What a lesson!

This jar contains nothing, rendering the label deceptive. As there is

---

♦For those not in the know, a random walk is a hypothesis about the stock market. Is the market efficient or inefficient? All this is explained in Burton Malkiel, *A Random Walk down Wall Street*, rev. ed. (New York: Norton, 2003).

no marmalade, much less orange marmalade, an accurate label would more truthfully read "empty."

One way to determine if a statement (in this particular case, the label) is correct is verification. In the case of the marmalade, verification would entail opening the jar and inspecting the contents directly. Physical verification of the truth or falsity of statements is just about the most important thing we can do in this wide world to get to the truth. It is the heart of the matter. Direct examination of evidence can convey a high truth straight to the soul. This kind of empirical testing of reality by experiment is fundamental to our scientific understanding of the world.

Once empirical truths are known, it is the job of logic to determine the truth-preserving properties of interactions of those truths. Thus science is concerned with truth discovery and logic is concerned with the evidentiary links in truth preservation.

The purpose, I believe, of Carroll's lifetime of teaching logic is: Analysis of the truth-preserving qualities of clear thinking. Alice should learn that lesson now. She should remember it for life. But, as we soon will see with her approach to the label "DRINK ME," she hasn't learned much—yet. And that's a fact.

Lewis Carroll made the idea even more explicit in a May 23, 1864, letter to Mary MacDonald:

> This hot weather has made me very sad and sulky: I can hardly keep my temper sometimes. For instance, just now the Bishop of Oxford came in to see me—it was a civil thing to do, and he meant no harm, poor man; but I was so provoked at his coming in that I threw a book at his head, which I am afraid hurt him a good deal.—(Mem: this isn't quite true—so you needn't believe it—Don't be in such a hurry to believe next time—I'll tell you why—If you set to work to believe everything, you will tire out the believing muscles of your mind, and then you'll be so weak you won't be able to believe the simplest true things.

Wow! For a churchman like Carroll this sounds like a strong argument against faith as the basis of belief. Carroll's skepticism (and his personal struggle against it) comes out in his introduction to *Pillow Talk*:

Perhaps I may venture, for a moment, to use a more serious tone, and to point out that there are mental troubles, much worse than mere worry, for which an absorbing subject of thought may serve as a remedy. There are skeptical [sic] thoughts, which seem for the moment to uproot the firmest faith; there are blasphemous thoughts, which dart unbidden into the most reverent souls; there are unholy thoughts, which torture, with their hateful presence, the fancy that would be pure. Against all these some real mental work is a most helpful ally.

FAITH VERSUS DOUBT: WHAT'S IT ALL ABOUT?

In Carroll's case we know from his diary that he was tortured at night by doubts about his religion. He admits that he invented mental puzzles and tasks to divert his own mind from thinking about these unsettling religious issues and notions. That method is Carroll's approach to a subject sticky for him—essentially an attempt not to think about or deal with the real issues, just the way Alice does not deal with the real issues entailed by her falling down the rabbit hole. Alice's faith in a benign fate is an example of faith-based rather than reality-based thinking. Whether it works or not is hit or miss. Stick to the reasonable and the real. That approach will serve you better.

By now it should be blindingly obvious that faith-based strategizing doesn't work. It is highly probable that the great religions began at a time when we knew a tiny fraction of what we know today about the origins of earth and human life. It's understandable that early humans would develop stories about gods to salve their ignorance. But people now have no such excuse and should have no such need. If they continue to believe in the unbelievable, or say that they do, they are morons or lunatics or liars or lazy thinkers with FAT MINDS. To modern people faith-based anything should be out. Reason should take the place of faith.

But how?

Instead of thinking based on faith, Descartes had a different approach based on the opposite of faith: doubt.

Thinking Based on Doubt versus Thinking Based on Faith

In 1629, a twenty-eight-year-old man sat in deep thought in an empty room. His name was René Descartes. Uttering a single word that would reverberate for the next four centuries, the young man exclaimed, "Doubt!" This word was the gauntlet thrown down by the scientific age. Descartes found doubt more useful than faith. And so, on the winds of doubt, Western science came into its own, adding one new absolute criterion: What is believed must be consistent with observed fact. Otherwise it must be doubted.

Stunning advances followed that were and continue to be mutually reinforcing. Carroll's lesson is clear: Don't strain the believing muscle of your brain. Would that he could have followed his own advice. Later he mentions that Alice often gave herself good advice but seldom followed it. Hummm, that sounds familiar. Me too. I seldom follow my own good advice. The famous Latin poet Ovid said famously, "I see what is best. I do what is worse." How about you?

IN ALL FIELDS BUT RELIGION CARROLL BELIEVED IN THE POWER OF DOUBT, AND THAT IS WHAT HE MEANT IN HIS ADVICE TO MARY MacDONALD

He's right. We tend to believe too much and doubt too little. One of the great American philosophers, Charles Sanders Peirce (1839–1914) spent the last twenty-six years of his life in seclusion thinking. Among the ideas he came up with were the warrants for belief. The warrants for belief are the inferential links that people use to hold on to or to justify their conviction and confidence in something. According to Peirce the usual warrants are four in number: tenacious, authority, a priori, and verification.

Tenacious

In the tenacious mode, the idea or belief or whatnot is for reasons unknown or perhaps for no reason whatsoever seized on and grappled to the soul with hoops of steel. It is kept there regardless of the evidence and regardless of how the situation changes or evolves. People in this mode just know that they are right. They don't care who thinks what or what evidence supports or doesn't support their position. When new evidence turns up that tends to indicate that they are wrong, they ignore the evidence, minimize it, or deny it completely. "Tenacious" is the right word for this stubborn, obstinate, outmoded mode of thinking. In AAW the Queen of Hearts and the Duchess illustrate this mode of thinking vividly. In real life, President Bush illustrates this mode of thinking.

Authority

In the authority mode, some authority is recognized and obeyed no matter what. The authority mode can present significant problems when the authority is wrong. About that, more later. In AAW the King of Hearts illustrates this mode of thinking. In real life, blind obedience to the authority of Hitler and the Nazis led to disaster.

A Priori

A priori is based on the application of a general and previously accepted principle to the particular situation. Thus, its dependability is uneven.

A PRIORI MODE ILLUSTRATED

After multiple observations, Charles Darwin concluded that all white cats with blue eyes are deaf. This is a subtle generalization that arose by induction from a series of hundreds of observations from which he ascertained that in every known case white cats with blue eyes just can't hear a blessed thing. If he had contented himself with the results of his own observations, and what he could discover from the observations of others related to this issue, the most that could have been said was that many white cats with blue eyes were deaf. Darwin was prepared however to go beyond his own experience and say that he had discovered a condition that was true of all blue-eyed, white cats, past, present, and future, which incidentally, is true.

Thus, via multiple specific examples, Darwin arrived by induction at the generalization that could then be applied as a general rule to particular situations. And for the most part his generalization was true. By the way, those white blue-eyed cats, you may know, that hear are not entirely white. Check in back of their external ear (pinna) where there is usually a black spot. Those cats are not truly white. Hence they do not fall within the purview of Darwin's rule. Modern biology has discovered the embryonic and genetic mechanisms that control cat color and hearing so that we now understand in molecular terms the reasons for Darwin's striking generalization about white cats with blue eyes. The details are not important for us. What is important is the fact that after multiple careful observations, the a priori mode works.

So, in the a priori mode we would conclude that the next entirely white blue-eyed cat that we see would be deaf, which, incidentally, it will be.

And speaking of cats—in AAW the Cheshire Cat often illustrates this mode of a priori thinking, sometimes defectively and sometimes with great effectiveness. In real life, we routinely operate by applying this mode of thinking. As a general rule you stop at the red light and go on green, else you risk a crash. As a general rule, don't gamble with money you need for food, else you risk starvation. As a general rule, don't go in deep water unless you know how to swim, else you might drown. And so forth.

Verification

Verification is the mode whereby all the evidence is examined. That is, ideas are tested against reality. Alice discovers that the jar is empty by lifting the lid and looking in. As there was no marmalade, she decides to get rid of the empty jar. As we will soon see, Alice most often illustrates the verification mode of thinking at the end of her journey during the trial of the Knave of Hearts. Alice's character arc is thus from naive blind faith to an insistence on evidence that she herself can verify.

Peirce liked the verification mode best because it gave the best chance of understanding the truth (truth is what is as opposed to what is not) and therefore gave the best protection from the unexpected, the unreasonable, the improbable, and the unexpectable. Scientists like the verification mode also. Much of the success of Western science is based on the certainties conferred on those who think in this mode.

Few scientists today would claim that science has keys to the ultimate problems of the universe, though such claims were characteristic of the optimism of nineteenth-century science and linger in the lay mind today. Scientists know that the methods of science are not adapted to the formulation of answers to the questions "Why?" and "What is the value?"

Scientists have, however, not only devised improved methods to obtain quantitative accuracy but have also thrown new light on the problem of the nature of evidence. At this point, science requires relevant and adequate evidence to support any conclusion. Relevant evidence must relate directly to the conclusion and adequate evidence must be sufficient in number, kind, and weight to justify the conclusion.

AMERICAN PRAGMATISTS
THINK REALITY COUNTS A LOT

And so, Alice, in opening the jar and actually looking in and finding that the jar contained nothing, proved that the label was wrong and that the jar did not contain marmalade, much less orange marmalade. In fact, the jar contained nothing. In voicing concern for results obtained by direct observation, Alice positions herself in the camp of Charles Sanders Peirce, William James, Benjamin Franklin, and Ralph Waldo Emerson, the founders of America's first indigenous philosophy—pragmatism. These gentlemen thought that reality counts. Reality certainly counts if you want some marmalade and the jar that you have in hand has none. Alice, we feel your pain.

What's the lesson?

Reality counts more than words and must remain the controlling influence on conclusions. No belief mode is perfect, but the verification mode works best under most circumstances. When there is a conflict betwixt the words (as in the label of this jar) and the fact, fact always wins. Fact trumps all arguments to the contrary.

Anything else?

Labels can be wrong. Don't just believe them. Verify!

Anything else?

Reality can be tough and verification can disappoint us when the reality turns out differently from what we wanted. But in the long run, we are probably better off knowing the reality (the truth) than we would have been continuing to believe in what doesn't exist. Alice didn't like the idea that the jar was empty. She would have much preferred something sweet to eat. But she is probably better off in the long run facing up to the bitter fact that she cannot look to that particular jar for marmalade or for anything else edible.

Anything else?

This is a stretch, but it is possible that Carroll was hinting here about one of the most important discoveries in the history of human thought, the discovery of nothing. Alice opens the jar and discovers it is empty, has nothing in it. This revelation raises an important question: Is the nothing in that jar something or is it nothing? Is nothing something or is nothing nothing?

This concept of nothing, of the null set, of nonexistence, of emptiness, of zero enables a modern computer to function and a modern school kid to do calculations (on that computer) or, when the computer is not at hand, on a sheet of paper, that our ancient Greek and Roman ancestors could do only on an abacus.

As Carroll was a nominalist, he believed that nothing did not exist. He thought "nothing" was just a word that indicated in shorthand form that no thing was in reference. About nothing, and Carroll's thoughts about nothing, and lots of fun about nothing (I almost said much ado about nothing), more later. In fact, much more ado about nothing later, especially when we consider why Alice wonders about where *does* the flame go when a candle flame goes out.

By the way, where *does* a flame go when it goes out? Think about that question. Think about why that question bothered Christian philosophers so much. Think about it. Answers appear shortly.

Anything else?

It is possible that Carroll was aware of the multiple meanings of ORANGE MARMALADE. He loves multiple meanings as we shall see. So it is possible that he intended multiple meanings here as another demonstration of the difficulties with language.

What might they be, those difficulties?

"Orange" is both a color and a fruit. An orange marmalade could be an orange-colored marmalade or a marmalade made from oranges. Apricot marmalade is the color orange for instance and most orange marmalade (from Seville oranges with loads of sugar) is actually colored a blotched, dark russet-orange shade—a color that the *Oxford English Dictionary* appropriately calls "marmalade." In context, the distinction is without a difference as the jar contains neither an orange marmalade nor a marmalade made from oranges. The jar contains nothing. Distinction without a difference, an error in clear thinking, will return again in chapter 2 when Alice tries to figure out who she is.

Meanwhile do we actually know what kind of orange marmalade was not in the jar? Do we actually know what kind of orange marmalade was in the jar? Do we know if there ever was any marmalade in the jar? Answers: No. No. No. We don't know and we never will.

* * *

> *"Down, down, down. Would the fall never come to an end? . . . —but then I wonder what Latitude or Longitude I've got to?"*
>
> *Alice had not the slightest idea what Latitude was, or Longitude either, but she thought they were nice grand words to say.*
>
> *"How funny it'll seem to come out among the people that walk with their heads downwards! The Antipathies, I think—" (she was rather glad there was no one listening, this time, as it didn't sound at all the right word).*
>
> *"— but I shall have to ask them what the name of the country is, you know. Please, Ma'am, is this New Zealand or Australia?"*

The joke here is that 99 percent of the people on this planet don't know what latitude and longitude are. Most of them are probably too lazy to look it up and get it straight.

Alice is right about *Antipathies*—that isn't the right word in this context, as it means "settled dislikes." *Antipodes*, which mean persons living directly on the opposite side of the globe, is more likely, if she wants the word to work as a common noun, which she clearly doesn't. As a proper noun, Antipodes refers to New Zealand and Australia, which she clearly does mean, hence her question.

On the most elementary level, one might say, the silly level, Antipathies is a malapropism (misuse of words caused by similarity in sound), a mispronunciation of Antipodes. On a deeper level, the difference between the two words, Antipathies and Antipodes, demonstrates an important truth about language: its signification is pretty much arbitrary because a single syllable difference may alter the meaning entirely. Even a single letter change can make a giant difference. "Real crap spring rolls" were advertised at our local Kroger supermarket. Putting a *p* where there should have been a *b* made all the difference, the difference between a crap spring roll and a crab spring roll. Lesson: Generally speaking, language is slippery and unless people agree upon a word's meaning, its use will be meaningless.

HOW CAN WE DISCOVER THE MEANING OF WORDS?

When you don't know the meaning of a word, whether the word is Latitude or Longitude or Antipathies or Antipodes or any other word of that ilk—or you aren't sure of the exact meaning of a word including its denotation, connotation, etymology, and word atmosphere—follow Alice's advice: Don't display your ignorance; keep your mouth shut.

And when you can, look the word up in a good dictionary. Correct your lack of knowledge. Don't live with it. And for heaven sakes don't use a word you don't know the meaning of. If you do, you will quite literally not know what you are talking about.

* * *

"Down, down, down. There was nothing else to do, so Alice soon began talking again."

Advice: If there is nothing to do, it doesn't mean you should fill the air with idle chatter. Patter and chatter—all gimmicky distractions, double talk, chit-chat, babble, banter, small talk, prattle, raillery, twaddle, nattering, drivel, blather, click-clacks, empty talk, and junk talk (junk talk is talk of no intellectual value, just as junk food is food—empty calories—of no nutritional value).

The ancients considered talking too much a great vice. Plutarch's tractate "On Talkativeness" combines all the standard features of the topic in a typically charming fashion. Yet it is marred by its own length and loquaciousness. It is, of all his tractates, the longest.

Garrulousness is a vice that is difficult to deal with reasonable words because the compulsive talker never listens to anyone else. Indeed, here

Alice has no audience and is talking to herself. Unlike other vices (love of pleasure, money, fame), it can never, according to Plutarch, achieve what it most desires, namely, attentive hearers, because it drives them off. The Spartans were renowned for their strength and self-control, and they were notoriously "laconic" in their speech. The wisdom of the past is shown by the brief adages of the sages. Even the oracles of the god Apollo are brief and direct—"Know thyself," "Nothing to excess," "Follow God," and so on. Come to think on it, the same argument can be made for books, especially, I suppose, books about books. The virtue of brevity? Mea culpa. Mea culpa. Mea maxima culpa.

So what's the lesson?

The lesson is save your breath. If you don't have something to say, keep the sanctity of discourse intact. Keep your mouth shut. As yet, Alice doesn't know this great truth. So she ridiculously starts to mutter and putter: "'. . . *But do cats eat bats? I wonder.' And here Alice began to get rather sleepy, and went on saying to herself, in a dreamy sort of way, 'Do cats eat bats? Do cats eat bats?' And sometimes 'Do bats eat cats?' for, you see, as she couldn't answer either question, it didn't much matter which way she put it.*"

It might not matter to Alice if cats eat bats or bats eat cats, but it matters to the cats and bats as there is a major difference between eating and getting eaten, just as there is a world of difference between getting paid and paying.

Subject and predicate are two different things as Lewis Carroll repeatedly shows us. They can't be interchanged without a change of meaning. The Hatter tells Alice the same thing in chapter 7: "'*Why, you might just as well say that "I see what I eat" is the same thing as "I eat what I see"!*'"

Converses are not necessarily true. The contrary example proves the Hatter's point. His might be madness, yet there is method in it.

But there is more to it than that. Alice's understanding of the equality of "bats eat cats" and "cats eat bats" is simple, unschooled, and incorrect. We forgive her because her mind is not functioning at peak efficiency as she is (again) drowsy.

But what's the real error? Think about it. What's Carroll's point? What's the deeper meaning?

Alice's error: She is treating the question as an algebraic equation rather than a sentence in English. In this instance, Alice equates the bat-cat question with 1+2=2+1, or A+B=B+A, or A&B ≡ B&A, which is correct because the order of conjunctive statements is irrelevant to the truth value of those statements. We can easily prove 1+2=2+1 by showing logical equivalence with a truth table:

Let P=1
Let Q=2
Let & = the arithmetic function "plus."
Let Þ = the biconditional: if and only if.
P&Q is true, if and only if, P is true and Q is true.
That is, P&Q=T Þ P=T and Q=T.

If P is false, or Q is false, then P&Q is false. Of course, P&Q is false if both P and Q are false. Thus, we can set up a truth table for P&Q and for Q&P:

	P	Q	P&Q	Q&P
Case 1.	T	T	T	T
Case 2.	T	F	F	F
Case 3.	F	T	F	F
Case 4.	F	F	F	F

Because column P&Q has the same truth value as column Q&P, Q&P is logically equivalent to P&Q (Q&P ≡ P&Q) and vice versa. Therefore, 1+2=2+1. However, cat eats bat is not equal to bat eats cat as cat eats bat is not a conjunctive statement but a statement that is making a definite claim, the claim that cats eat bats, which is probably true. The claim bats eat cats is different and is probably not true. So in one little package Carroll shows us the profound difference between a language statement and a mathematical statement. I think that is so cool. How about you?

* * *

Alice lands quite well and continues on her quest of the White Rabbit.

Note: Once Alice safely completes this fall, the event is closed and she cannot ever be hurt by that particular fall. That is the beauty of the past and also a major problem with the past: Once it's over, it cannot change.

* * *

There were doors all round the hall, but they were all locked; and when Alice had been all the way down one side and up the other, trying every door, she walked sadly down the middle, wondering how she was ever to get out again.

Laying aside the obvious nature of this frustration dream, the lesson here is that reality can treat us harshly, sometimes for no apparent reason. Alice soon finds a key. But alas! Alack! Alice is off the track: She finds that either the locks are too big or the key was too small (which amounts to the same thing and is logically equivalent). Logic equivalency is a big deal in some schools of philosophy that hold that two statements are logically equivalent if they both have the same truth value. In symbolic logic we write $\equiv$ to indicate logical equivalence, meaning statements on either side of this symbol have the same truth value and for every truth table assignment are identical.

Again Alice has come against the frustration of dealing with a reality contrary to her desires.

Me too. I have had that feeling. I have that feeling when reality seems to be ganging up on me and making my life rough and tough. How about you? Have you had that feeling?

MISMATCHES BETWEEN REALITY AND
HUMAN DESIRES ARE COMMON

Finally, Alice pulls aside the low curtain, finds the little door, and opens it with the key. Alas! Alack! Welcome back—welcome back to the desert of the real. The key works and the door opens, but Alice is too big to get more than her head through or (and this is $\equiv$) the door is too small for her to get her head through. Ugh! Yet another mismatch between the external reality and human need and desire.

Reality! Don't you hate it? Have you ever been in a situation like Alice's where nothing seemed to go as planned, everything goes awry? As Djay, the rapper, explains: "Things don't always come together just because you want them to."

And soon the final lesson occurs (and this one is the killer). As you doubtless remember, Alice gets small enough to get through the door. Hooray! Hooray!

But alas! Alack! She's off the track. Alice forgot the key on the table! She can't go back. She is now too small. She can't go back because she is too small to reach the key.

What does this prove? It proves that sometimes there is a certain sequence of action that solves the problem, which, if it is omitted, leaves the problem unsolved. Thus there exists a sequence that would have solved Alice's problem, but as she is not yet aware of that sequence, she's stuck. Pause here and think. Can you suggest a sequence that would have enabled Alice to deal effectively with the reality of her situation? Hint: Later Alice gets the sequence correct and successfully gets through without trouble. If she can get it right, so can you. And what's the moral of that?

Moral: There's a right way of doing things, and there's a wrong way of doing things. (And, of course, there's also the army way.)

Consider this gem of Viking advice: Pillage first. Then burn! If you burn first, there will not be much left to pillage.

"Can I be on top?"

"That's not the first question. The first question is are we going to have sex or not?"

First you ask question one and then you may get to ask question two.

BACK TO ALICE

Alice is stuck because the reality situation has changed. And the main reason that the reality situation has changed is because Alice has changed. She is small enough to get through the door. But she is still unable to get what she wants because she doesn't have the key. "What is actual is actual only for one time and one place," said T. S. Eliot. He was right. And Eliot's point is that what is true is true only for a particular time and place.

Here Carroll is making that exact point: Despite our best efforts to conform to the reality situation, by the time we do, the reality may have changed or we may have changed or, more likely, we have screwed up so badly that the opportunity has been lost. Recall Heraclitus? You can never step into the same stream twice. For the same reason, you or I can't buy Microsoft stock for two dollars a share.

> BRUTUS: There is a tide in the affairs of men which, which taken at the flood, leads on to fortune, omitted, all the voyage of their life is bound in shallows and in miseries.
>
> CASSIUS: The fault lies not in the stars, but in ourselves for we are underlings. ♦

What's the lesson? Not only does reason compel us to admit the existence of the external world and its ever-changing nature, it also requires us to face that world, deal with it effectively if we can, build for ourselves meaningful lives within its boundaries, and engage the

---

♦ Shakespeare, *Julius Caesar*, act 1, scene 2.

serious business of living intelligently by sizing things up and seizing opportunities. That's what Alice tries to do to get around her current problems and get what she wants. And to get what she wants she must confront the problems posed by EAT ME and DRINK ME. Let's consider DRINK ME first.

* * *

. . . tied round the neck of the bottle was a paper label, with the words "DRINK ME" beautifully printed on it in large letters. It was all very well to say "Drink me," but the wise little Alice was not going to do that in a hurry. "No, I'll look first," she said, "and see whether it's marked 'poison' or not"; for she had read several nice little stories about children who had got burnt, and eaten up by wild beasts, and other unpleasant things, all because they would not remember the simple rules their friends had taught them: such as, that a red-hot poker will burn you if you hold it too long; and that, if you cut your finger very deeply with a knife, it usually bleeds; and she had never forgotten that, if you drink much from a bottle marked "poison," it is almost certain to disagree with you, sooner or later. However, the bottle was not marked "poison," so Alice ventured to taste it, and, finding it very nice, . . . she very soon finished it off.

Q: Any problems with Alice's thinking?

A: Aside from being hilarious, this passage is chock full of errors in thinking. I'll just mention a few:

DRINK ME

Because a bottle is labeled DRINK ME does not mean Alice should drink it. In its assertion the label begs multiple questions among which are "Is it safe?" "What is it for?" "Why should I drink it?" "Who made the sign?" "Who filled the bottle and why?" "Why do they want me to drink the contents of the bottle?"

Note: The Victorian medicine bottle had neither a screw top nor a label on the side. It was corked, with a paper label tied to the neck.

Therefore, this is a medicine bottle. God knows we shouldn't take medicine unless it is specifically prescribed for us. Sometimes, dear reader, we shouldn't take medicine that is specifically prescribed for us. Lincoln, our sixteenth president, gave up on his little blue pills because they were making him sicker. They were mercury salts prescribed for his depression. Now we know those pills had no therapeutic value. Mercury salts would have made Lincoln feel worse, which, incidentally, they did. Good thing that Lincoln gave them up, otherwise we might have had a presidential suicide.

* * *

Alice was not going to do that in a hurry. "No, I'll look first."

I will argue that Alice had already decided that she would drink the stuff. Despite her gesture toward closer scrutiny, her decision is prefigured and is not dependent on careful analysis of the evidence, pro and con. Her decision is an ill-considered rush to judgment. Alice has (irrationally) decided that she will drink. She will drink after she looks at the bottle. Thus, she has dismissed the question of "Should I drink?" and substituted the question "When shall I drink?" To the latter question she has a ready answer: as soon as I look. This is weak sense thinking at its very worst. Alice wants to drink and has constructed reasons to justify her wish. She is arguing, not from the data or from a reasoned analysis, but from the conclusion that she has already arrived at. That is wrong, wrong, wrong. Deciding something time ahead and then fishing around for an excuse to do that thing is wrong, wrong, wrong. The consequences of this kind of wrong reasoning can be disastrous. The consequences can be fatal. In science such reasoning is called arguing from the conclusion. This is a sin because you are supposed to argue from the data (evidence). Your conclusion should be no stronger and no weaker than is justified by the evidence. Let the evidence justify the conclusion, not vice versa. Do not put the cart before the horse. Reality doesn't work that way.

Moral: Never plunge into any major action without due deliberation. Keep your options open. Never decide important issues time ahead. Try not to decide important issues time ahead especially if you do not have in hand all of the available facts and evidence.

The narrative shows that Alice just needed to go through some rationalizations before proceeding to the action. Her thinking is way off the point and defective. Those nice little stories she mentions were not nice. They were the traditional fairy tales, filled with episodes of horror and usually containing a pious moral. They told about children who got burnt, eaten up by wild beasts, turned into gingerbread by witches, and other unpleasant things. All that is true but it hardly seems relevant to the issue, which is to drink or not to drink from the bottle in hand.

OTHER IRRELEVANT ISSUES

A red-hot poker has nothing to do with the question of the danger lurking in the bottle. Besides, a red-hot poker will burn you any time you hold it. You don't have to hold it, as Alice said, *too* long to get burned. How long is *too* long anyway? The same minimization of danger is present in Alice's discussion of the knife: To bleed it is not necessary to cut *very* deeply. Deep will do.

That the bottle is not labeled poison is neither here nor there. A poison can be a poison whether labeled or not. Nevertheless, Alice concludes that since the bottle is not labeled poison, it is safe to taste. Stated more formally Alice's thinking would go:

(premise 1) All poisons are labeled "poison."
(premise 2) This bottle is not labeled "poison."
(conclusion 1) Therefore, the liquid in this bottle is not a poison.
(premise 3, based on conclusion 1) It is not a poison.
(premise 4) Things that are not poisons are safe to drink.
(conclusion 2) Therefore, it is safe to drink.

Premise one is false. Therefore, it does not follow for any conclusions derived from it are true. Premise 2 is true but not entirely relevant to the question because a poison could be present even if a poison label is absent. Premise 3 is true, but Alice didn't know that fact until after she drank. As premise 4 is not true, conclusion 2 isn't established.

Even if premise one were correct and the liquid was not a poison, the conclusions don't ring true. There are lots of substances that, though not poisons, would not be safe to drink—polluted water, for instance. Other substances are not poisons, but would be unpleasant to drink—vinegar, for instance. Other liquids are a food, a poison, or a drug, depending on the definition and the amount imbibed—alcoholic beverages, for instance. Some of those might not be suitable for a little girl to drink—Irish whiskey, for instance. The class of undesirable things to drink is much larger than the class of poisons.

Another way of examining this situation is by using John Stuart Mill's Property Tables.♣

Let P=present
Let A=absent
Let E=effect, which in the case of poison would be death.
We can construct a table showing the four possible combinations of P&A (present and absent) and the resultant effect:

Case	(Label-says-Poison)	(Bottle-has-poison)	(Effect-death)
1.	P	P	P
2.	P	A	A
3.	A	P	P
4.	A	A	A

The table shows that there are only four combinations. Either the label says poison or it doesn't and either the poison is in the bottle or it isn't. Thus, 2×2 makes 4 possibilities.

♣ John Stuart Mill (1807–1873) invented property tables (more or less). Cf. *System of Logic* (1843).

As depicted we get: Case one has the label and the poison. In that case, the result is death. Case three has the poison but no label. That's the killer. In that case, Alice would think it safe to drink when in fact drinking would cause death. Case three is the case that Alice did not consider but should have. Case two assumes the bottle has no poison but has the poison label. In that case, no death. Case four has no label and no poison, consequently there will be no death.

In symbolic logic, the four combinations would look like this.

Let ~ = not, ⊃ = entails, D=death, L=label, P=poison. Therefore, ~L= not labeled poison and ~P=no poison:

Case 1. P&L⊃D
Case 2. ~P&L⊃~D
Case 3. P&~L⊃D
Case 4. ~L&~P⊃~D

Inspecting the property chart or the symbolic summary of the possible combinations, we discover that the pattern distribution of P and A in the effect column is exactly the same as that in the poison column: only cases 1 and 3 entail death. Therefore, the death effect is (what else?) entirely dependent on the presence of poison. Death has nothing to do with the label. This makes sense. Recall the marmalade label. Words count. But not that much. They don't count as much as facts. The controlling reality in this poison or not poison problem is whether the bottle has poison or it doesn't.

Right?

Not only does this make sense, but it also is the perfect reason for not drinking from a bottle labeled DRINK ME. To focus attention only on the label is to focus attention away from real possibility of case 3, and possibly make an error that would prove fatal. Alice should have already learned, if she were a one-step learner, that labels can be false. She should have learned that brutal fact from the empty marmalade jar. But she didn't. Consequently, by drinking DRINK ME, Alice risks death.

Another way of looking at this DRINK ME situation is via a truth table. If L=labeled poison and P=has poison, then L is either true or false: T or F. Ditto P. P is either T or F. Hence:

	Labeled	Poison Present	Death
1.	T	T	T
2.	T	F	F
3.	F	T	T
4.	F	F	F

Note that column "Death" has the same truth value as column "Poison Present." As having the same truth value is the definition of logical equivalence, we can confidently say that Poison Present ≡ Death. This logical equivalency of course applies only in this particular hypothetical situation. There are other causes of death besides poison and there are effective antidotes to some poisons. Therefore, in real life death doesn't necessarily follow from ingestion of poison and failure to ingest a poison doesn't mean you will live forever.

Carroll's main point: To focus on the label would be to focus on a side issue and miss the important fact that it is the poison that controls the result, not the label.

By focusing on side issues that are off the point, Alice convinces herself that drinking the stuff in the bottle is O.K. This is a rationalization to justify what she wants to do. The real reason for her action is CURIOSITY. Alice is curious. She wants to know what would happen.

DEATH IS BAD

Is death bad? Isn't that a value judgment? What's the evidence that death is bad? Socrates pointed out that it is not reasonable to assume that death is bad, as we have no evidence one way or the other. He said that either death is an extinction in the which case it doesn't matter or it is not an extinction in the which case it doesn't matter. Hence, the logical equivalence of the statement either death is an extinction and does not matter or it is not an extinction and does not matter is that death does not matter.

Oh, I don't know about that. Extinction matters to some people. It certainly matters to me. It would hurt me to say good-bye forever to my family and friends. It would hurt even more to say good-bye forever to my (very entertaining) self. I think death is just about the worst thing that can happen to me. Woody Allen said, "I don't mind dying. I just don't want to be there when it happens." Me too, I don't want to be there *and* I don't want it to happen.

WHY DEATH IS BAD

Another consideration: From what I have seen of dead people (as a physician I've see hundreds of dead people and hundreds of real deaths), death doesn't look all that great. In fact I am prepared to assert, based on evidence, that death spoils your weekend. Not a single dead person I've known ever had a great weekend. Furthermore, not a single one of all the dead people that I have seen appeared in any way to be having any fun. Would any of you, dear readers, want to exchange places with any dead person? As for me, I would rather be an alive Patten than a dead Beethoven. How about you?

Woody Allen again: "Is there sex after death? I sure hope so. I wouldn't want to miss out entirely." Holy cow! Death might entail NO SEX! Socrates also missed that important point.

* * *

Because the bottle was not marked poison, Alice drinks the contents. She shrinks to ten inches and is now the right size (as mentioned) for going through the little door into that lovely garden. Before entering the garden, however, she waited for a few minutes to see if she was going to shrink any more: she felt a little nervous about this.

"... for it might end, you know," said Alice to herself, "in my going out altogether, like a candle. I wonder what I should be like then?" And she tried to fancy what the flame of a candle looks like after the candle is blown out, for she could not remember ever having seen such a thing.

Good for Alice! She is looking at her own experience to determine whether something might be true or might not be true. When she does that she again joins Benjamin Franklin, Ralph Waldo Emerson, Charles Peirce, and host of pragmatic American philosophers in America's first and probably only truly indigenous philosophy, pragmatism.

Alice can't remember ever having seen a flame after it had gone out. That is great!

Me too. I can't remember ever having seen a flame after it had gone out. How about you?

Why can't she **remember** seeing a flame after it has gone out? Why can't I remember seeing a flame after it has gone out? Why can't you?

She can't remember because she never saw a flame that had gone out. Neither have I. You can't see what doesn't exist. You can't (truthfully) remember seeing what you haven't seen.

Alice is being honest. She's not like those people who remember what they have not seen, many of them bearing false witness in the process. Because it can do such great evil, divine command comes down heavily against that false witness thing.

When you haven't seen something, admit it. Don't try to fool yourself. Don't try to fool others. And for heaven's sake, don't get up in a court of law and pretend to have a knowledge or experience that you don't have. There are too many fake things in this wide world. Don't add to them.

WHERE DOES THE FLAME GO WHEN IT GOES OUT?

By the way, where *does* a flame go when it goes out?

Alice wonders about that. So should we. Where, exactly, does the flame go when it goes out? To the mall? To heaven, hell, or limbo? Where?

Do we know?

The pre-Socratics were the philosophers before Socrates. Anaximander of Miletus (c. 610–547/546 BCE) and Anaximenes of Miletus (fl. 546 BCE) are the most famous pre-Socratics. They enjoyed discussing that problem. But as far as I know, they did not come up with a satisfactory answer. To say that the flame goes nowhere seems to beg the question. But actually it doesn't. The flame that goes out doesn't go anywhere. Our thoughts on the matter are simply being preconditioned (channeled) in the wrong direction by the words of the metaphor that describe the extinction of the flame.

Some language, as in the case here, comes to us with implied commitments, commitments so deeply ingrained that it is easy to overlook them or be fooled by them. Overlooking implied elements in language may lead to a simple-minded or (as in this case) a wrong view of nature. The problem of the flame is one of those pseudoproblems that arise, as Ludwig Wittgenstein observed, when language goes on holiday. If we had simply said, "the flame became extinct" or "ceases" or "ceased," there would be no further discussion or conclusion, for put this way, the question doesn't get off the ground.

So when you are asked next, "Where does a flame go when it goes out?" reply that the flame goes nowhere. It joins the null set, the class of nonexisting things that includes secular churches, square circles, four-sided triangles, whales that fly, married bachelors, and so on.

There is nothing wrong with the null set (pun intended). Carroll even thought that, in some respects, people that don't exist, are much nicer than people who do. For instance, he wrote in a letter to Sydney Bowles (May 22, 1891): "People that don't exist are never cross; and they never contradict you; and they never tread on your toes! Oh, they're ever so much nicer than people that do exist! However, never mind; you can't help existing you know; and I daresay you're just as nice as if you didn't."

What's the big deal about the flame anyway?

Lewis Carroll knows that this problem of the flame also haunted medieval scholastics. Here might be an anagorical (mystical) meaning. For if a flame could become extinct, disappear forever as part of nothing, then isn't it possible that the same dismal fate could happen to the human spirit or to the human soul? Isn't it possible that persons, when they died, just became nothing, joined the null set of nonexistent things? That is the hidden meaning of Alice's concern for the flame and the concern for her shrinking self. She is worried about becoming as extinct as an extinct flame. It is hard to say good-bye to family and friends. But to say good-bye to yourself, oh boy! That is harder. Many senior citizens, myself included, share the same anxiety as Alice. We don't like the idea that we might cease to exist. We don't like it one bit.

Thus, in her own childlike way, Alice is asking a daunting human question about death. The extinction of the candle is here compared to the extinction of life. Shakespeare used the same metaphor: "Out, out, brief candle. Life's but a walking shadow."

By the way, where does the human soul go when a human dies? Does it go out like a candle? Or does it continue to exist as some sort of immaterial spirit?

Alice wonders. So do we. Alice is concerned about the possibility of her own extinction, the disappearance of herself. We worry about the same issue. Where, exactly, do the souls (or the spirits or the vital elements that make the difference between the living and the dead) of people go when they die? Do we know?

Friends, about the soul, I know nothing. In fact, I can't remember ever having seen a soul after a person died. I can't remember ever having seen a soul after a person died because I have never seen a soul at all. If I have never seen a soul, I can't possibly remember seeing one. Thus, I can't say that I know there is such a thing as a soul. But I can assure you, there is such a thing as a flame. And I can assure you that when a flame goes out, it ceases to exist. The reason I know this is that while a flame exists it will burn my finger. But after it goes out, it won't. Therefore, the essential quality that distinguishes a flame from a non-flame disappears when the flame "extincts." An extinct flame can be neither seen, nor felt, nor heard, nor smelled, nor tasted. A real flame on the other hand can be seen, felt, heard, smelled, and tasted (don't try this with a real flame. You will burn your tongue).

SEMANTIC PROBLEMS ARE COMMON AND EASY TO FIX

It was nearly eleven-thirty, and I had just put the cat out. It hadn't been easy. For over twenty minutes, and more fiercely than anticipated, and smelling god-awful, with lots of dreadful black smoke, she had burned to a crisp.

Get it?

Putting the cat out and putting the cat out can be two different things. Hence, the semantic fun. When the cat goes out we know where it went. When the fire on the cat goes out, the fire goes nowhere.

Think about this: Is nowhere somewhere or is it nowhere. Is nothing something, or is it nothing. Lewis Carroll, as nominalist, has a clear answer. Nowhere and nothing do not exist. They are words that denote in a succinct, almost shorthand form: nonexistence.

HOW TO RESOLVE SEMANTIC PROBLEMS

The real test for Alice's flame problem and other problems of that ilk is to ask whether disagreement over the problem would be resolved by changing the terminology or would the disagreements persist despite changed language. For instance, no one could reasonably oppose the above resolution of the flame pseudoproblem by objecting that the expressions "the flame extincts" or "the flame ceased" leave out relevant facts captured by "the flame went out." With the case of the flame, there is no substantive fact under dispute, as became clear when the linguistic confusion was pointed out.

On the other hand, a problem that cannot be resolved by changing the language that views it or changing the angle in which it is viewed by that language, is not a purely semantic difficulty and must be resolved by examination of relevant and adequate evidence.

* * *

. . . she remembered trying to box her own ears for having cheated herself in a game of croquet she was playing against herself, for this curious child was very fond of pretending to be two people. "But it's no use now," thought poor Alice, "to pretend to be two people! Why, there's hardly enough of me left to make one respectable person!"

This reasoning, like most of Alice's postulations, is an error. She mistakes an individual's size for his or her individuality. A big person may be as respectable as a small person, as size is irrelevant to the moral value judgment of respectability. Dr. Suess is right: A person's a person no matter how small.

Did Carroll intend a pun on the adjective *curious?* Alice is curious (different) and she is curious (eager to explore). Curious and curious, though she might be, there is no evidence that the real Alice, Alice Pleasance Liddell, liked to pretend or ever pretended that she was two people. However, in keeping with the contention that Carroll injected much of himself into his fictional Alice, we must remember that Carroll was always careful to keep separate Charles Dodgson, the Oxford mathematician and logician, and Lewis Carroll, writer of children's books and lover of little girls. The two-persona idea, therefore, more likely reflects the psychology of the author; not the psychology of the person after whom the author patterned his protagonist.

* * *

EAT ME.
Everything that applies to DRINK ME applies to EAT ME.

Soon her eye fell on a little glass box under the table which had in it a small cake, on which the words "EAT ME" were beautifully marked in currants. "Well I shall eat it," said Alice, "and if it makes me grow smaller, I can creep under the door and if it makes me grow larger, I can reach the key."

THE ERROR OF FALSELY LIMITED ALTERNATIVES

Either-or thinking, black-and-white assessments, and falsely limited alternatives (although they are often cited in current American politics) don't work because they exclude multiple other possibilities. So why do we fall for this kind of silly thinking so often?

Who knows?

Academic scholars have pointed out that either-or reasoning resembles the disjunctive syllogism. This resemblance is superficial and the conclusions from either-or do not have the logical deductive certainty of the disjunctive syllogism.

One of the alternatives that Alice failed to consider is the one that is reasonable and expected: When she eats cake, her size will not change. Alice failed to consider the very real possibility that eating the cake would neither make her grow nor make her shrink. She failed to consider the most reasonable and expected result of eating cake, which is, and has always been, that there will be no immediate or dramatic change in body size.

Always bet on the reasonable, the expected, and the probable, for that is your best protection against the unreasonable, the unexpected, the improbable, and the seemingly unexpectable (which has a nasty habit of coming up now and again).

* * *

She ate a little bit, and said anxiously to herself "Which way? Which way?" holding her hand on the top of her head to feel which way it was growing; and she was quite surprised to find that she remained the same size.

To be sure, this is what generally happens when one eats cake.

Carroll has just presented us with the first of twelve occasions in AAW on which Alice alters in size. The first metamorphosis occurred after she obeyed the bottle's sign DRINK ME. Because of that single experience, Alice got into the erroneous idea that since drinking the stuff in the bottle had made her small, eating the cake would change her size in some way or other. Her conclusion is based on inadequate evidence, the case of N=1, an inadequate sample of only one instance. That is hardly sufficient to counter the experiential fact that every little girl knows or should know: one's size doesn't immediately change by eating cake. Over time, if you eat too much cake, you will get fat but you won't necessarily shrink or expand lengthwise.

Alice's thinking is again a false analogy: Because her size changed after DRINK ME doesn't mean there is a reason to think that EAT ME would do the same. Drinking and eating, though similar in some respects, are different in others. Drinking and eating do share the same property of taking things into the body via the mouth and so forth, but the mere fact that they share some properties does not mean they would share other properties as well.

If X has properties a & b, and Y has properties a & b, it does not follow that if X has property c, Y has c.

Whether DRINK ME and EAT ME share the properties in question of size alteration would have to be proven by more evidence than one trial of DRINK ME.

Post hoc reasoning like this is often defective, as this episode might prove. Alice knows her size changed after DRINK ME, but she doesn't really know that the DRINK ME was the causative agent. Loads of other data might be required to establish the causal connection. Just because one event follows another does not necessarily mean the second event was caused by the first or that the events are connected in *any* causal way.

The rooster crows and the sun rises. Does that mean that the rooster made the sun rise?

Of course not.

To think that it did is to think wrongly. The error is called *post hoc, (ergo) propter hoc,* Latin for *after this, (therefore) because of this.* Post hoc propter hoc (often abbreviated to "post hoc") is an error in thinking because the class of events that follow other events yet are not related to the event they follow is much much larger than the class of events that follow the event that caused them.

Just because two events are linked in time does not mean they are linked as cause and effect. The two might have happened together or closely together by chance alone, or they might be indirectly related to a third item. In the case of the rooster, the coming of dawn has caused him to call the hens to mate. If we kill the rooster, the sun will still rise. If you try this, that is, if you kill the rooster and the sun stops rising, write me for a complete refund.

ERRORS OF SCALE IN CHILDHOOD

No doubt many of you who have children and grandchildren have noticed that some of them do commonly make errors of scale. I believe Lewis Carroll knew this from his vast experience playing with children and that he put the frustrations of Alice in dealing with these errors in his story (many times she is too big or too small for her play place) as multiple examples of this phenomenon.

In adults and older children, the perception of an object and the organization of actions on it are seamlessly integrated. However, as documented by scientists, eighteen- to thirty-month-old children sometimes fail to use information about object size and make serious attempts to perform impossible actions on those objects. They repeatedly try, for instance, to sit in a dollhouse chair or to get into a small toy car or put doll shoes on their own feet.

Neuropsychologists have interpreted scale errors of this type as reflections of problems with immaturity in the inhibitory control mechanisms of the brain and with the failure to integrate visual perception with motor action.

Visual perception and motor action are, neurally and functionally, distinct brain systems that one must, through trial and error, learn to coordinate. Thus, scale errors involve a dissociation in young children's use of visual information for planning versus controlling their actions, as well as a failure of inhibitory control.

Whenever a child encounters a replica of an object from a highly familiar category, visual information from the replica—its shape, color texture, and so on—activates the child's representation of the category of larger objects that the replica stands for. Seeing a doll's or a toy chair, for instance, activates the child's representation of the category of larger objects that the category stands for, that is, the general category of typical chairs. In most cases this would be a representation of a chair much larger than the small doll's chair in question. Included in the child's primitive motor program would be the usual behaviors associated with sitting in the big chair. Hence, the difficulty.

What typically happens in older children and adults is that the visual representation of the miniature-size replica will inhibit the motor program as inappropriate for that size. However, once the inhibition fails, as it often does in children, especially small children, the child performs the motor program for the miniature chair precisely based on a mental representation of a different, larger chair. Multiple movies have shown, for example, a twenty-one-month-old persistently trying to sit down in a too-small chair. In trying to perform this impossible act, the child will repeatedly fall off the miniature object.

Currently, the theory that explains scale errors best is one that posits two neurally and functionally distinct visual systems underlying perception and action. A ventral stream of projections from primary visual cortex to inferotemporal cortex is involved in the identification of objects and in the formation of action plans. A dorsal stream of projections to the posterior parietal cortex provides online control of the movements required to execute those plans. Dissociations have been shown between those two systems, both in brain-damaged individuals and in normal adults' response to visual illusions.

The scale errors in children may reflect immaturity in the interaction of the dorsal and ventral streams manifested in occasional break-downs in the integration of visual information processed by the two systems. A scale error occurs when information about the identity of an object processed by the ventral system is not integrated with the information about its size processed by the dorsal system. The precise nature of such breakdowns and the factors that influence their occurrence will become clear only after further research. What is clear, and what is truly amazing, is that Lewis Carroll understood the phenomenon and sympathized with the frustrations that children must endure because of it.♥

Of course, we learn later that size transformations and the frustrations attached to them, as well as the bizarre events with DRINK ME and the other transformations that Alice undergoes, might have a more rational explanation:

Question 2. Which is what?

Answer 2. Alice is dreaming.

And in that dream, she is exercising her free will. The real cause of Alice's decisions is curiosity. She is curious to find out what might happen if she obeys the injunction EAT ME.

And speaking of curiosity, chapter 1 is now at its end, and I am curious about what the next chapter will contain. Of course, by now you know that I am also "curious" in the other sense of the word. But mainly I am curious since, as I write this, I don't know. And because I don't know, I can't tell. How about we get into the verification mode? How about we turn a few pages and see? But first:

THINGS TO REMEMBER— PROGRESS BOX FOR CHAPTER 1

- A conclusion must be justified by evidence. If the evidence is relevant and adequate, then the conclusion is justified. If the evidence is not relevant and adequate, the conclusion is not justified.

♥ For further discussion see Judy S. DeLoache et al., "Scale Errors Offer Evidence for a Perception-Action Dissociation Early in Life," *Science* 304 (May 14, 2004): 1027.

- The narrative asserts that free will exists by showing us that Alice can decide to do something (follow the White Rabbit, obey EAT ME, etc.) and she can decide not to do something (not make a daisy chain, not follow her own very good advice, etc.).
- Because free will exists, we should try to make choices that most closely relate to the reality situation in which we find ourselves.
- Thinking done while you are bored or tired is likely to be defective.
- Fact trumps all arguments to its contrary. Ignoring contrary evidence leads away from truth toward error.
- Because one event follows another, it does not mean that the second event was caused by the first event. To assume that it does is to commit the post hoc error in thinking.
- Don't use words if you don't know their meanings. Otherwise, quite literally, you don't know what you are talking about.
- Linguistic confusions arise because some aspects of language are wrong or misleading. A candle doesn't go anywhere when it goes out, although the language suggests that it does.
- The future is contingent. To assume that something must happen in the future is wrong. The future is tomorrow still; this is today. Events in the future predicted with confidence as facts can't possibly be facts. They might become facts at some future time. Then again, they might not ever be facts. To treat future contingent events as fact leads away from the correct perception of reality toward error.
- Past, present, and future, though they share some elements, are not the same. To consider them the same is to neglect a rather large body of evidence and therefore to risk error.
- Reality can be damn inconvenient. And dealing with reality can be inconvenient because we and it may change with time. What is real is real only for one time and one place. Therefore, carpe diem (seize the day).
- Make decisions on the basis of the evidence: Avoid premature, hasty conclusions based on rationalization or an apparent minimization of risk.

2

The Pool of Tears

"Curiouser and curiouser!" cried Alice (she was so much surprised, that for the moment she quite forgot how to speak good English).

*C*uriouser sounds like good English to me. According to the *Oxford English Dictionary*, it is correct. Therefore, the author (Carroll), whose comments always appear in parentheses, must be making a subtle point about using two curiousers when only one would do. Or perhaps this is another exploitation of the multiple meanings of the adjective "curious" (twelve in my dictionary) including "exciting attention or surprise" and "marked by desire to find out."

The first curiouser could apply to Alice and the second to the situation in AAW or vice versa. Or is this a negative example, an instance showing how reiteration adds no weight to statements? Or perhaps I don't get the point or the joke. If you do, send me an e-mail: Dadpatten@aol.com.

The important thing is not to stop questioning: "Curiosity has its own reason for existing. One cannot help but be in awe when he contemplates the mysteries of eternity, of life, of the marvelous structure of reality. It is enough if one tries merely to comprehend a little of this mystery every day" (Albert Einstein).

And talking about curious: The pool of tears has evoked some curious commentary. The literary critic William Empson referred to the theory that Alice's pool of tears represented the primitive ocean, the whole passage being supposedly associated with evolution and the emergence of tetrapod life from the sea.

Freudians associate the pool of tears with amniotic fluid and the trauma of birth. Others consider the pool of tears an allusion to the initial river journey that Lewis Carroll and the Liddell sisters had made to Nuneham on a very wet day in July 1862. Still others think this is a Carrollian reification, an attempt to treat an abstraction as if it substantially existed. In this case, the metaphor reified (that is, transformed into a concrete experience) has to do with the expression *drowning in one's own tears*. That is an interesting idea, except that Alice wasn't drowning. She was swimming.

Anyway, it is probably misguided to apply this kind of fantastic analysis to a work of imaginative literature. It may well be that, far from heightening appreciation, this curious dissection tends to belittle the author's creation and impair our enjoyment of it.

Oh hell, let's give credit where credit is due. The academic and psychotherapeutic redactors are just trying to unweave, unravel, unwind, and piece together this masterpiece the way I am. They, most of them, anyway, are usually harmless professors of English somewhere trying to make a living in an uncertain world.

* * *

"You ought to be ashamed of yourself," said Alice, "a great girl like you," (she might well say this).

Alice is castigating herself yet noting that she is old enough and developed enough for a more mature poise ("great girl" meaning "big girl" in Victorian British English).

Blame and praise in the same sentence and both self-addressed and followed by an authorial comment. What's up?

Blame and praise are both irrelevant to the consideration of an issue unless we know the reasons for the blame or praise. As no reasons are supplied, the two probably represent flip sides of the classically irrelevant emotional arguments known as insult and flattery.

Insult: Insulting people and calling them names is a diversion, totally irrelevant to the rational consideration of any issue. Whether Alice is great or should be ashamed makes no sense unless we get the reasons that she is great or the reasons she should feel ashamed.

That I am simple or unschooled has nothing to do with whether I am right or wrong. About a particular issue, a simple and unschooled person can be right or he can be wrong, just as an intelligent and educated person could be right or wrong about a particular issue. Calling me names or subjecting me to abuse is irrelevant. In the same way, whether I am sympathetic, unsympathetic, or even biased does not demolish my argument. Prejudiced, unsympathetic people can be right, and impartial people are sometimes wrong. Calling me a communist or a terrorist or another name is just another attempt to distract attention from the real point at issue, which is, all too often, the weakness, or in many cases the nonexistence, of the opponent's argument. Thus, if people call me unpatriotic for opposing the war in Iraq, they are arguing off the issue. Whether I am patriotic or not patriotic is not relevant to the question of whether or not the war in Iraq is justified. Calling me unpatriotic is just a low-down weasel way of diverting attention away from the real issue onto something fake.

Flattery: Our need to have our egos flattered makes us vulnerable to the flattery of con men, sycophants, and all sorts of hangers-on. Entertainers and some newspaper and magazine editors prey upon the same human (irrational) need to think well of ourselves, to think that we know more than we actually do. Flattery is a form of emotional argument. All appeals to emotion are irrelevant, including appeals to tradition, personal circumstance, innuendo, obloquy, guilt by association, use of or appeal to pity, shame, or charity.

Watch out! Because we are so influenced by affirmation, we can be easily manipulated by the cheap trick of flattery: "I really hate to ask you this because you have been so kind and generous to me in the past, but would you mind loaning me another hundred thousand dollars? I feel that I can venture this because, unlike those other stingy bastards, you possess the true spirit of Christian charity."

The petitioner has used flattery rather than reason for his request.

In fact, other than the dubious moral argument that a true Christian would make the loan, no evidence of need is mentioned, nor are we advised about the interest on the loan, payback conditions, collateral, insurance, and so on.

ARGUMENTS THAT APPEAL TO
VIOLENCE OR THREAT ARE IRRATIONAL

All threats of violence, all acts of violence—though sometimes effective in getting things that are wanted—are not relevant to the conclusion, are related to emotions and not reason, and are therefore unreasonable. Emotions may influence us to help or to do something, and there is a growing body of philosophic information indicating that emotions may have epistemic value, but that is beside the point here. The point is that a punch in the nose or the threat of a punch in the nose is not a reasonable argument.

EMOTIONAL ARGUMENTS DON'T MAKE SENSE

The point is that emotional appeals are not relevant to a reasoned conclusion. Emotions are poor substitutes for real evidence. Use of emotion to get to the truth is a poor substitute for thinking. Alice shouldn't do it. Neither should you.

"Trust me. You have nothing to fear."

Unsupported by reasons, the command to trust is irrelevant. When coupled with the above assertion, one might do well to be on guard. If someone keeps repeating "*trust me*," the implication is that there might be some reason to doubt that he or she is trustworthy because the attempt is to convince us of something that may in fact not be true. Just watch a few dozen Hollywood movies and see how often the villain utters "*trust me*" just before he does something dirty.

"You are not going to pass this course unless you sleep with me."

Attempting to persuade others of a position by threatening them with some undesirable state of affairs instead of presenting evidence for one's view is irrelevant. This ploy might work, but it is wrong and it is not a reasoned argument. Furthermore, punishments for this kind of unethical behavior are severe.

* * *

"Let me think: was I the same when I got up this morning? I almost think I can remember feeling a little different."

Most of us, like Alice, can remember feeling different (not just a little different) when we woke up this morning, as that is the usual case when we first awaken. In fact, I never feel quite like myself until I have had my morning cup of coffee. But does feeling different have anything to do with basic identity?

If it doesn't, then Alice has given us a non sequitur, of which there will be many more as her story continues. A non sequitur leaves us flat because the connection between it and what had been said before is nonexistent or obscure. A non sequitur passes through us just like a neutrino—no effect.

Or maybe this is another distinction without a difference. Orange (the color) marmalade is different from orange (the fruit) marmalade. But as the jar was empty, the distinction makes no difference. The fact that we feel (not just a little) different or that Alice feels a little different now compared to how we felt this morning or how she felt in the morning is a distinction without a difference. Our essential real nature has not changed.

The fact that Alice has changed since this morning doesn't mean that the essential self, the real Alice, is not the same person this afternoon who she was this morning. The reason for this is that the changes that occurred are minor and have little or no effect on or relationship to the overall personality. The change is there. But the change is not important.

Trivial things stand as trivia and are not to be overblown or assigned more weight than they are worth. Frequently, citing trivia is a diversionary argument designed to focus attention away from a real issue onto something fake. It is a distinction without a difference.

"I wasn't cheating. I was just looking over her shoulder at her paper to jog my memory, to check my answers, and to improve my grade."

This student is cheating. Whether he acted for the reasons specified is irrelevant to the issue. He is making a distinction without a difference.

"I didn't lie to you. I told you what you wanted to hear."

She did lie. Whether one did it for such a reason or not, it is still a lie. She is making a distinction without a difference.

Alice is different in the afternoon compared to the morning. But the difference doesn't make a difference in her overall functioning. It is a distinction all right. But the difference doesn't amount to a hill of beans.

Another form of the same diversion is to refute some trivial point of an opponent's argument and then suggest that his whole position has been undercut. Whether the argument is undercut by the discovery of some incorrect and relatively trivial fact referred to in support of it would depend on how much the conclusion is dependent on the incorrect statement of fact and not dependent on the discovery of the misstated fact per se.

"Britney Spears is not beautiful because her hands are too small."

Whether Britney is beautiful or not would not depend so much on the size of her hands as on the overall impression of her beauty. In reaching a reasonable conclusion, we should consider all the relevant evidence for her beauty and not make crucial a partially selected part of the evidence such as the size of the woman's hands. Her hand size might be small and her hands might not be beautiful, but that might be unrepresentative evidence of the whole beauty scene and insufficient evidence to draw the conclusion that she is not beautiful.

* * *

"But if I'm not the same, the next question is 'Who in the world am I?' Ah, that's

the great puzzle!"

Yes, that is the great puzzle. Multiple books in psychiatry and psychology have been written on the subject. And a great deal of modern literature concerns itself with this same question. My experience, however, is that this question almost never occurs to a child. Children know who they are. In fact I would wager that children never have a doubt that they are someone and that that someone is important. Anyone who has a granddaughter (I have four: Callie, Shae Mia, Arden, and Miranova) knows that's a fact.

Children don't question their existence. Children may pretend they are someone else or something else, but that's just pretend, a recreation. My granddaughter Callie Patten is fond of pretend:

> "Real is nice, but pretend is nicer."
> —Callie Patten

> "Today I'm a hedgehog and will spend the day in my burrow."
> —Callie Patten

"Who am I?" is really an adult question—made by, for, and about adults. The proof that an adult is asking this question is Carroll's immediate Oxford donnish textbook-type launch of the discussion into the classical Aristotelian examination of similarities and differences—the kind of thinking that underlies all classifications related to genus and species. The genus represents the similarities and the species represents the differences. And both genus and species, similarities and differences, enable us to classify individual types. Furthermore, according to Aristotle, if the genus and species of two things are the same, then the two items can be compared by quantity. His illustration: money is the same as other money. So the way to compare one pile of money with another is by quantity. About money, incidentally, Aristotle concluded that it was better to have more money than less. Most of us would agree with the master.

COMPARING ITEMS BY SIMILARITIES, DIFFERENCES, AND AMOUNTS

With similarities and differences in mind, let's look at how our little Alice manages the similarities, differences, and amounts involved in separating her identity from that of others: *"Alice began thinking over all the children she knew that were the same age as herself, to see if she could have been changed for any of them."*

Thus Alice comes up with the idea that she is similar to other children her age. If she is similar to other children in multiple relevant respects, then she might belong to the genus child, which, incidentally, she does.

What about the differences? Will the differences make enough difference to establish her identity? The quote is Carroll's. The shout type in brackets is mine to illustrate the points:

> *"I'm sure I'm not Ada," she said, "for her hair goes in such long ringlets, and mine doesn't go in ringlets at all [**distinction based on quality and on form difference**]; and I'm sure I ca'n't be Mabel, for I know all sorts of things, and she, oh, she knows such a very little [**distinction based on differences and amount of knowledge**]."*

So Alice knows that she is not those two girls. But this mental process doesn't address the real question. Alice didn't want to know who she isn't; she wanted to know who she is. Negative definitions are like that—rather limited.

In fact, negative assertions are hard to prove. Can you prove that you are not a communist? They can prove you are by finding the card in your wallet. But you can't prove you aren't. Can I prove I am not a child pornographer? The FBI might prove I am by finding certain stuff on my computer—provided they didn't plant the pornographic pictures there. But I can't prove that I am not a child pornographer.

The reason that a negative assertion is so hard to prove is that by its nature there is no evidence to support it. The lack of evidence, however, is never evidence of absence. If we see it, we believe it. If we don't see it, we don't know. The evidence could have been there and we missed it or maybe it wasn't there at all. The fact that the evidence is not there now doesn't mean it won't show up later. Perhaps at some time in the future the evidence will surface. Perhaps not. Meanwhile, in the absence of evidence, we just don't know.

Senator Lloyd Bentsen used a negative definition when he told Dan Quayle on TV: "I knew Jack Kennedy. You're no Jack Kennedy."

Whew! That was a good thing because if Quayle were Jack Kennedy, then it would have meant that Kennedy came back from the dead or didn't die in the first place, in the which case LBJ shouldn't have become president, history would have to have been rewritten, and so forth.

But you know we have to be practical: Sometimes negative definitions are acceptable without definite proof. Most of us would grant that Quayle was not Jack Kennedy. But neither was Bentsen nor anyone else for that matter. Quayle is Quayle and Kennedy no longer exists as he was killed.

So what?

Bentsen's remark was just a low-down sneaky way of insulting Quayle by comparing him to the then-exalted JFK. That was the negative spin Benson was trying to put on it. But actually, I would rather be an alive Quayle than a dead JFK. And although I don't know this for sure, it seems highly probable that Quayle himself would rather be an alive Quayle than a dead JFK. How about you?

For exercise, try proving that Santa Claus doesn't exist. Then compare my answer, which appears at the end of this chapter, with yours. Do your comparison the Aristotelian way by looking at similarities, differences, and amounts. Hint: Assume that Santa does not exist and that, consequently, there is no way to prove he doesn't exist. Nevertheless, adduce evidence that will show that the probability of Santa existing is mighty low. We will come back to this question soon. Meanwhile, THINK!

BACK TO ALICE'S QUEST FOR HERSELF

Alice continues her quest for herself by talking about what she knows. In the process Alice exhibits a vast ignorance of mathematics (she says four times five is twelve) and geography (she says London is the capital of Paris, etc.), all of which are particular examples of particular kinds of knowledge that are provable and capable of being known absolutely. Because they are capable of being known absolutely, they should be, when true, absolutely defended as true. And when they are known to be false, as here, they should be absolutely stated to be false. Let the record show that now and forever four times five is twenty and London is not the capital of Paris. London is the capital of England.

Alice's search for a personal identity by demonstration of her misinformation on multiple subjects is funny but not relevant to the important question "Who am I?" which remains at this instant not answered because it is, as Lewis Carroll knew, fundamentally unanswerable.

Unanswerable?

Whoa! Why is that question unanswerable?

There are multiple reasons for why this question is not answerable, but the main one is, I think, that the "I" asking the question would have to not know the answer. How else could it reasonably ask the question? Dig?

If the "I" asking the question doesn't know the answer, then how could that same "I" know the answer? It either knows or it doesn't. If it asks the question sincerely, then it doesn't know. If it doesn't know and asks, it can't know and answer. This is a logical contradiction that as far as I can see cannot be resolved.

ARISTOTLE: ON THE PROBLEM OF
PERSONAL IDENTITY

Aristotle considered the question of personal identity one of the first principles. That is, Aristotle thought we are ourselves and know it as a matter of fact even though we do change throughout our lives. Aristotle, as usual, is probably right: I know I am the same person that I was in high school and you know you are fundamentally the same person. If you are like me, you probably think that you—that is, the essential you, the deep heart's core of you—hasn't really changed your whole life long.

The problem was that Aristotle was in the same boat as Alice. He couldn't prove who he was. He certainly couldn't prove that, despite the obvious changes with aging, the essential person he was—the essential he—had not changed. This is especially difficult when one looks in the mirror as the changes are obvious. How did Aristotle get around that fact?

Aristotle believed those external changes were superficial and not significant. He thought they were distinctions that make little or no difference.

Hence, Aristotle declared personal identity one of the first principles. He considered a first principle any truth that can't be proven and must be accepted (like an axiom in geometry) as self-evident. This is, of course, old school. The modern approach recognizes that the most we can hope for is a set of postulates that we choose to accept as true. Euclid's axiom that things equal to the same thing are equal to each other might be therefore accepted as self-evident. But modernists might say that you really can't prove that is true. Therefore, it is really a postulate, not a self-evident truth. Postulate or axiom, the idea of personal identity will surface again many times in AAW, but about it, I intend to say no more because it's too nitty-gritty and twee.

Marcus Aurelius (121–180 CE), the Roman emperor and philosopher, pays tribute in his sole literary work, *The Meditations*, to the nephew of Plutarch, a professional philosopher from Chaeronea called Sextus, who taught the emperor not to think too much about "trivial things." What's good enough for the emperor should be good enough for us. But it is not enough for our poor little Alice who will return to the question of personality in chapter 5 when she confronts (yes, confronts—there is no other word) the Caterpillar.

For now, Alice starts reciting the famous "How doth the little crocodile" poem. But as soon as she has finished, she admits, *"I'm sure those are not the right words."*

This poem about a crocodile welcoming little fishes in with gently smiling jaws is nonsense. But it is nonsense that makes a good deal of sense in terms of the ruthless world Alice has entered, not to mention the one she has left. The poem is a parody of a (previously well-known and now not famous and virtually forgotten) poem by Isaac Watts concerning the busy bee who improves each shining hour with books, work, or healthful play. Carroll has stripped this Watts poem of its piety. For as the busy bee gathers food, so likewise does the crocodile, but instead of honey, the crocodile eats fishes. There is no talk of improving use of time in the crocodile's case, but there is plenty of talk of direct self-improvement by eating. Self-interest rather than a fake altruism is exposed as the basic motive (a good lesson for anyone to learn and keep in mind). And self-interest is clearly represented as antithetical to the interest of others. Thus with this crocodile-eats-fish fact, Carroll puts the lie to the many moralistic children's lesson book verses that children like the real Alice had to learn, lessons that simply don't come out right either underground or above ground, in Wonderland or outside of Wonderland, or, for that matter, anywhere: They are not in line with the reality principle. What is more, and this is the killer, one creature may eat another not just out of need but for the pleasure of eating. That's a shocker. Regrettably, it's true.

And the moral of the croc poem is: It's a harsh, cruel world out there full of primitive terror. The sooner children learn that lesson the better.

By the way, if you don't believe that it is a harsh, cruel world out there, try walking around Houston or any other American city without a dime in your pocket.

* * *

As she said these words her foot slipped, and in another moment, splash! she was up to her chin in salt-water. Her first idea was that she had somehow fallen into the sea, "and in that case I can go back by railway," she said to herself.

Ho! Ho! Ho!

This is a fine example of elliptical thinking where a conclusion is reached too fast and without rational justification.

For want of a nail, the kingdom was lost. If you don't know the poem and the connecting events, you don't get it. If you do know the poem, it makes sense because a chain of reasoning has been supplied.

Alice omitted a chain of reasoning. But her conclusion is not justified because her premise is contrary to fact. She can't go home by railway because she hasn't fallen into the sea. She isn't at Brighton. There is no railway.

The type of reasoning displayed here is called *sorites* (saw-rye'-it-teas) from the Greek meaning "heap." A sorites is a series of premises (stated or implied) followed by a conclusion arranged so that the predicate of the first premise is the subject of the next, and so forth, the conclusion uniting the subject of the first with the predicate of the last in an elliptical series of syllogisms, the entire false sequence of which is based on Alice's emotional need to go home.

Going home is an important topic. Like Dorothy in *The Wizard of Oz*, Alice is trying for that. Home base, home plate, homecoming, no matter what we call it, home is that special place at the end of a journey. Why is going home so important? Is it because being home is relaxing and makes us feel warm, safe, and cozy? Thus, the saying "Home sweet home"? Home, according to Robert Frost, is the place where they have to take you in.

Home is a lot more, of course. Our home is where we feel secure and keep our prized possessions, raise our family, and spend most of our time. Home gives us a social identity. The location, type, and condition of our homes reflect what's going on in our life and what matters most to us. No wonder that, on tasting the salt water, Alice's first idea was that she was at the beach and therefore would likely find the way to go home.

AVOID CONCLUSIONS FROM FIRST IMPRESSIONS

First ideas or first impressions to the extent that they are emotionally based and not reasoned are often in error. Such error is compounded when linked to a series of other ideas that seem to follow from the first impression.

Here Alice's reasoning is truncated. If it were spelled out in textual steps, Alice's chain of assumptions (her sorites) might be depicted as follows: The water that I have fallen into is salty. All salty water comes from the ocean. Therefore, I'm in the sea. Since I'm in the sea, I must be near a seaside resort. Seaside resorts always have railroad stations. Therefore, there must be a railroad station nearby. If this is a seaside resort, it must be like Brighton. Last time I was at Brighton, I came home by railway. Therefore, I shall be able to return home this time in the same fashion, by railway.

Let's look at Alice's statement again now that we understand it, because now that we understand it we can appreciate what a great insight Lewis Carroll had into the thinking of children: *"Her first idea was that she had somehow fallen into the sea, 'and in that case I can go back by railway,' she said to herself."*

The kind of thinking in steps sometimes goes by the name of domino theory. Correct reasoning like this has to have a separate justification for each item and a separate justification for each link in the chain of connected items. Some logicians call the justification for the link the warrant of inference. Warrant or whatnot or whatever it's called, if there is no justification for the link, the conclusion is not justified.

"Once you start smoking cigarettes, you'll smoke weed. Once you smoke weed, you'll start using cocaine and all the hard stuff. After that it's all down hill either to jail or to the cemetery."

Recognize the domino theory as applied to tobacco cigarettes? The overwhelming majority of tobacco users (and there are 71 million in the United States right now, according to the Centers for Disease Control and Prevention) never advance to cocaine or heroin. They do, however, end up in the cemetery, just like everybody else.

Another example: In the 1960s, President Johnson told us that if Vietnam fell to the communists, then Laos and Cambodia would fall to the communists and then all Southeast Asia would fall, and then the Indian subcontinent and then perhaps the whole Western world. His reasoning on these issues was called the domino theory. The idea was based on the false analogy that countries are like dominoes, that when one country falls, nearby others will fall in succession like dominoes, and that all the countries mentioned are similar to each other as similar as dominoes are to each other.

What's the defect in LBJ's thinking?

Countries are not dominoes. When their government changes, they don't fall anywhere. Even dominoes don't behave like dominoes unless meticulously set up on their narrower sides in metastable equilibrium.

In the harsh retrospective glare of history, we now know Johnson was wrong. Vietnam did "fall," but even that single nation didn't become communist, not entirely. Vietnam has a mixed economy, as do most countries of the world. Vietnam is now one of the most favored trading partners of the United States. Furthermore, when Vietnam fell (that is, when it won the war it was fighting with the United States), it subsequently fought a war with China and a war with Cambodia. In both those wars, Vietnam was fighting for its independence. Communism had little to do with it. Not only was the domino theory wrong in itself, it led to a wrong prediction about the future.

* * *

True, Alice had been to the sea once in her life, and had come to the general conclusion that, wherever you go on the English coast, you find a number of bathing-machines in the sea, some children digging in the sand with wooden spades, then a row of lodging-houses, and behind them a railway station.

This paragraph explains that there was no evidence, however skimpy, for Alice's thinking. She found none of the above listed items near the pool of tears. Hence, she soon realized she was in the pool of tears and not at the beach. The main thing that had fed her distorted reasoning was her emotional need to go home. Danger alert! When your emotions are involved, clear thinking often goes out the window.

To her credit, Alice figured out that her imagination had overgeneralized from her limited seaside experience. She then correctly perceives the reality: She is not in the sea. She is in the pool of salty tears that she had wept when she was nine feet high.

* * *

Alice emerges from her self-wrought sea to meet a menagerie of animals including the Dodo, the Duck, the Lory, and the Eaglet.

As discussed, much has been made of that. William Empson claimed that the emergence of Alice from the sea reflects Lewis Carroll's interest in evolution—for all life evolved from the sea. Charles Darwin published *The Origin of Species* (not, as many say, "Origin of the Species") in 1859, six years before the publication of AAW, so the timing is compatible with Empson's theory. Empson also suggested that the inclusion of the Dodo (a large flightless bird extinct since 1681, long before the publication of AAW) refers to Darwin's theories of the stronger species surviving longer than the weaker species.

This is an unschooled simplification of the theory of natural selection and, as such and to that extent, is wrong. It is also an unschooled misunderstanding of the textual history of AAW. We will see in the next chapter that there is a much more reasonable explanation for the presence of the Dodo and his friends. In fact, in the next chapter we will find out who the Dodo is. Can you guess? Hint: Lewis Carroll stammered and so did five of his sisters. When he gave his name at the beginning class, he often stammered, "Do, do, Dodgson."

* * *

"I dare say it's a French mouse, come over with William the Conqueror." (For, with all her knowledge of history, Alice had no very clear notion how long ago anything had happened.)

This is tongue-in-cheek. But the point is clear: When Alice doesn't know, she should find out. Most, if not all, English school children would know or should know that the Norman conquest started in 1066. As the daughter of the dean of Christ Church, Oxford, the real Alice would have known this date and that fact. Therefore, this is an underhanded way for Carroll to try to flatter the real Alice, just as some authors make the readers know more than the characters do. Showing characters that are silly, stupid, or ignorant flatters readers into thinking well of themselves. And that helps make sales.

By the way, the Norman conquest was not all bad. It led to the very language we speak, through a fusion of Norman French with Anglo-Saxon. And it led to the *Domesday Book*, a population and property survey of England in 1086. Much historic fact about economic, social, and political conditions in England of the time has come out of the *Domesday Book*.

THINGS TO REMEMBER—
PROGRESS BOX FOR CHAPTER 2

- A conclusion must be justified by evidence. If the evidence is relevant and adequate, then the conclusion is justified. If the evidence is not relevant or not adequate, the conclusion is not supported.
- All emotional appeals, including appeals to shame or the use of flattery, are irrelevant as they avoid consideration of the facts.
- Facts are important. Get them straight before using what you think you know to make decisions. Always check what you don't understand or haven't verified.
- All threats and all appeals to the use of force are irrelevant arguments.
- When considering evidence, all the available evidence must be taken into account, not just the elements that suit emotional

needs or prefigured conclusions. Selecting only part of the evidence is likely to skew the view of reality and lead to error.

- Chains of reasons must provide warrants for the links as well as support for the premises, otherwise the chain of reasoning is defective and likely to prove wrong.
- First impressions are often wrong because they are based on hunches and emotional elements and not based on evidence and reason.
- Sorry, kids, no Santa.

3

A Caucus Race and a Long Tale

Indeed, she had quite a long argument with the Lory, who at last turned sulky, and would only say "I'm older than you, and must know better." And this Alice would not allow, without knowing how old it was, and, as the Lory positively refused to tell its age, there was no more to be said.

Whether or not the Lory is older than Alice is not relevant to the argument because age does not make a person's argument correct or incorrect. An older person can be right or wrong. Therefore, age is irrelevant to the truth. Obviously the Lory (a type of Australian parrot and also a concealed reference to Alice's older sister, Lorina) is trying to appeal to authority, in this case the authority supposedly imputed to age.

Citing an authority is often a diversionary technique designed to focus attention away from the real issue and onto something fake. Appeals to authority are among the classical false arguments. This one, like the other classical false arguments, has an honorable Latin name: *argumentum ad verecundiam*. *Verecundiam* in Latin means something like "out of respect for." Thus an argumentum ad verecundiam is an argument out of respect for something, usually a respect for authority. The problem is that an argument out of respect for authority is sometimes an argument that is "all out of" respect for reality, that is, not respectful of reality.

WHY THE CRYSTAL BALL IS CLOUDED

Need proof when I say don't trust authority? Good! That's the spirit. Skepticism is better than blind belief. As C. P. Snow said, "When you consider the long and gloomy history of man, you find more hideous crimes have been committed in the name of obedience than have been committed in the name of rebellion."

Want me to prove that authorities can be and are often wrong? My pleasure: It is always disturbing to learn that authorities, even those who are highly trained and professional, can be wrong. Unfortunately, this situation is not unusual. Let's take medicine. If economics is the dismal science, medicine is the abysmal science.

George Washington died of the quinsy, a severe acute suppurative infection of the faucial tonsil and surrounding tissues of the throat. What did mainstream medicine at the time offer him as the treatment? If you guessed incision and drainage, you were wrong. If you guessed tracheostomy to bypass the obstruction to his breathing, you were wrong. If you guessed antibiotics, you were wrong, as they didn't exist. If you guessed repeated bleeding, you were right.

Repeated bleeding does nothing for infection except make it worse. Yet that was the official treatment for old George. Predictably, he got weaker and weaker. The infection spread. George died.

Well, at least our first president was spared some of the other standard treatments of the time: emetics, ointments, amulets, purgatives, spatula mundani (for constipation), clysters, and hog's flesh. Yes, lady, I said hog's flesh. In 1626, a certain Doctor John Potts of Jamestown, Virginia, was sued for denying hog's flesh to a woman who miscarried. This was probably America's first malpractice suit.

A century later after George Washington, as mentioned, Lincoln stopped those little blue pills because they were making him feel lousy. They were mercury salts prescribed for his depression. And lucky he stopped them, otherwise the Great Emancipator might have ended as a suicide.

Consider the estrogen story: Not long ago estrogens were routinely prescribed to women from menopause to death with the view of saving them from heart attacks, stroke, dementia, hot flashes, and almost everything else that goes wrong with women as they age. The more recent studies show estrogens cause strokes and heart attacks. Therefore, they are no longer prescribed because on balance they do more harm than good. Recent evidence from epidemiologists shows a significant decline in breast cancer and other endocrine-dependent cancers in women. Perhaps the hormones were also causing cancers.

How about objective studies of a simple thing like knee surgery? No difference was found in pain, function, recovery, and so on in men getting complete knee operations versus those who get only a sham incision over the knee.

Take tonsillectomy: There was a time when tonsillectomy was fashionable. I had one. Did you? The American Child Health Association surveyed a group of 1,000 children, eleven years of age, from the public schools of New York City, and found 611 of these had had their tonsils removed. The remaining 389 were then examined by a group of physicians, who selected 174 for tonsillectomy and declared the rest had no tonsil problem. The remaining 215 were reexamined by another group of doctors, who recommended 99 of these for tonsillectomy. When the 116 "healthy" children were examined a third time, a similar percentage were told their tonsils had to be removed. After some more examinations only 65 children remained who had not been recommended for the operation. Today, tonsillectomy is considered dubious surgery of no value in most cases. Numerous other studies have shown similar results about all sorts of medical procedures, from appendectomy and hysterectomy to interpretation of chest x-rays (error rate: 30 percent). Professional staff in psychiatric hospitals have been proven unable to tell the sane from the insane. And so forth.

Don't get me wrong. I am not beating up on doctors. Why should I? I am a doctor. So is my wife. So are my two children. But my son, Craig, is not a "real" doctor. His is a PhD in biophysics. Nevertheless, he has a doctorate and therefore is a doctor. So I am not beating up on doctors. I am just telling you the facts, the reality.

The point is that we should not take for granted the reliability and accuracy of medical authority. Demand proof! Demand evidence! Empower yourself! Judge and think for yourself! Ask questions. Read. Consult others.

THE KEY TAKE-HOME MESSAGE

All arguments in accord with reality are right. All arguments not in accord with reality are wrong. They are wrong because they are likely to get us into trouble with reality. You either deal with reality realistically or you don't. If you don't, then reality may harshly deal with you.

Arguments citing authority ignore that point, divert us from full consideration of the evidence and therefore, to that extent, divert us from consideration of the full reality. Therefore they are wrong. Such arguments tend to overgeneralize, prevent rational thinking, and prove simplistic and unreasonable.

From which follows:

Lesson: When someone like the Lory puts on the cloak of authority, treat him or her with suspicion, if not disdain. Experts can be wrong. They can be right too. Whether they are right or wrong depends not on their authority as such but on analysis of the facts and their reasons. Whether such facts or conclusions or whatnot apply to us or can be otherwise generalized must be demonstrated by evidence and not from the mere assertion of authority. Who the authorities are doesn't count. Their evidence (if relevant and adequate) and their contact with reality does count.

In the case of Lory, the supposed authority of being older is asserted by her as the reason that Alice should believe what Lory says. Mere assertion is no reason to believe anything. If you ask someone why you should do such and such or believe such and such and he says, "Because I say so," just laugh and walk away. Because someone says something, even if he is older, or wiser, or in a position of authority or power, or a famous movie star, or (God help us) a TV commentator, the president of the United States, or whoever, does not automatically render true what he says. Mere assertion does not make it so. Demand proof.

APPEALS TO AUTHORITY ARE IRRELEVANT

All appeals to authority are irrelevant because they do not concern evidence. What counts is not the person making the assertion, but the assertion itself and the evidence supporting it. We should believe something only if the evidence tells us to believe it. The evidence must be relevant and adequate. Adequate evidence should be sufficient in quantity, kind, and weight to justify the conclusion. Respect for authority is wrong when it is based on disrespect for evidence. Respect for authority is wrong when that gestured respect might involve disrespect for reality. I emphasize this point because it is key to keeping us out of trouble. This kind of clear thinking is not just fun. It also tends to keep us safer, make us more efficient, and generally give us an edge.

Sadly, the sorry history of blood-soaked Europe from 800 BCE through the twentieth century shows that too many people put too much trust in too many authority figures much too often, as C. P. Snow pointed out above. Compliant men and women did much to the detriment of humanity. They still do.

Alice missed the above points. She wanted to make her evaluation of the Lory's argument contingent on Lory telling her age. Her statement shows that she has uncritically accepted the Lory's unsupported and unwarranted assumption that if Lory were older, then Lory would know better. Too bad Alice's courage, which seemed to be on the rise, crumbled in confrontation with this arrogant bird. Alice should never accept unsupported statements without proof from a Lory or from anyone. Nor should we.

Note also that Lory could have won the argument by telling her age. The fact that she did not suggests that she feared she was younger, not older, than Alice. How else can we explain her sulkiness and her refusal to tell? Unless Lory is just one of those people who refuse to be amenable to argument.

Carroll disliked such people and suggests (in a letter) that "They must be restrained, like brute beasts, by physical force." Here Carroll is joking of course. He knows that the use of force is the ultimate bad argument, the *argumentum ad baculum.*

Argumentum ad baculum: Appeal to force; a grave error, wherein the argument has degenerated into a fight. Might doesn't make right, despite the maxim to the contrary. Because someone defeats another person by force doesn't mean he was right or wrong, noble or ignoble, supported by God or by the Devil, and so on. It merely means he won the battle, no more and no less. Resort to force is not among the rational forms of argument. It is quite the opposite.

Unless, unless, Lory's age is already known to the real Alice. That would be the case if Lory is Alice's dream representation of her older sister, Lorina. In fact, a case could be made that the Duck in this scene represents the Reverend Robinson Duckworth and the Dodo is Dodgson himself who, we have seen, had a bad stammer and often stammered his name (Do-Do-Dodgson). For that reason, the Oxford crowd called Dodgson "the Dodo" after the extinct flightless bird. After a while Dodgson called himself the Dodo probably because it was easier for him to say than his full last name. Perhaps he identified with the Dodo, the flightless bird from Mauritius that became extinct in 1681. Dodgson wasn't extinct, of course, but I'll bet he felt anachronistic in front of those Oxford students and when talking with the other Dons.

How do we know for sure that the Dodo represents Lewis Carroll? Crucial evidence: Lewis Carroll inscribed his gift edition of AAW to Duckworth: "To the Duck from the Dodo." Such an analysis would, by reductive elimination, make Edith, Alice's younger sister, the Eaglet. If this is true, we shouldn't wonder why Eaglet complains that the others in the party are using big words that she doesn't understand!

In the first version of the story, *Alice's Adventures Underground,* Alice remarks that she, the Lory, and the Eaglet are just like sisters, that the Duck sang nicely as they came through the water, and that the Dodo fortunately knew the way to a cottage where they dried off. That narration of events in time closely corresponds with what happened on the actual story-generating boat trip according to the recollections of the real Alice and according to the recollections of Canon Duckworth.

Another point: Lory's statement is truly diversionary because we never learn what she is arguing about. Therefore we can't judge anything. Older sisters, I am informed, are like that. And that indeed may be Carroll's not-so-subtle point here. In effect, he is siding with the fictional Alice against a representation of Alice's older sister, a position likely to gain him a certain degree of affection from the real Alice. This tactic would curry favor, for most people believe (without supporting evidence) that the enemy of my enemy is my friend.

One last point: Carroll may also be savagely parodying the Victorian attitude toward children and the ways in which adults in many times and places patronize and treat children intellectually. The Lory is a kind of pedant who refuses to come to terms with proper discussion of issues or inform the child of the reasons for things. Creatures of that sort insist that we accept what they say without question and at face value merely because they said it. They claim to know best but they don't support that claim with evidence. In so doing such pedants show a single fixed self-serving rigid standard, inimical to children but characteristic of this type of adult mind.

HOW TO TELL WHEN
YOU HAVE WON AN ARGUMENT

About sulkiness: When the opposition turns sulky (as Lory did), it is a good sign that they feel defeated and you have won. Another important sign comes when they start shouting, especially if the shouting includes calling you names. But perhaps the usual way of determining you have won is when the opposition shifts its argument. Remember, inconsistency is the classic way of determining if someone is handing you bullshit.

A splendid recent example of inconsistent shifting arguments occurred in the justifications promulgated for the Iraq war.

First, the war was to find the "massive stockpiles" of weapons of mass destruction. When the wheels fell off that argument, the war was to get rid of Saddam. That argument over, the war was to bring democracy to Iraq. The abuses of prisoners, the fake parliament, rigged elections, and so on, demolished that idea. So now it seems that we are there to repair the damage we did (this is General Powell's bull-in-the-China-shop argument—you pay for what you break) or we are there to vaguely "continue the mission and stay the course." When arguments shift grounds like that, they are, dollars to doughnuts, inauthentic and the arguers are arguing in bad faith. Several more examples of bad faith arguments appear later in AAW as we shall see.

* * *

"Ahem!" said the Mouse with an important air. "Are you all ready? This is the driest thing I know. Silence all round, if you please! 'William the Conqueror, whose cause was favored by the pope, was soon submitted to by the English, who wanted leaders, and had been of late much accustomed to usurpation and conquest.'"

That passage from the history of the Norman conquest is unlikely to dry Alice, who is still wet from her swim in her tears. The confusion (and the fun) arises from the two meanings of the word dry. A dull, boring, and dry history of the Norman invasion has nothing to do with another meaning of the word dry—to remove moisture.

RECITATION AND MEMORY TRAINING ARE PASSÉ

Modern education forgets to teach young people how to remember. No doubt, the real Alice memorized and recited by heart this drier than dust history of the Norman conquest. We know Carroll lifted the passage directly from Alice Liddell's history book. Sure the real Alice didn't understand some of the words (usurpation, for instance), but she could say them quite well. Just as I could, at age six, recite the Apostle's Creed without knowing what was meant by the phrase "conceived by the Holy Ghost."

The Victorian ideal of exact encyclopedic knowledge, parodied in the Mouse's tale, has fallen away. Oration and recitation, staples of the school system that trained me, where everything was memorized, not just poetry, have largely been phased out. Consequently, Britney Spears forgot the words she meant to lip-sync at the MTV Video Music Awards. Thus Britney joins the absent-minded ranks of Katharine McPhee (American Idol runner-up), who dropped a whole line from "Hound Dog," and President Bush, who couldn't recall the punch line of the "Fool me once" aphorism: Fool me once, shame on thee; fool me twice, shame on me.

The *New York Times* reported that Miss Teen South Carolina Lauren Caitlin Upton completely forgot what she was saying in a pageant interview in a clip that became a hit on the Web site YouTube.♠

Why blame them? They are products of a culture that does not enforce the development of memory skills. The older heritage in American education, where recitation was the standard pedagogical mode, has gone the way of the buggy whip. No one even knows phone numbers anymore.

Yes, all that's gone in this age of multitasking, except for poetry memorization, which held on because it supposedly helped develop the mind. Then there were slews of psychological tests that discovered that memorizing poetry doesn't do much more than help you memorize poetry. Still poetry held on. More recent neurobic science says poetry memory exercises stave off dementia and that memory needs a workout as much as abs do. So, once again, poetry hangs on.

♠ Jenny Lyn Bader, "That's All She Rote," *New York Times*, September 16, 2007.

BEWARE POMPOSITY AND POMPOUS PERSONS

Times have not changed: for even today, lots of absurd solutions to problems are proposed to us "with an important air." And with that important air, the Mouse continues the dry history of England:

> *"Edwin and Morcar, the earls of Mercia and Northumbria, declared for him; and even Stigand, the patriotic archbishop of Canterbury, found it advisable—"*
> *"Found what?" said the Duck.*
> *"Found it," the Mouse replied rather crossly; "of course you know what it means."*
> *"I know what it means well enough, when I find a thing," said the Duck: "it's generally a frog, or a worm. The question is, what did the archbishop find?"*

The Mouse did not notice this question but hurriedly went on. Did the Mouse not notice the question? Or were there other reasons he did not respond? 1. Perhaps he didn't know the answer. 2. Perhaps he was too involved with the sequence of his poll-parrot recitation and didn't want to get bollixed. 3. Perhaps he just wouldn't brook an interruption. All, one, or any combination of 1, 2, or 3.

"As wet as ever," said Alice in a melancholy tone: "it doesn't seem to dry me at all."

Good for Alice.

She proves the dry talk has had no effect on wet clothes. Alice had a perfect right, some would say an obligation, to take her own experience seriously. In voicing concern for results, she again positions herself in the camp of the pragmatists and the logical positivists, people who think that reality counts.

By denouncing the dry words as ineffective in drying *her*, Alice is telling us that reality counts more than words and that events (results, effects, actions, etc.) must remain the controlling influence on conclusions. Things in themselves, not what we say or think about them, are more closely congruent with reality because the things in themselves have an existence independent of what we think of them.

Don't believe me? Not convinced? Listen to the master, Aristotle:

"True statements are extremely useful, not only for knowing but also for living"; "Arguments about emotions and actions are less trustworthy than the facts themselves."♠

Well? What, in fact, did the archbishop find when he found it advisable? The officious mouse ignored the question. When one ignores the question, you know you are on to something important; you know you've hit a sore spot. The mouse has mounted one of the most primitive of defense mechanisms. He has ignored a valid inquiry.

By the way, "it" can have many meanings. For the duck it's usually a frog or a worm. For those who sport the following bumper stickers, it is usually a crude reminder of basic sexuality:

FARMERS DO IT IN THEIR WELLIES
WATER SKIERS DO IT STANDING UP
HOOT IF YOU HAD IT LAST NIGHT
HANG GLIDERS DO IT IN MIDAIR
CURRENCY TRADERS DO IT BACK TO BACK
WHY DO IT YOURSELF WHEN YOU CAN DO IT WITH ME?

Many words besides "it" in English have confusing or vague referents that depend on context. Take for instance the word *took* as in "The passengers took the boat up river." In the ordinary sense, the passengers would pay the captain for their trip. But in another sense the captain might take after them for theft. Here is yet another example of equivocation, multiple meanings of the same word.

Literature is often a matter of multiple meanings embedded in the text. The Prophet claimed that each verse of the Koran has seven meanings, the last meaning of which is known only to God.

Here's an example from George Eliot's immortal novel *The Mill on the Floss*:

"I know what Latin is very well," said Maggie, confidently. "Latin's a language. There are Latin words in the Dictionary. There's bonus, a gift."

♠ Aristotle, *Ethics*, bk. 10.

"Now, you're just wrong there, Miss Maggie!" said Tom, secretly astonished. "You think you're very wise! But 'bonus' means 'good,' as it happens—bonus, bona, bonum."

"Well, that's no reason why it shouldn't mean 'gift,'" said Maggie, stoutly. "It may mean several things—almost every word does. There's 'lawn'—it means the grass-plot, as well as the stuff pocket-handkerchiefs are made of."

Maggie is trice right: bonus means gift; almost every word means several things; lawn refers to a grass-plot as well as to a kind of fine linen resembling cambric from which handkerchiefs are made. The additional embedded meaning here is that Maggie is three times smarter than Tom, which, not incidentally, the text clearly indicates she is.

Here is an example more subtle: (Did you get it when it went by?) Argument out of respect for authority may be out of respect for reality. The play on the two meanings of "out of respect" will become obvious if you think about it. In one case, I mean showing respect for and in the other case I mean out of line with or showing disrespect for. Dig?

Carroll makes much of the double meanings of words later on in passages where "knot" and "not" are confused, and "draw" (as in sketching) and "draw" (as in water from a well), and "axes" (as in chop off your head) and "axis" (as in what the Earth and other planets rotate on), and where flamingoes and mustard both have a bite, and "mine" (the absolute possessive form of "my") gets crossed with "mine" (a place where minerals come from), and so forth. In *Looking-Glass*, the Frog can't understand why anyone would answer the door unless it has been asking something. Get it?

The Bard of Avon himself plays on the double meaning of the word "call" in *Henry IV, Part 1*, where Glendower boasts to Hotspur, "I can call spirits from the vasty deep." "Why, so can I or so can any man," says Hotspur, unimpressed; "but will they come when you do call for them?"

Dig?

"Bob wanted salad for supper. Because the recipe said 'serve without dressing,' I didn't dress. What a surprise when he brought home a friend for supper and they found me naked."

There are two ambiguities here: One is dressing for a salad and the other is dressing meaning putting on clothes. Is there not also a possible confusion about the idea of bringing home a guest to eat and bringing home *a guest to eat?* Eating people, by the way, is wrong.

Pretty stupid stuff, right?

Sometimes funny and often confusing, such examples are always illustrations of the limitations that language imposes or can impose on human thought, expression of thought, and consequent communication. This flexibility in expression is a vice all right. Symbolic logic was invented to clear up the muddle that afflicts human thinking in language. But the ambivalence and nuance of language is also a virtue, especially in poetry, where it expresses beauty and truth succinctly in interesting ways.

Sometimes the ambiguity in language has nothing to do with multiple meanings of words but arises from an uncertainty in construction of a sentence or clause in which the individual words are unequivocal. When that happens it is called amphiboly as distinguished from equivocation, though in popular use the two are confused.

Example: Bob likes tennis more than his wife.

From the construction itself, some of us don't know if Bob likes tennis more than he likes his wife or if Bob likes tennis more than his wife likes tennis. Professors of English tell me that the sentence as constructed and strictly interpreted means that Bob liked tennis more than he liked his wife. But how can that be? Bob's wife is a babe.

Another example from the *New York Times:* "[They] did not pester their parents to buy things they saw advertised, never smoked or drank alcohol, and knew more about wildlife than the leader of a trip to Kenya."◆

It is highly unlikely that these paragons of excellence know more about wildlife than the mentioned expert. And it would be highly unusual for anyone to smoke alcohol as the usual thing is to drink it.

Congressional Quarterly quote of the day: "They never stop thinking

---

◆ Jane E. Brody, "TV's Toll on Young Minds and Bodies," *New York Times,* August 3, 2004.

about new ways to harm our country and our people, and neither do we." That's President Bush's remark referring to al Qaeda at a bill signing on August 5, 2004.

People who use "never" speak at their peril. If, just for one moment, al Qaeda did stop thinking about new ways to harm us and thought about old ways, or about anything else, or just stopped thinking even for a moment, then the presidential statement would be proved wrong.

The same reasoning applies to the president and his buddies: If they should stop thinking about new ways to harm our country and thought about old ways, or about anything else, or just stopped thinking altogether even for a moment, that odd part of the statement is proved wrong.

Actually, from an adult (especially an adult in high office) we expect greater clarity of expression. But imagine children just beginning to learn the language. What confusion! How the devil do they ever get it straight?

But what's the real point? What's Carroll's point in logic? Why do the two different meanings of "dry" in the Mouse's episode add up to nonsense? And why does Carroll go for so many examples of ambiguity? Answer: He is illustrating the importance of the identity principle.

THE IDENTITY PRINCIPLE IN LOGIC

In a bit of reasoned discourse the terms that occur several times must retain their same sense throughout. They can't keep changing their reference. They can't keep changing like the Cheshire Cat. Otherwise, there will be confusion. An argument will clearly be cogent and convincing if and only if in each of its occurrences the word in use retains a fixed meaning with the same name and the same reference frame for the same kind of object or idea. This requirement, that in a given context a term must continue to be used in essentially the same manner, is expressed as the principle of identity. When the identity of a word shifts (that is, when it equivocates), confusion occurs, as AAW so well illustrates.

Humpty Dumpty in *Looking-Glass* says in a famous passage: "When

I use a word, it means just what I choose it to mean—neither more nor less. 'The questions is,' said Alice, 'whether you can make words mean so many different things.' 'The question is,' said Humpty Dumpty, 'which is to be master—that's all.'"

This last statement is a rebuke to Alice, who has not understood the problem: it is not to make words mean so many different things. It is to make a word mean just one thing that its user intends and that the listener understands and nothing else. Which is to be master?—the system of language that says "glory" means "a brilliant radiance" or Humpty, who says "glory" means "a nice knock-down argument"?

"I'm not drinking any more, then again I'm not drinking any less." This joke plays on two meanings of the phrase "any more." Carroll exploits the same problem when the Hatter tells Alice to have more wine when she hasn't had any. Alice chides that she can't have more when she hasn't had any and Hatter opines that you can always have more wine but you can't have less if you have had none. The fun of this exchange is based on the two equivocal meanings of "have more." One meaning relates to having more of what you have had already and the other relates to the possibility of having more to make up for not having had any.

The problem of double meanings and unclear referents and identity shift is exploited in that Abbott and Costello skit wherein Abbott proves that Costello is not there in the studio in New York City:

Abbott: I can prove to you that you are not here.
  Costello: You can't.
Abbott: Not only that. I will get you to say you are somewhere else.
  Costello: Impossible! I am here.
Abbott: You're not in San Francisco, right?
  Costello: Right, I'm not in San Francisco.
Abbott: You're not in Chicago, right?
  Costello: Right, I'm not in Chicago.
Abbott: Well, if you are not in San Francisco and you are not in Chicago, you must be somewhere else, right?
  Costello: I am somewhere else!
Abbott: See, I told you! If you are somewhere else, you can't be here.

What's the confusion?

The confusion is change of context with loss of the identity of the expression "somewhere else."

The expression "somewhere else" is never used in a vacuum or in a context-less way. It always is expressed within a frame of reference. No one can be somewhere else because there is no such place. "Somewhere else" means either not here, where "here" is specifically or implicitly defined, or it means not there where "not there" means somewhere other than the place or places explicitly mentioned. Abbott mentioned San Francisco and Chicago, exploring meaning #2—not there. Costello is somewhere other than San Francisco or Chicago. That's true. Abbott then exploits meaning #1 thereby shifting in this context the identity of the phrase "somewhere else."

Clearly, Costello's admission would in no way imply that Costello is not in New York City, where, incidentally, he was. Costello's admission just means he recognized that he wasn't in San Francisco or Chicago. The problem relates to deictic references: when I say "here" it means something near me; when you say "here" it means something near you. My "here" is your "there"; your "there" is my "here." To Abbott "somewhere else" is not "here" when actually by deictic reference it should be. To Costello "somewhere else" is not in San Francisco or Chicago, but here in the studio in New York City. This mistake is the error of the fourth term (discussed in chapter 1) all over again.

* * *

"... the best thing to get us dry would be a Caucus race."

"What is a Caucus race?" said Alice; not that she much wanted to know, but the Dodo had paused as if it thought that somebody ought to speak, and no one else seemed inclined to say anything."

Lesson: Silence is O.K. If you don't want to know, don't ask. Just keep your mouth shut.

"Why," said the Dodo, "the best way to explain it is to do it."

Those of you who have suffered through tea parties (I am a veteran of seventeen) hosted by your daughter or granddaughter know that the caucus race is often the final event in the party. My granddaughter Callie Patten, after having directed the party for a while, will often stand up and announce, "Let's practice our running!" She will direct us to run in a circle for a variable period of time. The first time I heard this announcement, I almost fell over with delight. Callie had not yet then been exposed to Alice or her story. So Callie's vision of a caucus race was actually a spontaneous demonstration of a basic type of childhood play. Informal, unstructured, and fun, it has no winners and no losers—a game, in which satisfaction comes from playing itself, rather than from winning.

The caucus race is the first game in AAW. In a way it represents the best kind of play, if not the most primitive. There are no clear rules. The play area is vaguely defined—"a sort of circle (the exact shape doesn't matter)." There is no fixed starting point for the runners. There is no finish line. Kids begin when they want and stop when they wish or when their oxygen-deprived, lactic acid–soaked muscles scream out for relief. In effect, it is the kind of play found at Gymboree. Individually, the kids do as they like and yet the game is social in that it includes the notion of having fun in a group—together. Of course everybody wins. All must have prizes.

Notice Alice supplies the comfits (fruit candies) for all participants and accepts her thimble as the reward for her contribution. In a sense, the tax system works this way. The rewards, distributed in the way of benefits from the government, come from the citizens themselves. The usual direction of rewards and benefits is from the haves to the have-nots, as in this case Alice has the candy and the others have not. Recent corporate scandals have temporarily reversed the usual direction of benefit transfer, taking from the have-nots and giving to the haves.

The caucus race and similar sorts of pointless play can also be good for adults—a welcome respite from the rat race. This kind of play is what happens when I enjoy myself in the garden, or take the boat out for a spin, or have fun in any other informal way. It is the kind of play where I set my own rules, begin and leave off when I like, and am aloof (temporarily) from the incursions of others. I would argue that the "free-play" game model of the caucus race is not a mind relic of the play of presocial children. Instead it is a realm of unrule-bound fun and self-expression that can be and often is enjoyed by most people of all ages.

In all, the caucus race demonstrates the arbitrary nature of games. One wins when the rules say so. When there are no rules, there is no winner. The rules themselves are arbitrary inventions of mankind in the sense that they have no real external existence apart from the human significance assigned to them. You can't find the rules of baseball in the forest no matter how many stones you overturn. Nor are they written in the sky on the clouds. The arbitrary nature of games is an insight that recurs throughout AAW, especially in the croquet game at the end where the rules keep changing so quickly that Alice can't figure them out. As she can't figure them out, she cannot play rationally.

Do these games with their arbitrary rules reflect the arbitrary nature of our lives? How about the arbitrary administration of power in AAW? Is that a warning? How about the general chaos during the trial of the Knave of Hearts? A warning? Thanks to the harsh experience of life, supreme mistress of all disciplines, these cautionary indications, I think, take on real meaning. But what is the real meaning behind the meaning? What is the real meaning of life?

Ah, that is a question! That is a question that would require too much time, energy, and work to address, all of which are tasks I don't care to undertake. But I have no objection to your working on that question. Let me know the answer when you get it.

GAMES COME FULL CIRCLE

Returning to the matter in hand: The shape and form of the caucus race demonstrates another aspect of the nature of games: their circularity. In spite of all the purposiveness displayed by the players, the game literally does not get anyone anywhere. Circularity is demonstrated not only in the caucus race, but also in the tea party game (chapter 7) and in the lobster quadrille (chapter 10). Most novels and movies return to the place of the beginning. And I just love it when, at the end of Arthur Clarke's *2001: A Space Odyssey*, Dave sees himself as a fetus.

GAMES—WHAT'S THE POINT?
WHERE DO THEY GET US?

The only place a game gets you, if there are rules, and if winning is permitted, is in front of your opponent. At the tea party, the Hatter, March Hare, and Dormouse keep shifting positions, moving around the table. Alice wants to know what happens when they arrive back at the same place they started. The answer is a clear and resounding— NOTHING!

DEFINITIONS

Among the many kinds of definitions, we find a definition by example especially valuable for motor activities, such as the caucus race, which would be otherwise difficult to explain in words. Try explaining how to ride a bike. Much easier to demonstrate it. Try explaining a caucus race. Much easier to demonstrate it.

Other ways of defining things include generic definition, divisional definition, synonym, or specific criteria. For instance, how can we define anxiety?

Anxiety is a state of being uneasy, apprehensive, or worried about what may happen. This definition is generic as it is expressed in a complete sentence. The same definition could be recast into divisional components to get a divisional definition. Anxiety is a state of being 1. uneasy or 2. Apprehensive or 3. Worried or any combination of 1, 2, or 3.

Anxiety is what I feel when they take my blood pressure at the doctor's office. This is a definition by example.

Anxiety is feeling nervous. This is a definition by the criterion of synonym.

Anxiety is the subjective feeling of nameless dread associated with increased activity of the autonomic nervous system. This is a definition by psychological and physiological criteria. The matter of definitions, and the important problems associated with them, will surface later in AAW, especially in conversations with the Duchess and in the trial of the Knave of Hearts.

THE BATTLE OF LABELS IS
A BATTLE OF DEFINITIONS

Many labels are hidden definitions. Some of these labels have been coined to prejudge the issues or to channel our minds in one direction. Modern linguistics calls this a "frame."

How a problem or question is framed often determines how we think about the problem or question. For example, "partial birth abortion" makes it sound as if this is a medical procedure wherein a birth is taking place and that the birth is being aborted. The official medical term for this procedure is much more neutral: "dilation and extraction."

"Compassionate conservative" is a label designed to appeal to a larger group of voters than either the label "conservative" or "compassionate" would draw in. The conservatives latch onto the conservative part, the liberals to the compassionate part, and bingo—you have two groups of people for the price of one label.

"Casual elegance," as a form of evening attire, is popular: The people who like the casual go for the first part and the people who like the elegant (that is, more formal attire) go for the second. With that in mind, what idea does "pro-choice" encompass? How about "pro-life"? How about "tax relief"? What about the term "tax relief" channels your mind toward the idea that taxes are a burden? And what about the "death tax"? People who want it repealed would like us to think that every poor slob who dies is being punished. "Estate tax" is the more neutral term. Estate taxes are designed to prevent inherited wealth from holding sway over those who don't have it.

WHAT'S A CHICKEN-HAWK?

How about the moniker recently applied to President Bush: "chicken-hawk." On one level, the metaphorical level, it implies that Bush is both a chicken and a hawk. How can that be? He acts like a chicken by his behavior—avoiding combat service in Vietnam, for instance—and talks like a hawk—in making war on Iraq. Thus the term implies a contradiction between behavior and speech. The fun is increased by our knowing that there is another type of chicken-hawk, a real chicken-hawk, a raptor bird that specializes in stealing chickens.

WHAT SHOULD YOU DO IF YOU DON'T UNDERSTAND A WORD?

Whenever you don't know the definition of a word, the best thing to do is look it up. Otherwise, you quite literally don't know what you are talking about. Alice, you will recall, didn't know what she was talking about when she mentioned Latitude and Longitude, Antipathies and Antipodes. No wonder the Eaglet complains to Dodo: "Speak English! I don't know the meaning of half those long words, and, what's more, I don't believe you do either!"

* * *

"Mine is a long and sad tale!" said the Mouse, turning to Alice and sighing.
"It is a long tail, certainly," said Alice, looking down with wonder at the Mouse's tail; "but why do you call it sad?"

"Long" can mean extended in time or extended in space (that is, length). The sound for "tail" and "tale" is identical in oral speech, so the meaning of that sound can only be deduced by examining the context. In written speech, of course, one can examine the spelling.

The Mouse's tale is the best-known example of emblematic, or figured English verse: poems printed in such a way that they resemble something related to their subject. This conceit goes back to ancient Greece. My hero, Charles Sanders Peirce, the American logician and philosopher, was much interested in the visual representation of poetry. In his unpublished papers there is a copy of Poe's "The Raven," written with a technique that Peirce called "art chirography," the words formed so as to convey a visual impression of the poem's ideas. This notion is not as absurd as it may first appear. The technique is used in lettering of ads, book titles, titles of magazine stories, cinema titles, and so on. Don't believe me? Take a look at the opening title cards in Oliver Stone's movie *Alexander*. Alexander's name is stylishly displayed in Greek, English, Persian, Aramaic, Sumerian, Hindi, Latin, and in Egyptian hieroglyphs.

* * *

At the end of chapter 3, Alice makes the mistake of talking about Dinah (her cat) in front of a host of birds, who promptly begin to excuse themselves and move to exit: *"... one old Magpie began wrapping itself up very carefully, remarking 'I really must be getting home; the night, [sic] air doesn't suit my throat!' And a Canary called out in a trembling voice, to its children, 'Come away, my dears! It's high time you were all in bed!' On various pretexts they all moved off, and Alice was soon left alone."*

Napoleon said men are motivated by fear and self-interest. Here the departure of the birds appears motivated by both. But the reasons the birds give for departing are not real reasons. They are rationales. The fox says the grapes are sour, not because the grapes are sour, but because, through a deficiency in himself, he can't get them. The birds leave not for the reasons stated but because of the anxiety engendered by Alice's mention of her cat.

RATIONALES ARE OFTEN NON SEQUITURS

Arguing off the point gives the appearance of reason but is really just a rationale thinly disguised. It is an attempt to thicken proofs that do demonstrate thinly.

Question 3. What famous play does "thicken proofs that do demonstrate thinly" come from?

Answer 3. If you don't know, stop reading this book right now and start reading your Shakespeare.

"Don't touch me. I'm a Catholic." That the lady doesn't want to be touched cannot be doubted. But that she is a Catholic is not a reason that she should not be touched. Her failure to stick to the point is the mark of a confused thinker who is distracted (or is trying to distract) from the relevant issue. We have already mentioned other forms of diversion arguments that are non sequiturs including *argumentum ad hominem* and *argumentum ad verecundiam*. Both of those assert false reasons and distract us from the truth.

"I subscribe to *Hustler* because of the great articles." That statement is likely a rationale. I have never seen a great article in *Hustler*, but the magazine does have great pictures of beautiful women in various stages of undress.

THINGS TO REMEMBER—
PROGRESS BOX FOR CHAPTER 3

- Oh hell, you get the points and don't need a progress box anymore. Instead, take some time off and stretch your legs or give yourself a small reward for your due diligence in wading through all this stuff. Psychologists tell us that we learn better when we reward ourselves for reaching goals. The reward works on the brain to cement the memory of what was learned. If true, that's great. If not true, it's fun to get a reward anyway.

4

The Rabbit Sends in a Little Bill

Much of this chapter has a tacked-on quality that doesn't lend itself to serious discussion of logical or philosophic issues. The White Rabbit ordering servants around seems inconsistent with his previously displayed timid character. The multiple changes in Alice's size are now ho-hum.

Many commentators have felt that the puppy is out of place in Wonderland (a gratuitous puppy at the end of lots of gratuitous violence?) as if it had wandered into Alice's dream from some other story or perhaps from the real world. This puppy is the only important creature in Wonderland who does not speak to Alice. It barks. It chases a stick (yawn!). It pants (big deal). It jumps in the air (so what?). By its conventional behavior this puppy disfigures the character of Wonderland that has already been established. Also: The dog is the only character living in Wonderland who is not (at least a little) mad. Unlike other characters in AAW who dress (at least in part) like humans, this puppy is not dressed in anything but its own fur.

For the above reasons and many others, I offer the conclusion that chapter 4 is the weakest chapter of AAW, for it comes close to abandoning nonsense and the language of play for ordinary discourse, for ordinary slapstick, and for ordinary sadism (forcing poor Bill the lizard down the chimney, for example).

The texture of chapter 4 is thin: Contextually, it does not complicate or develop any of the earlier motifs, save that of Alice's confusion about her identity. There is a little too much second-rate *Gulliver's Travels* in this chapter to make it memorable, and one is happily relieved when Alice finally (in the beginning of chapter 5) comes upon the mysterious large blue caterpillar quietly smoking a long hookah. For here, indeed, is Wonderland again.

And so without further comment let us pass to chapter 5 to the advice from a caterpillar who seems to be in a very unpleasant state of mind and whose main advice, uttered in a quite grumpily angry tone, is "Keep your temper."

5

Advice from a Caterpillar

"Who are you?" said the Caterpillar.

This was a popular question in Carroll's day and remains popular in ours. Who are you? What do you do? Where are you from? Or the question I get most often: Are you married?

These questions are routine at cocktail parties, job interviews, and dances for seniors. In Houston, we have a retired physicians club where everyone knows who's who and what he or she did (and if you are married or not), so the most popular question at the club is "Where you been?"

"Where are you going?" is probably the question husbands most frequently put to their wives, the other being "Where have you been?"

"Who are you?" was not an encouraging opening for a conversation. Alice replied, rather shyly, "I—I hardly know, Sir, just at present—at least I know who I was when I got up this morning, but I think I must have changed several times since then."

"What do you mean by that? Explain yourself!"

"I'm afraid I ca'n't explain myself, I'm afraid, Sir," said Alice, "because I'm not myself, you see."

"I don't see," said the Caterpillar.

Double meanings again and double fun. This time the fun revolves around the word *myself* and the phrase *I don't see*. Alice can't explain herself, meaning she can't explain who she is; and she can't explain herself, meaning the explanation can't be given by her. In the sense that the

Caterpillar doesn't get what Alice means, he doesn't see. Yet, as he is not blind, he does see. How can he see and not see at the same time and in the same place? This apparent contradiction is not a contradiction at all because the word *see* is used with two different meanings: 1. Understand and 2. Recognize, using the eye and associated parts of the visual system of the brain.

And so, as Alice is not getting anywhere, the Caterpillar in typical Oxford don fashion comes full circle to his original question: "Who are you?"

No motivation for the Caterpillar's aggressiveness toward Alice is apparent. His insults are gratuitous, funny, and intimidating—just the kind of obnoxious behavior expected from an Oxford don or a university professor. Those guys can be pretty insufferable, some of them. Others are quite nice. But by the Caterpillar's negative example are we getting a moral? Remember Carroll illustrates what's right by showing us what's wrong.

Social relationship skills make for more pleasant living, especially when the relation is as asymmetric as the one between a caterpillar and a child. By negative example are we getting a moral? Or is the Caterpillar's behavior an example of something positive? What's your take?

Professors often have an economy of speech that speeds up the conversation by quickly getting to the point without circumlocution. The Caterpillar's short, pointed questions can be a way of expressing interest and thoughtfulness. Yet these kinds of questions break social norms (some of them anyway)—albeit for a reason. Social norms should be broken when they interfere with clear thinking, obscure truth, or delay our quest for knowledge. The Caterpillar's short questions could simply be a signal that more information is wanted.

In this chapter, AAW and Alice are again concerned with the subject of growing up, with mysteries of the changes that occur in our bodies (especially around puberty). The Alice of AAW is seven and a half years old. The Alice of real life was, at the time she received the original handwritten version of "Alice's Adventures Underground," eleven years old. The focus of this child's interest (the real Alice and her fictional counterpart) is (probably) to some extent on becoming an adult and the anxieties of maturity attendant upon the necessity of entering the (usually inane and sometimes insane) world of adults. And indeed the "Who are you?" often morphs into (adult to child) "What will you become?" Or asked another way: "What do you want to be when you grow up?" For this later question and the one previous, Callie Patten has ready answers: "I'm a princess and when I grow up I will teach little girls how to become princesses." Ah, ambition is nice, but shouldn't it be made of sterner stuff?

On the other hand, the Caterpillar's repeating the question is not only contemptuous but also unnerving considering Alice's previous difficulty in answering that question. Has the Caterpillar read her mind (as he literally does later in the chapter), known her anxieties, and put this question to her again to torment her further?

Farther along in this chapter, Alice is hit with a similar problem (of identity) when Pigeon assumes Alice is a serpent: *"But I'm not a serpent, I tell you!" said Alice. "I'm a I'm a—"*

Part of the hesitation is based on Alice's sudden realization that it is awfully hard to prove anything. It is even harder (as discussed) to prove a negative statement. Perhaps this is the reason for our presumption in law that you are innocent until proven guilty. It is up to the prosecutor to prove the guilt beyond a reasonable doubt by providing evidence that is relevant and adequate.

So, sensing the difficulty of proving that she is not a serpent, Alice falls back on a positive assertion of what she is. Alice does this in the hope that it will be a sufficient demonstration that, if she is a little girl, she can't be a serpent as there is no case on record of a little girl being a serpent too.

This business of knowing who one is remains surprisingly tricky. We think we know who we are, but our common sense intuition has evaded definition by the philosophers. The best we seem to be able to do when asked, is to point a finger at ourselves or give our name. Alice could have pointed a finger at herself and said, "I am Alice Pleasance Liddell, daughter of Dean Liddell."

And yet, and yet, tons of psychiatric research indicates that there is no such thing as a self that can be pointed to or expressed in a name or in words. Language (as every real writer knows) fails us because of its inability to fully encompass the daunting complexity of exactly who we are and what is our real self. The French Dadaist Marcel Duchamp puts this bluntly: "As soon as we start putting our thoughts into words and sentences everything gets distorted, language is just no damn good—I use it because I have to, but I don't put any trust in it. We never understand each other."

The word "self" for instance can only be a shadowy reflection of the real self behind the label. The "I" is "another" according to the great poet Rimbaud, meaning that the first moment of the subject (the I) is socially produced or determined. Therefore the "I" must be another, separate, and distinct from the "me."

"A rose by any other word would smell as sweet," said Shakespeare, implying that the rose has an existence independent of any words used to describe it. By the same token, I would contend that "myself" and "yourself" have an existence independent of any words used to describe them.

Further complicating the matter is the fact that the self mutates and changes depending on multiple complex factors. For example, when I speak French, especially when I speak French in France, I find my personality is different: Different from what it would have been had I been speaking in English and much different from what it would have been had I been speaking Mayo Irish. My self actually changes with the language I speak. Weird, but true, as truly bilingual people will tell you.

MOST OF US ARE DIFFERENT IN DIFFERENT PLACES AND AT DIFFERENT TIMES, BUT NOT THAT MUCH

Rather than have a constant self, we constantly construct and reconstruct our selves to meet the needs of situations we encounter, doing so with the memories of our previous encounters and under the tutelage of previous instruction from our parents, friends, and culture. Therefore, the alterations that Alice undergoes under different circumstances can be understood in terms of her renewed and familiar well-worn (but not often consciously recognized) attempts to adapt her personality to the exigencies in which she has been placed.

The failure to recognize the fact that people are different in different social contexts is called by psychologists "the fundamental attribution error." It's an error all right, and an attribution error all right, but whether it is fundamental or not is debatable.

Interestingly, here in the West we tend to underestimate the influence of the social situation on our behavior and overestimate the influence of our individual personalities. In the East, the opposite is true: The individual's contribution is minimized and the social influence is heavily emphasized. So what's the answer? Who is right?

Answer: If you said, "That depends," then congratulations! You are catching on. What is true is true only for a particular time and place. Unless we know the details, we can't say for sure how much behavior is due to the individual and how much is due to the social context.

And which is more important, the individual or the group? My take is that the magic is in the mix. To neglect the interests of the individual would create a totalitarian society. To neglect the interests of the group would be to create a chaotic dysfunctional society.

MUCH OF THE MODERN AMERICAN APPROACH IS WRONG

It can be reasonably argued that modern American society has emphasized individual interest too much. This way of thinking was expressed by Fritz Perl at Esalen, home of the Get-into-Yourself movement: "I do my thing and you do your thing. I'm not in this world to live up to your expectations and you are not in this world to live up to mine. You are you, and I am I, and if by chance we find each other it is beautiful. If not, it can't be helped."

That sounds familiar. It's the me-me-me philosophy of the Ivan Boeskys, the Imelda Marcoses, the S&L presidents, subprime lenders, the Donald Trumps, and (sadly) most politicians. They, the corporate-takeover experts, the inside traders on Wall Street, and others of their ilk have been mentors to millions. Michael Douglas, portraying a Wall Street investment banker, summed it up: "Greed is good!"

THE LITERARY SELF, WHAT IS IT?

"What is the self?" can be a (real) literary question. One answer that is especially modern is that the self is a narration. At this point we might do well to examine what the narrative self is, the subject about which the narrative creation of Alice can be supposed to be. This is a good time to bring this up as the question has come up again as Alice confronts the Caterpillar: *"Who are you?" said the Caterpillar.*

Is there a self, an essential self that is just there inside us? Is that who we are? Or are we something else?

To review: Aristotle proclaimed the identity of the self as one of the self-evident principles. He said that although we are different now than we were this morning or last year, we still are identical to ourselves. Something did change, he admits, but those changes are not significant in relation to the core person who we were and are. He admitted that he could not prove this point just as he couldn't prove the principle of contradiction: That a thing can't be and not be at the same time and in the same place. I can't have a pickle on my White Castle hamburger and not have a pickle on my White Castle hamburger at the same time and in the same place. That is as impossible as my changing my identity. But as principles, identity and contradiction can't be proven. Carroll exploits this identity problem many times and we will note instances. About the principle, I have already said I would say no more. Therefore by saying more, I have contradicted myself. Whether

I did contradict myself or didn't would therefore devolve around what I meant when I said I would say no more. Did I mean in this entire book or did I mean at that point in the book?

PHILOSOPHIC PROBLEM NUMBER ONE:
DOES THE SELF EXIST?

If our self did not exist, then why do we talk to that self? Why would we need to talk to it? (Why, does it talk back?) And why would there be such injunctions as "Know thyself" or "To thine own self be true"? If our selves were just there, we would have no need to tell ourselves about ourselves. Yet we spend a good deal of time doing just that, either alone or with friends.

Pathetically, many of us, in making that explanation fall back on explaining who we are by giving information as to what we have achieved or our titles or our positions. All of these things are probably related to, but are not identical with, our true selves. Hence, I'm sympathetic to Alice in her difficulties in explaining who she is. How about you? Are you sympathetic? And by the way, WHO ARE YOU?

* * *

"Well! What are you?" said the Pigeon. "I can see you're trying to invent something!"

The question has changed in form but not in substance. If Alice can't explain who she is, perhaps she can explain what she is. At first glance, that seems easier as the class of what we are is much larger than the class of who we are. Or is it? Is this a distinction without a difference or not? Let's see how Alice handles the question.

"I—I'm a little girl," said Alice, rather doubtfully, as she remembered the number of changes she had gone through, that day.

"A likely story indeed!" said the Pigeon, in a tone of the deepest contempt. "I've seen a good many little girls in my time, but never one with such a neck as that!"

Is that true?

Does Alice have a long neck?

Looking over all the original drawings of Alice by Sir John Tenniel, I find no evidence that Alice's neck is long, except in chapter 2 where everything about her is long. Most of Tenniel's remarkable drawings create the visual framework through which the characters come to life for us. All drawings (that were published) were approved by Carroll. Hence, it is significant that most of the pictures show a normal neck or a small neck. In the picture showing the Dodo giving her thimble back to her, Alice doesn't have much of a neck at all. Ditto the picture of her at table with Hatter and Hare at the mad tea party. Conclusion from the drawings: Alice's neck is normal or short and is not long.

O.K., great. The conclusion from the pictures must be that Alice's neck is normal. Therefore, if Pigeon concludes that Alice is a serpent on the basis of her having a long neck, that conclusion must be based on a false premise. If the conclusion is based on a false premise, it does not follow.

Looking at Lewis Carroll's photograph of the real Alice dressed as a street waif, I find that the real Alice's neck is normal in size and configuration. Thus, it appears that Pigeon's observation is contrary to fact. In the book Alice doesn't have a long neck, and the real Alice upon which the book is based and for whom the book was written doesn't have a long neck. If Alice doesn't have a long neck, then the premise of Pigeon's conditional syllogism is wrong and Pigeon's conclusion (that Alice is a serpent) does not follow.

Furthermore, neck is defined as the body part between the head and the shoulders. So here's the kicker: By definition no serpent has a neck. A serpent has no shoulders as it has no limbs (this is the zoological definition of serpent—a limbless reptile), so it doesn't make a lot of sense for Pigeon to be looking at necks as a criterion for serpenthood.

Carroll knew this. Hence the inside joke. Pigeon is calling Alice a serpent because she thinks that Alice has a long neck. But that can't be right because serpents have no neck at all.

Of course, we know what Pigeon has in mind. She is thinking that the long (snakelike) body of a serpent is a neck.

Still Pigeon is convinced that Alice is what Pigeon says she is:

> *"No, no! You're a serpent; and there's no use denying it. I suppose you'll be telling me next that you never tasted an egg!"*
>
> *"I have tasted eggs, certainly," said Alice, who was a very truthful child; "but little girls eat eggs quite as much as serpents do, you know."*

The Pigeon's thinking is poor. Obviously, a little girl can have a long neck as well as a short neck. So neck size is no criterion of girlhood one way or the other. Neck size is irrelevant to the issue. Therefore, Pigeon would be wrong to conclude that Alice is not a little girl because of her neck size, even if her neck were long, which it isn't.

Having knocked down the neck argument, let's examine Pigeon's egg-eating criterion for serpenthood.

Here's the syllogism through which Pigeon reaches the conclusion that Alice is a serpent:

Serpents eat eggs.

Alice eats eggs.

Therefore, Alice is a serpent.

Any problem here with the reasoning?

Recall that in syllogisms there are assertions, called premises, and one conclusion that follows if the premises are true. In Pigeon's syllogism, the predicate of the conclusion contains the major term and the subject of the conclusion has the minor term. Thus "is a serpent" is the major term and "Alice" is the minor term. The major premise is the premise that has the major term and the minor premise is the term that has the minor term. Thus "Serpents eat eggs" is the major premise and "Alice eats eggs" is the minor premise. The term that is present in both the major and the minor premise is the middle term. Here the middle term is "eats eggs."

O.K., so let's examine, in a formal way and then in an informal way, the truth of the premises and the truth of the conclusion. Is the major premise true? Do serpents eat eggs?

Answer: Yes.

How about the minor premise? Is that true? Does Alice eat eggs?

Answer: Yes. Probably.

Alice admitted tasting eggs. While it is possible to taste eggs without eating them, it is unlikely that Alice tasted eggs without having eaten them. Alice may have equivocated here, put a little sugar on the dog eat dog. She did that in order to assuage the Pigeon, who seems very keen on this egg-eating issue. She admits tasting eggs and she asserts that little girls eat eggs, but she doesn't herself admit to eating eggs.

Attention, dear reader, STAY FOCUSED. I sense that your mind is tending to wander. I have a definite point in mind. Here it is.

If the major and the minor premises are correct, why is the conclusion wrong, as we know it must be? Alice is not a serpent. She is a little girl.

Answer: In formal logic, this syllogism is invalid (that is, wrong) because the middle term is not distributed (distributed means applies to each member of the class) at least once. That is, eating eggs, while done by all serpents, can also be done by other animals as well. The class of egg eaters is larger than the class of serpents and the class of serpents does not include all those egg-eating animals. Therefore, that Alice eats eggs doesn't exclude the possibility that she is not a serpent. The major premise says "Serpents eat eggs." It does not say that any animal that eats eggs is a serpent. Alice is quite right in her refutation of the Pigeon: *"Little girls eat eggs quite as much as serpents do, you know."*

That refutation should have stopped the argument dead. Instead of admitting defeat, Pigeon answers: *"I don't believe it"* . . . *"but if they do, then they're a kind of serpent: that's all I can say."*

This is Pigeon's confession that the major premise has to be changed in order for the conclusion to be justified. If anyone who eats eggs is a serpent, then Alice is a serpent. But changing the major premise makes it false. Here's the reason:

Pigeon's new statement would look like this:

Whatever eats eggs is a serpent.

Alice eats eggs.

Therefore, Alice is a serpent.

The previous problem of the undistributed middle term has been corrected. Now the middle term is distributed and encompasses all classes that eat eggs. In redistributing the middle term, Pigeon did correct the problem of the undistributed middle term. But Pigeon also changed the major premise so that it is no longer true. In fact, Pigeon has changed the major premise to an erroneous broadcast definition. "Whatever eats eggs is a serpent" is not true. Since it is a generalization, we can prove it not true by finding one exception. Since exceptions are legion, the premise is obviously false. Therefore, Pigeon's conclusion is probably false. Any conclusion based on a false premise does not follow.

Therefore, Pigeon is still wrong. Truth has once again triumphed: Alice is not a serpent. By sheer strength of correct thinking, we have proven that Alice is not a serpent.

Ladies and gentlemen, isn't that fantastic? We have labored long and hard, but we have finally proven something. See how hard it is to prove one simple thing? That's why we should have a great respect for fact. Robert Frost said the fact was the sweetest dream that nature knows. He was right.

More argument and more proof: We know Alice is a little girl. No little girl has ever been a serpent. That is a fact. Therefore, Pigeon is wrong. Pigeon is arguing contrary to fact. Arguing contrary to fact always puts you in a bad position vis-à-vis the truth. Pigeon shouldn't do it. Nor should you.

EMOTIONS OFTEN DICTATE OUR THINKING ON CRITICAL ISSUES

Can you guess why the Pigeon is so hung up on the serpent thing and the egg-eating thing?

Deep-seated fears and anxieties are often at the heart of poor thinking. Pigeon's is a typical example. Undoubtedly, at some time in the past Pigeon had had her eggs eaten by a serpent. Whenever pigeons (or people) persist in being irrational, suspect a deep underlying psychological basis adversely working from their deep heart's core on their perspective capacity, leading them away from truth and toward error.

DON'T ARGUE OFF THE POINT

But the heart of the matter is that both Alice and Pigeon are arguing off the point. Pigeon is not really concerned about whether or not Alice is a serpent. Pigeon is concerned about the possibility of Alice eating the Pigeon's eggs. Clear definition of the problem in the beginning would have avoided lots of wasted breath and time.

6

Pig and Pepper

In this chapter, the irrational behavior of the creatures in AAW gets worse and develops further. After a silly display of pomp and circumstance with the Fish-Footman and his giant letter and entangling curls, Frog Footman sat on the ground near the door (right in character and just like a frog) and started staring stupidly up into the sky. This is what frogs usually do, but why they do it is not clear. Alice tries to construct an explanation: "*He was looking up into the sky all the time he was speaking, and this Alice thought decidedly uncivil. 'But perhaps he ca'n't help it,' she said to herself; 'his eyes are so very nearly at the top of his head.'*"

Why do frogs stare at the sky? That's the question.

Aristotle had a ready answer: "It's their nature." That answer begs the question. My answer, though a little venial, is probably closer to the truth: They are looking for a nice juicy insect to eat. In fact, the desire to eat is a major motivation for frogs and for the behavior of a lot of other animals, including the little animals we call children. In including lots of eating and drinking in his book, Carroll blatantly caters to the interests of kids, who are highly stimulated by and often embrace anything edible.

Sidebar: Failure to make eye contact, closed body posture, and not smiling are the three things that, in Anglo-American culture, turn people off. Eye contact, open body posture, and a great big genuine smile are the three things that turn people on. Alice feels uneasy with Frog because Frog has violated the important social convention about making eye contact with whom you are making verbal contact.

Frog-Footman accepts the chaos around him. He takes it for granted as if it were a normal, expected part of the adult world, which, incidentally, it often is. When a plate flies out of the door and breaks against one of the trees behind him, he continues talking "exactly as if nothing had happened."

About plate breaking: At the annual meeting of the Lewis Carroll Society, there is a booth where Carrollinians may vent some of their frustrations by trashing crockery (the crockery smashing booth). This is altogether fitting and proper as it celebrates the chaos in "Pig and Pepper." But in a larger sense, senseless destruction is part and parcel of the human situation and is fun. Children love to build things up (sand castles, block houses, etc.) but they also love to knock them down. In his *Poetics*, Aristotle discusses the therapeutic effect of seeing violence in plays. The benefit is called catharsis, a purging of harmful emotions. An extension of that analysis would indicate that breaking things as a form of catharsis might vent anger and prevent actual aggression against others. *"'There is no sort of use in knocking,' said the Footman, 'and that for two reasons. First, because I'm on the same side of the door as you are: secondly, because they're making such a noise inside, no one could possibly hear you.'"*

These do indeed appear to be good reasons for not knocking. They are not reasons for not getting through the door. The first reason is true as the footman is on the same side of the door as Alice.

But so what?

It might be part of his duty as a domestic servant to greet (or confront) visitors—but in his absence many others might fill in. All his statement means is that it would not pay nor would it make any sense for Alice to knock for *his* answer from the inside as he is not inside. The second reason is probably true: knocking might be ineffective because all the noise might preclude anyone on the inside from hearing the knock and coming to the door.

Both these reasons illustrate the difficulties of thinking in terms of conventional and limited alternatives and possibilities. The assumption (and in a sense the Footman's presumption) is that he and he alone can open the door. And that he can open the door, if and only if, he is on the inside. That can't be true. In fact, if the Footman is on Alice's side on the outside, it is likely that the door is unlocked and that either the

Footman or Alice or both of them or anyone else for that matter could just open the door by pulling on the doorknob.

BEWARE ARTIFICIAL LIMITATIONS IMPOSED BY CONVENTION, BY OTHERS, OR BY YOURSELF: CONSIDER MULTIPLE ALTERNATIVES, OF WHICH THERE ARE USUALLY MANY

Footman is too much into protocol and habit and needs to think just a little out of the box. His reality is obvious to us, but not to him: He can open from the inside and he can open from the outside. He is wrong to artificially restrain his own behavior and limit his own powers by an erroneous mental construct.

* * *

"How am I to get in?" asked Alice again, in a louder tone.
  "Are you to get in at all?" said the Footman. "That's the first question, you know."

It was no doubt; only Alice did not like to be told so.

What is Alice's error in thinking?

Alice begged the question: She assumed she was to get in when that assumption is not supported by any evidence. When we assume something that needs to be proven, we are begging the question.

"What college are you going to, Pete?"

Here, Pete's uncle assumes Pete is going to college. Actually, Pete wants to join the navy and see the world.

"When we have sex, can I be on top?"

This also begs the question. First she should find out if he wants to have sex—that's the first question, you know. Then the lady should ask if she can be on top. This situation must come up all the time for this is, according to Shakespeare, a bawdy planet. We also saw it back when we discussed sequence. First the couple decides if they want to have sex. Then they decide who's on top.

* * *

"It's really dreadful," she muttered to herself, "the way all the creatures argue. It's enough to drive one crazy!"

Alice's query assumed she was to get in. Alice was begging the question. The Footman called her on it. Her frustration in dealing with the Frog-Footman and his logic is understandable. We feel your pain, Alice. But, oh me, oh my, oh Dear, what do you expect from characters in a book written by an Oxford don whose main mission in his professional life was to teach logic!

In like manner, thousands of Oxonian students probably got millions of headaches dealing with Carroll's lessons and lectures, so, in a sense Alice, is getting off easy.

By the way, did you get the multiple meanings of the word "tone"? A louder tone and a louder tone and a tone are (or can be) three different things: the musical or a vocal sound with reference to its quality, a style of speaking, and vocal expression indicating some feeling or emotion. These multiple meanings can't be accidental. Carroll put tone in there to illustrate (again) the problems with language.

And did you get by examining Footman's statements that he is not devoid of intellect, not utterly stupid, in short, not an idiot, and certainly not perfectly idiotic? And yet the next thing we hear from Alice is: *"'Oh, there's no use in talking to him,' said Alice desperately: 'he's perfectly idiotic!' And she opened the door and went in."*

Bad for Alice.

She has reached an erroneous conclusion. Frog is not idiotic and he is certainly not perfectly idiotic. To be perfect anything is rather hard. Callie Patten often says, "I don't believe people who say they are perfectly happy because perfect is a high standard. When my friend Rebecca said she was perfectly happy, I knew she wasn't."

Good for Callie.

And good (on other grounds) for Alice.

Alice is showing individual initiative, daring, and self-reliance. She proves that behavior does not have to have restraints imposed on it by language. She proves how matter and reality can escape the confines of the artificial and constraining categories imposed upon them by language and the human mind.

Alice's method is to verify whether or not the door is locked. Empirical verification proves the door is open and negates all of the Footman's statements about the impossibility of getting through the door.

Along these lines, I am reminded of one of the "Table Talks" of the great Roman moral philosopher Plutarch (45–120 CE). Table Talk Seven concerns a discussion among the men at the table on the important question (then): "Where does wine go after it is swallowed?"

While these guys are in their cups multiple points of view get aired. Their consensus: It seems that either the wine goes directly to the stomach or directly to the lungs.

The amount of information that the ancients did not know is voluminous. Their discussion is both cute and pathetic. It is cute because the resolution of the question is determined by which philosopher has the best reputation. His shall be the received and accepted position. Our ancient ancestors were inordinately impressed by character arguments like this. We are not, nor should we be. A philosopher's reputation is not as important as physical observation in determining where wine goes when we drink it.

The discussion is pathetic in that the question could have been easily resolved by the dissection of just one cadaver, especially if that person had just finished drinking some wine before he died.

ATTENTION: MAJOR LESSON COMING

Lesson: Fact trumps all arguments to the contrary.

Finding wine in the stomach and not in the lungs would prove all the philosophers who thought differently wrong. In the same way, discussions of special creation and so-called intelligent design are silly. Evolution is the cornerstone of modern biology. It occurred and continues to occur. Evolution is a fact and fact trumps all arguments to the contrary. It is not a matter for philosophical discussion, much less debate: Evolution is a fact.

Whoa! If evolution is a fact, how come people call it a theory?

The answer, my friends, goes back to the scientific definition of a theory, which is a detailed organizing set of principles that explains a large body of fact and knowledge. Evolution is a theory because it explains a large body of fact and knowledge, just as quantum theory explains a large body of fact and knowledge about subatomic particles, and music theory explains a large body of fact and knowledge about harmony, melody, cadence, counterpoint, modes, scales, meter, beat, dynamics, and rhythm.

Back to Alice.

O.K., good for her. She proved that the door was open and she let herself in. But bad for Alice. She made a statement that can't be true. Alice said that the Footman was "perfectly idiotic." Not only is this statement redundant and pleonastic (as the *Oxford English Dictionary* says, "idiotic" means devoid of intellect, utterly stupid, senseless, or foolish), but it is also supererogatory and contrary to fact. Frog shows a fairly good mastership of deductive logic in the form of contingents (known in the logic schools as the conditional syllogism):

If I am on the outside, I can't answer from the inside.

If the noise on the inside is too loud, they won't hear you knock.

Frog's speech and behavior prove he is not idiotic. And that's a fact. If he is not idiotic, he can't be perfectly idiotic. Therefore, Alice's statement that Frog is perfectly idiotic is false. Notice I did not say perfectly false as that would have made my statement perfectly suspicious and suspiciously perfect. Dig?

AVOID SUPERLATIVES AND PLEONASMS

Few things in this wide world are perfect. When you claim something is perfect, you open yourself up to the myriad darts of those who know differently. People who use superlatives are often trying to convince you (and sometimes themselves) about something that might not be true. If a woman says in a calm detached voice, "I am calm," we might be inclined to believe her. But if she says in a rising crescendo, "I am calm, I am calm, I am *perfectly* calm!" it is possible that she is trying to convince us and herself of something that might not be at all the case. Her behavior contradicts her words. Fact trumps all statements to the contrary.

The standard of "perfectly calm" is a much higher standard than just calm and is therefore more difficult to prove. Avoid getting yourself in hot water. Keep your statements moderate. Such statements will be easier to defend. They will also be closer to the truth.

Tom DeLay often got into hot water with implausible superlative claims. During the Terri Schiavo discussions, Congressman DeLay stated "pulling Terri's tube was an act of barbarism." Subsequently, some reporter discovered that years before, Tom DeLay agreed to have life-support discontinued for his own brain-damaged father. "My father's situation was completely different," DeLay told reporters in explaining the contradiction between his behavior in his father's case and his statements in Terri's case.

Work out on DeLay's statement in view of the following facts. Remember, DeLay said his father's case was *completely* different from Terri's:

1. Tom DeLay's father was brain damaged.
2. Tom DeLay's father was on life-support.
3. Tom DeLay father's prognosis for recovery was poor.
4. Terri Schiavo was brain damaged.
5. Terri Schiavo was on life-support.
6. Terri Schiavo's prognosis for recovery was poor.

Facts 1 and 4, 2 and 5, and 3 and 6 are the same. Therefore, DeLay's father's case is proven similar to Terri's in at least three respects. If it is proven similar in any respect, it cannot be completely different. If it is not completely different, then DeLay's statement is false.

President Bush must have caught the exaggeration bug too. I heard him say on NPR (6:00 PM, CDT, December 15, 2005), "[In Iraq] we will only accept complete victory." The president's statement is pleonastic, supererogatory, and predicts a future event with certainty when the future cannot be predicted with certainty. The statement also admits that we do not have victory in Iraq at the present time. The reporters rightfully asked what the president meant by victory. There was no reply. Can you tell why?

A more reasonable and more believable statement might have run like this: "We hope for victory in Iraq. When victory will come and what it will consist of when, and if, it comes, we don't know."

BEWARE OF PEOPLE WHO MAKE FALSE STATEMENTS

Catching someone in an exaggeration, a false statement, or a lie should alert us to the possibility that we are dealing with a person of poor character. Either Tom DeLay believes what he said or he doesn't. If he believes it, then he believes something false. That's not good because leaders are much more effective when their beliefs match up with the truth. If he doesn't believe what he said, then he is purposely deceptive. Either way, the reflection on his character, and consequently on his qualities as a leader, is bad. When people feed you misinformation or bullshit, don't trust them.

AVOID PLEONASM

Pleonasm is the use of more words than are necessary for the expression of an idea. Examples: "perfectly idiotic," "plenty enough," and "very unique." If a thing is unique, it is one of a kind by definition and doesn't need the word "very" to emphasize its uniqueness. To the sensitive mind, a statement claiming something is "very unique" raises the question of puffery.

AVOID AD HOMINEM (PERSONAL) ON THE OPPOSITION

So Alice opens the door and enters into the realm of chaos and the grotesque, the Duchess's kitchen, the desert of the real. Alice's effective action in opening the door herself shows that self-reliance can bear fruit, and that reality beats hypothesis, conjecture, and defective thinking. It beats it every time! That's good.

But Alice's ad hominem attack on Footman is not justified and is bad. Alice's derogatory statement about the Frog-Footman is as inductively weak as it is not likely to be true. The Frog-Footman is not idiotic and he is certainly not perfectly idiotic. The vitriolic attack on him probably had its origin in Alice's displeasure at being told that she had begged the "How shall I get in?" question. Humans are like that: when attacked, they attack back. When they attack back, the attack often takes the form of pejorative name calling.

LOGICAL ARGUMENT IS GREAT, BUT FACT IS GREATER

The Alice and the door situation reminds me of the famous Greek philosopher Zeno of Elea who argued that it was impossible to go from here to that stone over there. His proof was that you would first have to traverse half the distance, then half of the distance that remained, then half again of what remained after that and so on, by infinite regression, never quite getting to the stone. Another Greek, whose name is now (I think) lost to history, refuted the argument: He got up, walked over, and sat on the stone.

The more common expression of Zeno's Paradox relates to Achilles and the Tortoise:

Achilles and the Tortoise were to run on a circular course, and, as it was known that Achilles could run ten times faster than the Tortoise, the later was allowed a hundred yards head start. There was no winning-post, but the race was to go on until Achilles either overtook the Tortoise or resigned the contest. Now it is evident that, by the time Achilles had run the hundred yards, the Tortoise would have got ten yards farther; and, by the time he had run those ten yards, it would have got a yard farther; and so on forever. Hence, in order to overtake the Tortoise he must pass over an infinite number of successive distances. Hence Achilles can never overtake the Tortoise.

The problem is of course related to incompatible premises. Achilles can't be faster than the Tortoise and yet not catch up with him. If a man says "I am telling a lie," and speaks truthfully, he is telling a lie, and therefore speaks falsely: but if he speaks falsely, he is not telling a lie, and therefore speaks truthfully. Dig?

With this understanding in hand we are now prepared to answer that immortal question, "What happens when an irresistible force runs up against an immovable object?"

The answer is nothing.

The answer is nothing because an irresistible force and an immovable object cannot exist at the same time in the same place. They cannot exist because they contradict each other. An irresistible force is incompatible with an object that can resist any force. This is the equivalent of saying there is a force F and an object O such that F can move O and F cannot move O.

Now work on this problem: Why can't almighty God make a stone heavier than he can lift? (Answer appears below)

And here's another paradox (probably the root paradox of AAW): How can you make sense out of nonsense? After you have solved that paradox, work on this one: Can there be meaning in a meaningless world?

* * *

The door led right into a large kitchen, which was full of smoke from one end to the other; the Duchess was sitting on a three-legged stool in the middle, nursing a baby; the cook was leaning over the fire, stirring a large cauldron that seemed full of soup. *"There's certainly too much pepper in that soup!' Alice said to herself, as well as she could for sneezing."*

There was certainly too much pepper in the air. But Alice doesn't have any data to reach the conclusion that there is too much pepper in the soup. That reminds me of my mother-in-law who, without first tasting the food, is in the habit of accusing us of adding too much black pepper when we hardly ever use pepper at all.

Conclusions must be justified by the evidence. The evidence that is best is directly acquired through the pertinent sense and applies to the issue at hand. If Alice had tasted the soup, she might have been able to reach a reasonable conclusion about whether there was too much pepper in it, too little pepper, or just enough for her personal taste. However, since her conclusion would depend on personal taste, it would have to be quite limited in scope and not applied generally. Thus: *This soup has too much pepper for me* would be a reasonable assertion of personal preference. But, *This soup has too much pepper* might be too universal and overgeneral to apply at all times for all people. It certainly doesn't apply to the Duchess and the cook who must love pepper and for whom (it seems) there is never enough.

Well, what is the correct amount of pepper?

The correct amount of pepper according to Aristotle is just the right amount for a given place and time, not too much and not too little—the golden mean. Both the Duchess and the cook seem to be erring on the side of too much pepper in the air and possibly in the soup. But that's their choice. It takes all kinds to make a world. We should be tolerant of the personal preferences of others.

THE LESS THE BETTER AND THE MORE THE BETTER ARE BOTH BAD CONTINUUM ARGUMENTS

Let's examine these two defective arguments in turn.

The less the better is a bad argument

If too much cholesterol is bad for you, it does not follow that no cholesterol is good for you. Cholesterol is a natural body chemical needed in the construction of cell walls and many essential hormones. Too much cholesterol is bad. But too little is bad too. What is needed is just the right amount. Too much wine might be bad for you. But recent studies indicate that wine decreases the incidence of heart attack and stroke. So, too little wine might be bad for you also. The proper amount of wine is not too much or too little. Too much wine would make you drunk and, taken consistently, damage your health in other ways. But too little might deprive you of the health benefits of moderate drinking.

When I treat a patient with a kidney infection with Colistin, I give just the right dose of that antibiotic because I know too little will not cure the infection and too much will, itself, cause kidney failure. The proper dose is the amount of Colistin that will solve the problem of infection without causing too many other problems.

In the same way, too little pepper in the soup would make the soup taste flat. Too much pepper would make the soup taste too sharply peppery. What is needed is the right amount.

The more the better is also a bad argument

Vitamin A is good for you. Without it you will get sick. But too much vitamin A is toxic. Way too much vitamin A is fatal. Too little vitamin A is bad; too much is bad too. What is needed is the right amount. Some salt or pepper might improve the taste of a food, but too much, or too little might not improve anything.

Closely related to the less the better and the more the better fallacies is the tyranny of numbers and size.

BIG NUMBERS MAY NOT LEAD TO THE TRUTH
AND CAN LEAD TO BIG ERRORS

Large numbers tend to impress people more than small numbers. Add
this to the fact that most Americans don't understand statistics, percent-
ages, and fractions, and that it is usually more persuasive to quote the
large number rather than the percentage. Shifty rhetoricians and spin
doctors know that large numbers might obscure the truth and mislead
the naive. For example, in the 2000 presidential election, the winner,
George W. Bush, got fewer popular votes than the loser, Al Gore (due
to the operation of the electoral college and the US Supreme Court).
Therefore, the winner's total votes are often quoted (in the millions,
instead of percents) to obscure the fact that over half the voters voted
against the man who became the president. Conversely, just as large
numbers may be unreasonably impressive, so small numbers tend to be
overlooked like those credit card interest rates or the late charges. Once
I was charged a twenty-five-dollar credit card late fee on a balance due
of eleven dollars. This might look small, but as a percent finance charge
the twenty-five dollars looms large.

Another example: In discussing international politics, Saddam Hus-
sein pointed out that America has only two parties, whereas Iraq has
one. He implied that this was an insignificant difference because it was
a difference of only one party.

* * *

*"Please would you tell me," said Alice, a little timidly, for she was not quite sure
whether it was good manners for her to speak first, "why your cat grins like that?"
"It's a Cheshire-Cat," said the Duchess, "and that's why."*

No information in that answer. The Duchess's answer reminds me of a press conference that I attended as a boy.

A reporter asked, "President Truman, what are you going to do about the present economic situation in the United States?"

President Truman answered, "Why we're going to do something. And if that doesn't work, we'll do something else."

Truman said nothing substantive other than he was predisposed to action. Instead of answering the question, the president diverted our attention by giving us bullshit (and political pragmatism). His statement is irrelevant because he didn't answer the reporter's question.

Truman's statement leaves us flat. In that respect his statement looks tautological. A tautology is a circular argument made by repeating the same meaning twice.

President George W. Bush was asked, "What makes you think there's a relationship between Iraq and al Qaeda?" His reply: "I think there is a relationship because there is a relationship."

Simple repetition of the same statement is even worse than some of the other fallacies and by no means a reasonable argument. Repetition, rather, tips us off to the absence of a reasonable argument. And absence of reasonable argument often tips us off to the absence of reasonable thought. If there is evidence about al Qaeda and Iraq, let's hear it so we can effectively evaluate whether that evidence is relevant and adequate. Relevant evidence would relate directly to the issue and adequate evidence would be sufficient in number, weight, and kind to justify the conclusion.

Attention reader: Doctor Patten wants you to memorize that last sentence for he believes it will serve you well your whole life long: Relevant evidence would relate directly to the issue and adequate evidence would be sufficient in number, weight, and kind to justify the conclusion. Repetition is not a reasonable argument. Repetition often points to the absence of a reasonable argument, which often points to the absence of reasonable thought.

Here's another Bushism: "If you don't stand for anything, you don't stand for anything."

Some people like to have their ideas reinforced by repetition. Other people just like to hear themselves talk. Either way, repetitions are ineluctable tautologies that are easy to spot. They are often mere assertions like: "That's the rule." "It's against company policy." "That's the way we do things around here." "Like it or lump it." "It's tradition." "I talked it over with the staff and we all came to that conclusion." And so forth. Real reasons are omitted. All we get is bullshit.

The full exchange in repetition tautology looks like this:

Nurse: "Patients are not allowed out of their rooms during doctors' rounds."

Patient: "Why are we not allowed out of our rooms during doctors' rounds?"

Nurse: "It's the rule."

The nurse's explanation is not a clarification or elucidation of the reasons for the prohibition. It is merely a restatement of the rule in a different form. The nurse's second statement says nothing new, is off the point, and is tautological. The patient would have a right to say: "I asked for the reason for the rule. All you told me was the same thing twice. I already know that we are not allowed out of our rooms during doctors' rounds. I want to know why."

Nurse: "Ward policy."

Patient: (now exasperated) "I asked for a reason. And all you are doing is feeding me bullshit."

A tautology is an error in thinking because it merely restates an assertion rather than proving it. Any assertion, including those repeated, needs to be backed up by evidence, else there is no reason for us to accept it.

Urine is yellow because it contains yellow pigments. Did you learn anything from that statement about why urine is yellow?

Morphine induces sleep because of its somniferous properties. That statement is a tautology because the word somniferous means sleep inducing. What is being said is that morphine produces sleep because it produces sleep. The statement leads nowhere. It certainly doesn't enlighten us about why or wherefore morphine works.

Once I told an attorney who was cross-examining me that he was being Sisyphean. Whereupon, the opposing attorney jumped and said, "and needlessly repetitive as well." That's what tautologies do. They waste our time with needlessly repetitious or trivially obvious observations: They are Sisyphean.

"He's poor because he is always broke." "Our annual report comes out every year." "The homeless are homeless because they have no homes."

MORE TAUTOLOGICAL GEMS
FROM PRESIDENT BUSH

"A low voter turnout is an indication of fewer people going to the polls."

"It isn't the pollution that is harming our environment. It is the impurities in our water and air that are doing it."

"The vast majority of our imports come from outside the country."

On hearing those tautologies we are left blank. We are not one bit more informed than we were before. Since a tautology doesn't get us closer to the truth and doesn't inform us about reality, I consider it an error in thinking.

After hearing the last statement from Bush about imports, my three-year-old granddaughter, Shae Mia Patten, shook her head, frowned, and announced, "He tells us what we already know."

"Either George Washington died in 1999 or he did not."

On one level, the linguistic level, some people might regard that statement as true. I think it's just bunk. It's bunk because it doesn't inform us about anything. After we have read it, we remain just as unenlightened as we did before. In fact the statement is always true and therefore is a tautology. The formal proof of this is:

Let P equal "died in 1999."

Let not P or ~P mean "did not die in 1999."

Let T = true, F = false, and PV~P mean P or not P with the "or" meaning the inclusive meaning of "or": either one or the other *or both*.

Then all cases and possibilities would be described by the following truth table:

	P	~P	PV~P
1.	T	F	T
2.	F	T	T

Since PV~P is always true, no new information comes to us by the statement and the statement is a tautology.

I subscribe to six investment letters. One of these, the Dow Theory Forecasts, always hedges the bets by saying something like, "The major trend for this month is up but there may be a price retreat." In other words, the stock market may go up or it may not. That is a pretty safe bet.

Closely related to tautology are all gimmicky distractions, double talk, chit-chat, patter, and empty talk. For example:

Wednesday, April 7, Pentagon Briefing by Donald Rumsfeld

"We are trying to explain how things are going and they are going as they are going."

"Some things are going well and some things obviously are not going well."

"You are going to have good days, and you are going to have bad days."

"This is one moment, and there will be other moments. And there will be good moments and there will be less good moments."

ANALYSIS OF RUMSFELD'S STATEMENTS

The information density is slight. Most of the statements are platitudes, truisms, tautologies, or contradictions. The statements taken as a whole are simple and simplistic, overgeneralized, and irrelevant to the Iraq situation that he was supposed to be talking about. They present no evidence about external or internal (that is, the internal psychological and mental processes of the people who are in power: what they are thinking) realities. The statements cannot be denied. Yet they tell us nothing substantial.

Don't believe me? Review each of his statements and see if they could easily apply to North Korea, a baseball game, a horse race, a Telenovella, the latest issue of *Playboy*, or anything else for that matter.

See what I mean?

What is frightening about the statements is that either Rumsfeld believes he has said something or he doesn't. I don't know which of those two possibilities is more frightening. How about you?

* * *

"I didn't know that Cheshire-Cats always grinned; in fact, I didn't know that cats could grin."

"They all can," said the Duchess; "and most of 'em do."

"I don't know of any that do," Alice said very politely, feeling quite pleased to have got into a conversation.

"You don't know much," said the Duchess; "and that's a fact."

All arguments contrary to fact are weak arguments. Remember, a weak argument is one that is probably not true. Alice just saw a cat that grins and asked about it. She specifically noted the grin. It was a Cheshire-Cat, one of the most famous cats in history. Therefore, Alice knows or should know that cats can grin. She just saw one that does. Furthermore, her statement that she knows of no cats that can grin is contradicted by the presence of the Cheshire-Cat's grin, about which she just asked the Duchess.

The Duchess's statement that Alice doesn't know much is true, not only in this particular manifestation of failure to recognize as real something Alice has already seen with her own eyes but also in the larger sense that no human knows much. Isaac Newton said that what he knew was as a small pebble compared to the vast ocean of his ignorance. If that statement is true and applies to Newton, how much more does it apply to us? "The fact is the sweetest dream that nature knows," said Robert Frost. He was right. But more than that, facts are facts and only fools refuse to face them. Alice failed to acknowledge a fact and therefore is justly chastised by the Duchess.

* * *

"If everybody minded their own business," the Duchess said, in a hoarse growl, "the world would go round a deal faster than it does."

This non sequitur is a conditional syllogism that makes no sense. The conditional syllogism is a deductive form of logic that depends on the truth of the premises. If the premise is true, then the conclusion must follow. But is that enough?

Obviously not.

In a subtle way, Carroll is pointing out that there must also be, in the conditional syllogism, an evidentiary link (also known in the logic business as a warrant) that justifies the connection between the antecedent and the consequence. Without the warrant, the conclusion doesn't follow. As there is no relation between people minding their own business and the rotational speed of earth, the Duchess's statement can't be true. If it can't be true, it must be false. It is false because it is unwarranted.

There is another point here that is more subtle. See if I can explain it. The conditional syllogism resembles a hypothetical statement as in a scientific hypothesis. The hypothesis is advanced to give the basis for experiment. It is not accepted until proven by test. The confusion here with the Duchess is therefore twofold. 1. Her statement does not follow as there is no warrant, and 2. It channels our minds in the wrong direction as we are likely to be deceived because the statement resembles in form the form of the conditional syllogism.

Down the way, in chapter 9, the Duchess says, "Oh, 'tis love, 'tis love, that makes the world go round!" Whereupon, Alice whispers (pointing out the apparent contradiction), "Somebody said that it's done by everybody minding their own business!" To which the Duchess replies while digging her sharp little chin into Alice's shoulder, "Ah well! It means much the same thing."

If it means much the same thing, what the devil does it mean? One meaning is that both statements claim a human influence on nature that doesn't exist. Therefore, both statements are false. Since both statements are false, they do in fact share the same meaning of being not true. They have the same meaning: They don't correspond to reality. This very subtle point, I think, relates to the distinction between a contradiction and contraries. Two statements are contradictory if they can't both be simultaneously true. But two statements are contraries if they both are false. It is false that love makes the earth rotate and it is false that minding one's own business would speed up the earth's rotation. Therefore, the two statements by the Duchess are both false and are contraries. If this is not clear, consider the following two statements:

The present king of France is bald.

The present king of France is not bald.

While the two statements appear to contradict each other, they really do not. Both statements are false as there is no present king of France.

One more thing: Alice is making an error here. Can you figure out what it is? She is assuming that one and only one thing can make the world go round. This is the error of black-and-white thinking, where we limit our understanding by limiting our choices to either-or. Alice implies that the Duchess had contradicted herself because only one thing can make the world go round. Which is it anyway? Does love make the world go round or do people minding their own business? Or both? Or neither? As for me I vote for love. In a certain sense, love makes the world go round. But, mind you, muscle gives love the push.

This type of thinking is the trouble with most mythologies, which after all operate between two opposite poles. Either you go to heaven or you go to hell. There is no place in between, no gradation of guilt or reward. Pretty simple, right? And simplistic.

CLAIMS OF CONTROL OF NATURAL EVENTS MUST BE VIEWED WITH SKEPTICISM

This is a key point so let's work out on it: Both of the Duchess's statements imply a control of the forces of nature by humans. In the first place, she claims that human love controls the earth's rotation. In the second place, she claims that by everybody minding his or her own business, the earth's rotation will speed up. Either statement is wrong, of course, because what humans do or don't do has no influence on the rotation of the earth. At some time in the future, humans might be able to speed up the rotation or slow it down or do both. They might or they might not. At present, such a feat is logically possible and (I believe) physically possible. But at the present time it is technically impossible.

Egocentric views of the universe and false claims about human control of the forces of nature crop up often enough. At one time, most humans believed that the earth was the center of the universe. Galileo challenged that belief. He used a telescope to show that the moon was not perfect, as the church said it was (it had craters that marred its face), that there were literally millions of stars in the Milky Way, and that Jupiter had moons that rotated around Jupiter. This last point, the moons of Jupiter, for unknown reasons, became a big deal to the Catholic Church—really spooked it. So, in 1616 Galileo received a formal warning that the theory that the earth was not the center of the universe was contrary to church doctrine. He responded:

> I am inclined to believe that the intentions of the Sacred Scriptures is to give to mankind the information necessary for their salvation. But I do not hold it necessary to believe that the same God who has

endowed us with senses, with speech, with intellect, intended that we should neglect the use of these and seek by other means for knowledge which these are sufficient to procure for us, especially in a Science like astronomy, of which so little notice is taken by the Scriptures that none of the planets, except the sun and moon and once or twice only Venus, by the name of Lucifer, are so much as named at all. This therefore being granted, me-thinks that in the discussion of natural problems we ought not to begin at the authority of the texts of Scriptures, but at sensible experiments and necessary demonstrations.

A reasonable defense, but he was subsequently arrested and confined ten years for having "held and taught Copernican doctrine." Nearly 342 years later, Galileo was pardoned by Pope John Paul II. Better late than never but better still—never late.

Wasn't Galileo cool?

Question: What about Galileo bugged the Catholic Church?

Answer: Galileo adduced evidence that the sun, the heavens, and, for that matter, the entire universe did not revolve around us.

Notice how Galileo subtly took notice of how the scriptures didn't mention much about astronomy? They don't mention much about any other science either. No mention of the cause of infectious diseases, for instance. God let cholera, typhoid, and the plague wipe out entire cities without even telling us about the microscope or antibiotics. The Bible doesn't even know that the sun is a massive thermonuclear reactor or that matter and energy are the same physical thing. And so forth.

Question: What's the essential difference among the following three statements?

It rained in Clear Lake because the pastor of the Saint Luke's Catholic Church said a Mass for rain.

It rained in Clear Lake because the Chicahomminy elders did a rain dance.

It rained in Clear Lake because cold air from Canada met warm moist air from the Gulf of Mexico causing the air temperature to drop below the dew point and precipitated moisture from a supersaturated gas mixture of air and water.

Answer: All explain why it rained. Items a. and b. assume human intervention has something to do with the rain. Item c. ascribes the rain entirely natural causes. Items a. and b. imply humans might have some power over the forces of nature, which they do not. Item c. implies humans have no power over the forces that cause rain. But, and here's the advantage, knowledge of the conditions of the atmosphere at a given time and place *does* allow humans to make reasonably accurate predictions of where it will rain and when and how much. Such predictions can give a valuable heads-up on what is going to happen. Items a. and b. have no predictive value whatsoever.

TRUTH USUALLY COMES OUT

It might take some time, in fact it might take 342 years, but sooner or later, truth comes out and is properly recognized, even by the pope. Sooner or later, truth will out.

In a larger sense, the Duchess's claim represents a conceit that most humans secretly share. As a species we think we are pretty important. We think that what we do has major effects on the natural world. My belief is the opposite. I believe what we do, especially considering the vastness of the universe and the daunting extension of time, has little effect. The forces of nature are stronger, much stronger, than the forces of man. We are too puny to have any major influence or any lasting result. Compared to the indifferent forces of nature, we are not important. We are impotent.

Take the sun, for instance. No matter what we do, our sun, the nearest star, will continue converting hydrogen into helium at the thermonuclear rate of four million, three hundred thousand tons per second. And our sun is nothing special. It is just a medium-sized star in a common sequence of yellow star development. In the vast scheme of things even our sun is insignificant. Yet, nothing we do, nothing we can do, will affect its moil and toil. Nothing we do will affect the moil and toil of the other stars, billions of them, nuclear infernos, which flash across the vast blue wastes of our dark skies. Humans in the human scale might count for something, might count for some little thing. But massive evidence indicates that humans in the cosmic scale count for naught.

Most religions capitalize on the human need to control the blind forces of nature. Prayer may make us feel we are doing something to help our humble situation, but the sad fact is that prayer is likely to be ineffective. This idea was succinctly expressed by a character in the recent movie *The Island*. The character is trying to explain God to the two clones, Lincoln and Jordan, who have not had any theistic training. "God is the person who ignores us when we ask for something."

WISHFUL THINKING AND PRAYER ARE ALIKE— BOTH WASTES OF TIME

Major Point: You can't do much to alter reality by prayer, wishful thinking, or changing your emotional state. You can do something to alter reality by action. Cut down the rain forest, built a football stadium, destroy a Japanese city with an atomic bomb, donate your Steinway to the local high school, and so on. Action counts. Wishes don't.

CRITICISM—ADULT TO CHILD

The Duchess is harsh in her criticism of Alice. Criticism in any manner, shape, or form needs to be handled with extreme circumspection. Most people don't like it. As a general rule, don't do it. Certainly never criticize your mistress or lover, wife or spouse. That is just asking for trouble. Always think three times before even hinting at anything negative. Instead, accentuate the positive. Avoid the negative. Put yourself in the other person's Guccis. If you can't say something nice, keep your mouth shut.

Me too. I find criticism extremely annoying. This includes that oxymoron "constructive criticism." Some children, whom I call "porcelain kids," just can't take any criticism without falling apart. They need love, lots of love, not correction.

In the rare event that you must criticize a child, do it in a way just the opposite of the Duchess. Do it with respect and circumspection and reasonable explanation. Like this: "Alice, dear, you just saw my cat with a big grin. That proves cats can grin. And in my opinion most of them do."

* * *

"Talking of axes," said the Duchess, "chop off her head!"

Note a shift of meaning by way of clang association from the axis of rotation of the earth to axes, the executioner's tools. From axes to chop off her head is only one small step farther for the Duchess, but a giant leap for someone's head.

* * *

"Oh, don't bother me!" said the Duchess, "I never could abide figures!"

No comment. But this attitude does remind me of a prominent political figure in the United States government who said, "It must be a budget. It has a lot of numbers in it."

People like the Duchess who ignore evidence, who don't want to bothered with the facts or figures, who don't want to be concerned with knowing the reality situation, those who Charles Sanders Pierce would consider tenacious mode thinkers, are not only the bane of our civilization, they are hopeless. Sigmund Freud: "The less a man knows about the past and the present, the more insecure must be his judgment of the future."

We'll have more fun taking the Duchess to task in chapter 9. Meanwhile, let's see what the Cheshire-Cat is up to.

* * *

"Would you tell me please, which way I ought to go from here?"
"That depends a good deal on where you want to get to," said the Cat.
"I don't much care where—," said Alice.
"Then it doesn't matter which way you go," said the Cat.
    "—so long as I get somewhere," Alice added as an explanation.
    "Oh, you're sure to do that," said the Cat, "if you only walk long enough."

These eminently logical remarks by the Cheshire-Cat are among the most quoted passages in the Alice books.

According to Martin Gardner, a former editor of *Scientific American*, the deep meaning here involves the relation of science to ethics. The cat's answer expresses very precisely the eternal cleavage between science and ethics. Science cannot tell us where to go, but after this decision is made on other grounds (social, political, environmental, ethical, esthetic, etc.), it can tell us the best way to get there.

An echo of Cheshire-Cat talk is heard in Jack Kerouac's novel *On the Road*:

"... we gotta go and never stop going till we get there."
    "Where we going, man?"
    "I don't know but we gotta go."
    A passage in the Talmud is similar: "If you don't know where you are going, any road will take you there."
    I recently got a postcard that said, "I don't know where I'm going ... but that's the beauty of it."

That a Cheshire-Cat has been eminently logical in this one instance doesn't mean it will be logical in another or in the next instance: *"'In that direction,' the Cat said, waving its right paw round, 'lives a Hatter; and in that direction,' waving the other paw, 'lives a March Hare. Visit either you like: they're both mad.'"*

Misinformation is common, especially in directions given by locals to strangers. We don't really get a clear sense of the directions indicated by waving the right paw round. Does that mean the Hatter is on the right? Moving a paw around doesn't clearly indicate a direction and pointing with the right paw doesn't necessarily mean the paw is pointed to the right.

Anyway, the Hatter might live on the right but he can't be visited there. The Hatter is with the March Hare at the March Hare's house on the left, or in front of it, which is almost the same thing. Hence, both Hatter and Hare may be visited on the left.

The directions seem confusing so I know they are confusing on purpose. They are certainly proven erroneous by the facts disclosed in chapter 7. But, then again, the Cat didn't say the Hatter and Hare were in different places. He just said they may be visited. As the Cat didn't say when they may be visited on the right and the left, the information, though equivocal, might be true at some time in the future, even though it is not true at present.

The Cheshire-Cat indicated that Hatter and Hare live in different places. With a charitable interpretation of the meaning of the word "live" (the place of domicile rather than the act of existing), Cat could have been speaking the strict truth. In the truth table of contingent possibilities there is a case where the visit to the Hatter on the right is possible. Therefore that visit is possibly true. Hence, Cat's statement, though contingent, could be true or false at some time in the future.

And yet, and yet—the Cat is still misleading Alice. His (her? its?) statement that Alice may visit Hatter on the right or Hare on the left is contrary to the fact at the time that it was made.

As the directions seemed vague, Alice might well have asked for a clarification. When Alice arrived at the March Hare's and found both the Hatter and Hare there in the same place, she should have learned by deduction that the Cat's statements were not entirely trustworthy. And the moral of that is when someone feeds you misinformation, bullshit, or lies, don't trust them.

On the other hand, perhaps the Cheshire-Cat is a Jesuit who learned casuistry in the seminary—casuistry, the subtle but misleading sophistry of saying a thing one way but intending it to be taken another.

Cheshire-Cat certainly does sound like some of the Jesuits I knew when I was a boy. Their form of argument is well illustrated by the following passages:

> *"But I don't want to go among mad people," Alice remarked.*
>
> *"Oh, you ca'n't help that," said the Cat: "we're all mad here. I'm mad. You're mad."*
>
> *"How do you know I'm mad?" said Alice.*

Wonderful!

Alice is asking for evidence. She knows that all she needs is one counterexample to prove the Cheshire-Cat's generalization "we're all mad here" wrong. If Alice can show she is not mad, or better still if the Cat can't prove she is, then the Cat's statement will have been proven false. Let's review what we covered before and see how the clever Cheshire-Cat handles Alice's challenge.

"You must be," said the Cat, "or you wouldn't have come here."

In a sense this is an excellent example of circular reasoning. It is a tautology because it gives no further information and leaves us unenlightened. In effect, the Cat is saying Alice is mad because she is there and because she is there, she is mad. The second claim is a subaltern claim of the first and is therefore merely a restatement. It's like claiming "All whales are mammals" from which follows that most whales are mammals, some whales are mammals, this whale washed up on the beach in Galveston is a mammal, no whale is not a mammal, and so on. If the claim that "all here are mad" is true then the subaltern claim validly asserts that any person there must be mad. Dig?

But in a larger sense, the Cat speaks truer than he knows. He and Alice are in a dream.

DREAM THINKING IS PRIMARY PROCESS THINKING
—A PHENOMENON AKIN TO MADNESS

Psychiatrists tell us the type of thinking in a dream (primary process thinking) is close to, if not identical with, the thinking of psychotics. Lewis Carroll's diary in 1856 raises the same issue: "When we are dreaming and, as often happens, have a dim consciousness of the fact, and try to wake, do we not say and do things which in waking life would be insane? May we not then sometimes define insanity as an inability to distinguish which is the waking and which the sleeping life? We often dream without the least suspicion of unreality."

In Plato's *Theaetetus*, Socrates addresses the same problem:

Theaetetus: I certainly cannot undertake to argue that madmen or dreamers think truly, when they imagine, some of them that they are gods, and others that they can fly, and are flying in their sleep.

Socrates: Do you see another question that can be raised about these phenomena, notably about dreaming and waking?

Theaetetus: What question?

What question is Socrates driving at?
I have an idea it's about the nature of mental realities, but your guess is as good as mine.

WHAT MODERN PSYCHIATRY
TELLS ABOUT DREAMING

Modern psychiatry would hold that primary process thinking in dreams is normal. But the failure to distinguish the real from the unreal while awake is the characteristic ego disintegrative sign of psychosis. That consideration aside, let's look at the Cheshire-Cat's logic:

Premise: We're all mad here. (unsupported assertion)
Premise: I'm here. You're here. (assertions that are probably true)
Therefore, you must be mad. (conclusion)

Hey! Does that remind you of a catch-22 from the famous novel of the same name written by Joseph Heller? Doc Daneeka, the flight surgeon, explains it: He cannot ground a crazy man, despite the fact that the rules require him to ground anyone who is crazy. The reason is that the crazy man must ask to be grounded. But as soon as he asks he can no longer be considered crazy because according to the catch-22, "a concern for one's own safety in the face of dangers that are real and immediate is the process of a rational mind." Thus, Yossarian, the pilot who wants to be grounded, is looped in a paradox.

THE CHESHIRE-CAT MUST
OPERATE UNDER REJOINDER

Cartesian philosophy requires that we doubt all unsupported assertions. Under the classical debate requirement of rejoinder, it's up to the Cat to give his evidence. If the evidence is relevant and adequate, we might believe him. If it is not relevant and adequate, we should not believe him.

* * *

"and I wish you wouldn't keep appearing and vanishing so suddenly: you make one quite giddy!"

Alice resorts to an ad hominem argument to give herself time to think of a good reply to the Cat's circular reasoning. Her statement is an attack on the Cat's behavior and has nothing whatever to do with the issue under discussion, which was: are they all mad or not?

Diversionary arguments, whether our own or Alice's, are irrelevant. Also did you get the appeal to pity? Alice's reason that she doesn't like the Cat to disappear so quickly is that the disruption makes her giddy.

Appeals to pity are emotionally based diversionary arguments that are off the point. They, too, have a Latin name: *argumentum ad misericordiam.*

APPEAL TO PITY IS NOT A REASONABLE ARGUMENT

When the salesman at Conn's tells me that he's glad to see me because his numbers are behind this month and he needs to make a sale for the benefit of his wife and children, I could be a snot and ask him to prove that: 1. He is behind. 2. He has a wife and children. 3. They would be materially affected if he didn't make the sale. His argument is an appeal to pity, a diversionary argument focusing attention away from the real issues that are what features of high-definition TV are good enough for me to shell out several grand. What he told me might be valid reasons for his urgency to make a sale, but they are not good reasons for me to buy.

UNFAIR RECONSTRUCTION OF OPPOSING ARGUMENTS IS UNFAIR

"All right," said the Cat; and this time it vanished quite slowly, beginning with the end of the tail, and ending with the grin, which remained some time after the rest of it had gone.

Notice that the Cheshire-Cat unfairly selects part of Alice's request and gives that part of the request undue emphasis and importance. His changing slowly is not what Alice really wanted. Alice wanted him to stop changing and remain constant. But of course she opened herself up to the Cheshire-Cat's interpretation by not stating precisely what she wanted. General rule: Say what you want and mean what you say.

"Well! I've often seen a cat without a grin," thought Alice, "but a grin without a cat! It's the most curious thing I ever saw in all my life."

This shows us that if a statement is true, the converse of that statement is not necessarily true. This same point is hammered in farther along during the tea party where "mean what I say" is not the same as "say what I mean."

Modern academics might also inform us that it is impossible to mean what we say or say what we mean, because there is always a slippage between the I that speaks and the I that is spoken of. Such distinctions appear too rich for my blood—so we will not go there—for we probably wouldn't get anywhere even if we did. Dig?

> *"I see what I eat" is not the same as "I eat what I see" and "I like what I get" is not the same as "I get what I like."* To which the Dormouse adds:
>
> *"You might just as well say,"* added the Dormouse, which seemed to be talking in its sleep, *"that I breathe when I sleep is the same thing as I sleep when I breathe!" "It is the same thing with you,"* said the Hatter, and here the conversation dropped.

Sometimes the example comes right out of Carroll's lesson book: "All apples are red, but it does not follow that any red thing is an apple."

This emphasis on the nonequivalence of converses is important and relates to categorical syllogisms, disjunctive syllogism, and to If, then conditional syllogisms as discussed.

BACK TO THE MAIN ARGUMENT: ARE THEY ALL MAD IN WONDERLAND OR NOT?

> *"How do you know I'm mad?"* said Alice.
>
> *"You must be,"* said the Cat, *"or you wouldn't have come here."*
>
> *Alice didn't think that proved it at all; however, she went on: "and how do you know that you're mad?"*

Good for Alice. She knows that the categorical affirmative universal statement "All (persons) here are mad" can be refuted by demonstrating that there is one person here that is not mad. Alice is attempting to use the principle of counterexample to refute the Cat's assertion.

So Alice asks a key question consisting of eight words that weigh in at several tons: "and how do you know that you're mad?"

The Cat, by the debate requirement of rejoinder, must now answer the question with a reasonable argument. Here's what he offers:

> *"To begin with," said the Cat, "a dog's not mad. You grant that?"*
>
> *"I suppose so," said Alice.*
>
> *"Well, then," the Cat went on, "you see a dog growls when it's angry, and wags its tail when it's pleased. Now I growl when I'm pleased, and wag my tail when I'm angry. Therefore, I'm mad."*

The Cheshire-Cat's proof is based on yet more faulty reasoning: A dog wags its tail when happy and growls when angry and is not mad. But a cat wags its tail when angry and growls when it is happy. Just the opposite of the dog. Therefore, if the dog is not mad, then the cat that does the opposite of the dog must be mad.

The defect in the analogy is clear: A dog is not a cat. What a normal dog does isn't necessarily normal for a cat and vice versa. Dogs and cats may share some features but they don't share other features because they are different animals; they have, according to Aristotle, different natures. Because they have different natures, the analogy must break down. Aristotle points out that all animals need nutrition. All animals must extract from their environment organic molecules that provide energy and materials for growth and repair. That is true. But it doesn't follow that I could get along on bird seed. The bird and I are different animals. Because we are different, we have different nutritional needs.

Carroll knew that all analogies if carried far enough break down. They have to break down by their nature since the things compared, unless identical, can never by definition be exactly the same.

Also notice how Alice questions Cheshire-Cat's definition of "growl" and questions the slight change of meaning in context:

"I call it purring, not growling . . ." said Alice.
"Call it what you like," said the Cat.

Notice that our clever Cheshire-Cat, for his argument to succeed, needed to opt on the side of flexible definitions. The Cheshire-Cat, then, seeing Alice's reasoning getting too close for comfort, changes the subject: *"Do you play croquet with the Queen today?"*

BEWARE OF ANY DIVERSION THAT TRIES TO DERAIL AN ARGUMENT

Diversions are a common trick to derail cogent arguments and clear thinking. When you encounter a diversion like this one, just get the diverter right back on track by calling that Cat's attention back to the point. Chances are you have already won the argument just as Alice has. Remember that when people turn sulky, start shouting, call you names, or change the subject, the chances are good that you have won the argument and that by their behavior the other side is admitting defeat.

* * *

"Well! I've often seen a cat without a grin," thought Alice; *"but a grin without a cat! It's the most curious thing I ever saw in all my life!"*

We have already discussed the nonequivalence of converses. But we didn't discuss the fact that this inside joke comes straight out of Lewis Carroll's logic course. So if you are still awake, pay attention.

GRINS WITHOUT CATS EXIST—HERE'S THE PROOF

There is a class of animals called cats. All other animals are not in that class. Thus, the logicians say there are cats and there are non-cats. The class of non-cats most logicians would call not-cat or not-feline. In biological terms it's feline and not-feline.

If the not-cats (not-felines) had a grin, then they would be animals that had a grin without a cat.

All cats are detached as most cat owners know. But Cheshire-Cat is more detached than most. He is probably a very direct symbol of ideal intellectual detachment. He (She? It?) can disappear because it can abstract itself from its surroundings into itself. It can appear only as a head because it is almost a disembodied intelligence. It can appear only as a grin because it can impose an (unsettling) atmosphere without being (entirely) present.

According to Martin Gardner, the phrase "grin without a cat" is probably not a bad description of pure mathematics. Although mathematical theorems often can be usefully applied to the structure of the external world, the theorems themselves are abstractions built on assumptions that belong to another realm "remote from human passions." Bertrand Russell once put it as: "remote from the pitiful facts of nature . . . an ordered cosmos, where pure thought can dwell as in its natural home, and where one, at least, of our nobler impulses can escape from the dreary exile of the actual world."

(By the way, ever notice how much Bertrand Russell resembles the Hatter? No doubt this is a result of psychic anticipation and channeling by the AAW artist John Tenniel.)

Gardner's idea is probably pure hokum. But I will admit it has endearing features. The origin of the idea for the Cheshire-Cat character has been discussed ad nauseam especially by Katsuko Kasai. The explanation that I like the best is Kasai's conjecture that Cheshire cheese was once sold in the shape of a grinning cat. One would tend to slice off the cheese at the cat's tail and end up with only the grinning head on the plate. Furthermore, if the cheese came in the shape of a cat, then a rat could eat the cat—a Carrollinian idea that would probably appeal to Carroll, who should know something about Cheshire Cats as he was born in Daresbury, Cheshire.

CATS AND GRINS IN SYMBOLIC LOGIC

On another level, the idea of a grin without a cat is more basic: Carroll used cats in the logical discussion of the principal relations among categorical classes. In dividing the universe of creatures into cats and not-cats, logicians used the defining form $x \in$ cat, which defines the class of cats and states that x is in that class. This in turn determines the class of not-cats, which, I suppose, started with x is unfeline or x is not a member of the cat class. If this group was used as the class of not-cats and if not-cats is ~C, then "cats" is C. Using this concept let's work out on the truth tables to see if a cat can logically exist without a grin and vice versa:

Let C = cat

Let S = grin (Think of S as a smile, which is a kind of grin. S looks less like a C than a G does so S will serve better as a symbol for grin than G.)

& is the logical connective signifying conjunction meaning both

V is the logical connective signifying disjunction meaning either, or, or both.

Therefore, ~C = not cat; ~S means no grin, (C&S) means a cat with a grin, (C&~S) means a cat without a grin, (~C&S) means a grin without a cat and (~C&~S) means no cat and no grin. Thus, truth tables for such simple and complex statements would be:

	C	S	~C	~S	(C&S)	(C&~S)	(~C&S)	(~C&~S)
1.	T	T	F	F	T	F	F	F
2.	T	F	F	T	F	T	F	F
3.	F	T	T	F	F	F	T	F
4.	F	F	T	T	F	F	F	T

The table lists all possible combinations of the statements involving the simple terms C and S. There are only four cases. They correspond to the conditions 1. cat with a grin 2. cat without a grin 3. no cat but a grin 4. no cat and no grin. Column 3 is the no cat column and its truth values are the opposite of column 1. Column 4 is the no grin column, which is just the opposite of the grin column, column 2. The complex statements follow directly. For example: (C&S) is true in case 1 only because only in case 1 are C and S true. In the cases 2, 3, and 4 either C is false or S is false or both are false. If either C or S are false then the conjunction (C&S) must also be false.

So what?

Hold your horses. I have a point in mind. That will come out with the analysis of the more complex statements [(~C&S)&(C&~S)] and [(~C&S)V(C&~S)].

	(~C&S)	(C&~S)	[(~C&S)&(C&~S)]	(~C&S)V(C&~S)]
1.	F	F	F	F
2.	F	T	F	T
3.	T	F	F	T
4.	F	F	F	F

Thus we prove that you can't have a cat without a grin **and** no cat with a grin because all the cases of that conjunction are false. Such a statement is a contradiction. But the last column proves that we can have a grin without a cat **or** a cat without a grin. The complex statement reflecting those assertions, [(~C&S)V(C&~S)], is true in case 2 and in case 3. Situations that are true in some cases and false in others are contingent on the circumstances for their truth and are logically possible as indicated in the last column. As a teacher of logic, Carroll knew that. And that, I believe, was his rather obscure, but important, point in Alice's observation.

In the same way, with the same tables, I could prove to you that a cat without a grin or a cat with a grin is just a cat and a grin without a cat or a grin with a cat is just a grin. Carroll probably worked out these tables (just for grins?). That is why the eminently logical Alice mentions the truth value of [(~C&S)V(C&~S)], although she claims (contrary to fact) that she has never seen a grin without a cat. (Alice is looking at one as she speaks—looking at an immortal grin without a cat, looking at an immortal grin without a cat that belongs to the immortal Cheshire-Cat, who in turn belongs to the class of immortal characters in the general class of immortal stories.) And so I wonder if the Wonderland here depicted is not only the fabulous place of Carroll's imagination but also the Wonderland of truth, knowledge, and logic, the abstract world where that great man, the author of AAW, used to spend his time.

Carroll's point in this is (I believe) to demonstrate in the analogical matrix known as fiction that the grin can exist without a cat, and that, in the analogical matrix known as logic, the same grin can also exist without a cat. In nature such a thing is also possible, if the class of not-cat is defined simply as the class of all things that exist that are not cat. At least I think that true.

Who knows?

I do know that my wife, Ethel, has an excellent and endearing cat grin that she puts on when it suits her. In that case E! (E! is the logic symbol for "it is asserted as existing") (S&~C) might be justified since the grin in this particular case is attached to a human and not a cat.

In math the square root of −1 exists but in nature it can't exist.

Grins without cats, and math without reality: This is a distinction with a difference, a difference that we should not lose sight of.

WATCH OUT FOR MATHEMATICAL PROOFS

Math is one thing; the real world is another as my example with the square root of −1 proves. Only sometimes do the twain, the two great realms meet. At other times the two may be far, far apart.

Mathematical proofs can describe the real world or they cannot describe the real world, depending on how closely the assumptions, on which the proofs always depend, relate to the real world.

Math may be the queen of the sciences, but the history of mathematics proves that the queen is often in error (like the Queen of Hearts?), though (like the Queen of Hearts) rarely in doubt. Queen Math is often in error because she has been often contradicted by reality. The history of mathematics is a graveyard of reasoned "proofs" once thought perfect and later found defective. This leads to a clear lesson: Do not give undue weight or too much attention to supposed mathematical proofs. Mathematical proofs are only as good as the assumptions that underlie them and may not reflect reality or truth.

Example: When a mathematical analysis by AT&T scientist John Carson was quoted as conclusive proof that FM radio was not possible, the technical community committed the kind of error then that, unfortunately, continues to be quite common now: They believed it.

Someone proves a statement based on certain assumptions. Others forget those assumptions and remember only the conclusions. People then tend to apply such conclusions to all cases, even ones that do not satisfy the original assumptions. This is what had happened to FM, and it was tantamount to a prejudice against FM.

Edwin Armstrong, a Columbia University professor who was always suspicious of mathematical proofs of the impossible, in a brilliant moment of lateral thinking decided to challenge John Carson's wisdom, and he proved the math wrong. He proved it wrong not by challenging the assumptions but by actually inventing an FM radio that worked. Thus, we see here the same proof Alice discovered when she just opened the door to the Duchess's kitchen: Fact trumps all arguments.

7

A Mad Tea Party

The table was a large one, but the three were all crowded together at one corner of it: *"No room! No room!' they cried out when they saw Alice coming. 'There's plenty of room!' said Alice indignantly, and she sat down in a large arm-chair at one end of the table."*

Wow! Alice is forward here. One wonders if a Victorian child well trained in manners would sit herself uninvited at someone else's tea party. Later I may come back to this important ethical and moral question. Then again I may not.

* * *

"Have some wine," the March Hare said in an encouraging tone.
    Alice looked all round the table, but there was nothing on it but tea, "I don't see any wine," she remarked.
    "There isn't any," said the March Hare.

Alice is right and has once again resorted to the proof of her own senses. But there is something on the table that might interest a little girl.

Look again, Alice. There is no wine. But there is a milk-jug on the table. We know this because later on the March Hare spills it: *"Alice rather unwillingly took the place of the March Hare. The Hatter was the only one who got any advantage from the change; and Alice was a good deal worse off than before, as the March Hare had just upset the milk-jug into his plate."*

Failure to observe carefully is a cause of many incorrect conclusions. Failure to see the obvious is common. Many of our failures result from the mental set governing the search procedure at the time. In this case, Alice is looking for wine, not milk. She sees no wine, but she misses the fact that there is milk. Milk would have been a more appropriate drink for a girl seven and one half years old. But perhaps Alice was more interested in wine.

* * *

> *"Then it wasn't very civil of you to offer it," said Alice angrily.*
> *"It wasn't very civil of you to sit down without being invited," said the March Hare.*

In effect, the March Hare is saying that because Alice is guilty of doing the same thing that she is criticizing him for doing (i.e., being uncivil), her argument is no good. Thus, with this counterattack on Alice, the March Hare avoids the obligation to explain his own uncivil behavior. This is a violation of the relevance criterion. That some other person engages in a questionable practice is irrelevant to whether such a practice merits acceptance. Practice what you preach is sensible advice, but not logical argument. Two wrongs don't make a right. Shortcomings of your position cannot be defended by pointing out the errors or shortcomings of the opposition. This common fallacy has been dignified with a Latin name: *tu quoque* (you do it too).

Tu quoque thinking is a common and very powerful psychological response, which most of us have experienced since childhood. It is a natural emotional response, when you think about it, to the inconsistent behavior of a critic. It is human, terribly human for the Hatter to resort to this irrational argument.

HOW TO RESPOND WHEN SOMEONE HITS YOU WITH TU QUOQUE

We often feel no impulse to respond to criticism under such circumstances. Because tu quoque thinking is so emotionally convincing, its fallacious character is usually not fully recognized until pointedly brought to one's attention. And that, of course, dear reader, is your job.

PRINCIPLE: TU QUOQUE (YOU DO IT TOO) IS NOT A REASON AND IS OFTEN AN ATTEMPT AT DIVERSION

To reject criticism by accusing one's critic of doing the same thing (the same thing that is being criticized) diverts the argument to an irrelevant issue and then often proceeds to extend a false conclusion by overgeneralization. Example: "Clinton smokes cigars. So it must be O.K. for me too."

Whether the other party does something or does not do something is not materially related to the conclusion. It is often just a diversion to focus attention away from the real issue, which in this case is whether or not one should smoke cigars. An intelligent consideration would address the pros and cons of cigar smoking and decide the issue on the basis of the evidence.

"At your age you shouldn't be working so hard, Roy. You might get a heart attack."

"Look who's talking."

The questions of age and working hard were not addressed. Instead, it is implied that since the speaker does it too, it must be O.K. What others do or don't do, in so far as those actions are not supported by reason, is irrelevant to the implied conclusion that hard work is O.K. at a given age. Even if the mutual involvement were relevant, outside evidence would have to prove that the conclusion could reasonably be generalized to include the particular person or persons cited.

"Allegra hit first."

Children should not feel entirely justified in antisocial behavior if they can explain it away that way. Because someone else is bad doesn't give you general license to be bad back. If the guy ahead of me runs a red light does not mean it is O.K. for me to run it too.

"George, if I were you I wouldn't smoke so much."

"If I were you, Paul, I wouldn't smoke so much either."

The respondent knows that the other is not he and that, therefore, the statement is not only tu quoque, it is also contrary to fact. Contrary to fact statements ignore evidence and are therefore irrelevant.

"Mickey, I don't think you should be drinking. Alcohol tends to dull your senses, reduces your physical control, and may even become addicting."

"Pop, that's not very convincing with you standing there with a scotch whiskey in your hand."

A father has a duty to tell his son his concerns about his son's drinking. The father is under no moral requirement to follow such advice himself, especially if the father is staying at home and not driving.

"You must stop smoking or you'll get another heart attack."

"Nice of you to say that, Doc. But I saw you ditch that cigarette just before you came in the room."

The doctor has a perfect right, some say a duty, to advise patients about the hazard of smoking, especially after a heart attack. But it's a separate issue as to whether the doctor smokes or doesn't. In fact, from a strictly logical point of view, the doctor's advice appears more cogent given the fact that he does smoke.

* * *

"Take some more tea," the March Hare said to Alice, very earnestly.

"I've had nothing yet," Alice replied in an offended tone: "so I ca'n't have more."

"You mean you ca'n't have less," said the Hatter: "it's very easy to take more than nothing."

True. And an excellent explanation of the null case (the set with no members) known as nothing. It's hard to get less than nothing but easy to get more because nothing is the lowest you can go in the real world of material objects. About nothing, we and Lewis Carroll shall talk more (not less) later.

* * *

"Your hair wants cutting," said the Hatter. He had been looking at Alice for some time with great curiosity, and this was his first speech.

"You should learn not to make personal remarks," Alice said with some severity.

The Hatter's eyes opened very wide on hearing this."

Ah! Contradiction! It's delicious! Here Alice contradicts herself. And the Hatter knows it. That's why his eyes opened not just wide, but very wide—the sign of surprise. If Hatter had turned up his nose and squinted, he would have signaled disdain. To open his eyes wide, he must have raised his eyebrows. The eyebrows are powerful body language communicators. They are the first to announce surprise. When the eyebrows flash, two quick ups and downs, on the other hand, what they indicate is a delight nonpareil.

Alice is making a personal remark while telling the Hatter (in effect) not to make personal remarks. Is Alice one of those "Do as I say and not as I do" people? Is Alice a hypocrite?

I hope not.

Question: Any contradiction in imagining a God who commands "Thou shall not kill" and then goes ahead and floods earth for forty days?

Answer: You tell. It seems to me that this God is the kind of person who says do what I say but do not do what I do.

About Alice: What I like to believe is that Alice is just an innocent source of amusement for Lewis Carroll and not a hypocrite who says one thing and does another. Lots of jokes use contradiction this way. Here I believe Carroll is just making a joke. Alice's behavior is contradicting what she says and that is funny.

Here's one from Harrigan and Hart.

Harrigan: Hands up! Your money or your life?

Hart: Take me life. I'm saving me money for me old age.

People love this kind of contradiction and they like feeling superior to the *schlimazel* because they see the contradiction and he doesn't. Lots of comedy teams operate on this principle. The first was the toast of

Broadway, Weber and Fields, where Weber was the *schlemiel* in the Yiddish tradition and Fields was the *schlimazel*. Fields is the straight man and Weber the childlike, innocent, born loser. Abbott and Costello, Dean Martin and Jerry Lewis, Laurel and Hardy, and the Smothers Brothers follow the same comedy formula, amuse people and, in the process, make millions of dollars.

As Wonderland illustrates, the more weird and bizarre the characters and conditions, the funnier things can be. Weber and Fields spoke in what they and their audiences called Dutch, but it was really a twisted and strangled kind of Deutsch (German):

Weber: Who vass dat lady I seen you wid last night?

Fields: Dat vass no lady, dat vass mine vife!

Note the contradiction produces the humor. The effect is magnified because we are understanding what Fields does not.

Here's another example of contradiction producing humor: She had difficulty completing simple calculations. For example, when I asked her what three times three plus one equals, she said, "ten."

Get it?

Who is simple here? The speaker or the spoken of?

"When everything is coming your way, you're in the wrong lane."

Billboard sign (about Iraq) on Interstate Highway 45 into Houston: "No setback is a setback for us."

Get it? Either a setback is a setback or it isn't. Also consider this: The logical equivalent of this universal statement "All setbacks are not setbacks for us" is "No setback is a setback for us."

What they really meant to say is "for us no setback is a setback for long." But as the statement stands, it is a contradiction and a setback for clear thinking. It's funny because it shows that the people who made the sign didn't know that they were contradicting themselves. They in effect announced that they had experienced a setback and at the same time they denied that it was a setback. Dig?

About contradiction we should say a few more words as the concept of "unbirthday" is coming up soon in this chapter, unbirthday being the negation of birthday.

The concept of negation has occupied philosophers from day one. Yes or no, true or false, 0 or 1, + or −, go or no go, not, and, or, NOT, AND, OR, she loves me she loves me not, setback and no setback.

By the way, those readers who wish to write me a letter can. My address is always at the end of this book unless it isn't.

In a major way, contrast by negation is a major way that philosophers arrive at a vision of the truth. When Carroll shows us a bad king and a bad queen, he is telling us kings and queens can be bad and is showing us how. In effect, this is a stern rebuke to the Platonic concept of the (good) philosopher king as depicted in the *Republic*. Incidentally, Plato excluded poets and literary men from the republic because he thought they would corrupt the people. So in his rather negative depiction of royalty, Carroll may be getting a kind of poetic revenge on Plato.

END OF SIDEBAR AND BACK TO ALICE AND HER ADVICE NOT TO MAKE PERSONAL REMARKS

Either Alice believes what she says or she doesn't. If she believes it, then why does she not follow her own advice? Why does she tell Hatter not to make personal remarks at the same time that she is making personal remarks? If she doesn't believe her advice, then why does she tell Hatter he should not make personal remarks? See my point? You can't have your cake and eat it too. Alice's behavior contradicts her advice. Both the behavior and the advice cannot be simultaneously true. Ken Lay can't tell us that Enron is a great investment at the same time he is selling his stock like crazy. His behavior contradicts his words. One or the other can't be pointing to the truth.

To my mind, the reason Ken Lay couldn't admit the truth was because he has always taken the view that perception is reality. If he could convince people that Enron was the great company he said it was, then it surely was—and never mind that its profits were largely fiction. Ken Lay's belief in the power of public relations is the reason he gave a news conference the day after he was indicted. It's the reason he made that speech in Houston the week before Christmas 2005. He seemed to believe that if he said something often enough, and loud enough, it would come true. Fat chance of that.

Did Ken Lay know that he lied about Enron? Who knows? That is what his trial tried to determine. One thing is for sure: Once the trial started, Ken Lay had to leave the public relations dream world to face hostile questions from prosecutors. There was lots of hard evidence of fraud, double dealing, and cover-up. And the jury found him guilty. He didn't like that reality one bit. But then, reality had never been his strong point. Unfortunately for him, reality has a sneaky way of creeping up on people and wreaking its revenge. Lay went down because of the overwhelming evidence against him. (Note: Lay was convicted, but avoided punishment by dying of a heart attack. Ironically, this result harkens back to the English common law prevailing in the eighteenth and the early part of the nineteenth century wherein business fraud and accounting fraud were capital offenses.)

CONTRADICTIONS ARE COMMON

"There are two things I can't stand: Prejudice against other cultures . . . and the Dutch."

The overt meanings of that prejudicial statement from *Austin Powers 3: Goldmember* is clear—as is the hidden meaning that Austin's father, played by Michael Caine, is in fact prejudiced against the Dutch. Since he claims he can't stand cultural prejudice and yet actually has one himself, Austin's father is also telling us that he is a hypocrite. He is a hypocrite as much as Alice is a hypocrite when she tells Hatter not to make personal remarks and as much as Ken Lay was when he told us to buy Enron stock while he was selling.

UNBIRTHDAY: A CLASSIC CONCEPT
IN PRISTINE PURE LOGIC

Unbirthday is right out of Carroll's course in logic at Oxford: Unbirthday is the denial or negation of birthday. It is another way of saying not birthday. The concept is trivial, but the results are not trivial. The results underlie much of our Western civilization's quest for logical certainty.

You have one birthday a year. All the other days are unbirthdays. This could be formulated B or not B, or we could abbreviate the statement as logicians do by placing the sign for negation, the tilde ~, before the second B. Thus, ~B stands for the unbirthday.

Now it is obvious that when a statement is true, its denial is false. When a statement is false, its denial is true. Using the shorthand, we can symbolize this information in a truth table:

B	~B	
T	F	(case one)
F	T	(case two)

The truth table tells us that when it's a birthday, it is not an unbirthday (case one where B is true and ~B is false) and vice versa: when it is not a birthday, it is an unbirthday (case two where B is false and ~B is true). This is the same thing (that is the logically equivalent form) that Hatter tells Alice.

Truth tables like this have had a major effect on the development of computerized information processing and underlie most computer logic. They are the foundation of our mathematics, as proven in extenso by Alfred North Whitehead and Bertrand Russell in their book *Principia Mathematica*.

The probability of today being your unbirthday is 364/365 and the probability of this being your birthday is 1/365. Therefore the probability of ~B/B is 364 to 1. By the truth table above it is obvious that any statement of B is inconsistent with its negation, ~B. In other words B and ~B are mutually exclusive. If it is B, then it can't be your ~B and if it is ~B, it can't be your B. Hatter explains this in words alone. But he could have just given Alice the equation Probability(B or ~B) = 1 and therefore, probability(1− ~B) = probability(B).

By the way, Hatter isn't entirely reasonable: Hatter thinks it is much better to celebrate unbirthdays than celebrate birthdays because there are so many more unbirthdays than birthdays. This reasoning assumes celebrating is desirable. It might be from his perspective or the perspective of the kids, but it might not be true for others, especially adults. Hatter's reasoning disregards the utility factor that must be included in any value judgment. Any mother of a two-year-old knows, especially if she has suffered through even one birthday party, that some birthday parties are no fun at all for adults. I can't stand them myself. Some of the longest moments of my life have been spent at birthday parties for my children and grandchildren. How about you?

* * *

"It was the best butter," the March Hare meekly replied.

"Yes, but some crumbs must have got in as well," the Hatter grumbled: "you shouldn't have put it in with the bread-knife."

In the context of this exchange, one level of the lesson is clear: Don't use butter to fix your watch. But on another level, these two sentences are profound as they hark back to Aristotle's discussion of the proper use of things. Aristotle's idea was that each individual things has an individual nature. By examination of the particulars of a thing, its function and proper purpose can be discovered. Once discovered, that function is what Aristotle would call the "natural function." The natural function of a hammer, for instance, is to exert focused pressure (that is, to hammer). The natural function of a lyre is to play music. We could make a kind of music by hammering and we could actually hammer with a lyre. However, the hammer would do a much better job for the hammering purpose than the lyre would and the lyre would do a much better job of music making than the hammer. Furthermore, using the lyre for hammering might injure the musical instrument, rendering it unfit for its natural function.

Butter is good for bread and should be applied with a butter knife. But butter is not good for a watch and applying it with a butter knife can transfer crumbs that foul up the mechanisms. And so, by negative example, we learn this important lesson: To each tool its proper purpose and for each purpose its proper tool.

Old Chinese Proverb: Why do you kill chicken with cow knife? The idea is that you should use a small knife to kill a chicken. By extrapolation, you should use the proper means to get any task done and not over do it.

According to Aristotle's virtue ethics, there are two sins: excess and deficiency and only one virtue: the golden mean. By golden mean, Aristotle did not mean (pun intended) the arithmetic mean. He meant the exactly right and most excellent way available under the (ever-shifting) circumstances. Thus repairs to the watch should be done the best way possible. Excess and deficiency should be avoided.

Using the *best* butter for watch repair is irrelevant because Hare should not be using butter at all. Whether the butter was applied with a butter knife or not is also irrelevant because butter should not have been applied at all. Carroll must have had a field day dreaming up these examples of poor thinking for this spate of conversation.

Lesson: No butter in watches, please.

In the same way, it would be inappropriate for me to fuel my Lincoln Ultimate Luxury Town Car with the best beer. It might be the best beer, and it might come out of the best aluminum can with the best pull top, but even the best beer would foul up the engine. Gasoline is the only appropriate fuel to use in my Lincoln. Anything else would not work.

* * *

"You can draw water out of a water-well," said the Hatter; "so I should think you could draw treacle [treacle is British for molasses] out of a treacle-well— eh, stupid?"

Here Hatter interprets algebraic equations as absolutely universal— standing for all possible entities. The interpretation in words rather than symbols, in sentences rather than in mathematical formulas, does not guarantee meaning. "You can draw water out of a water well," the Hatter says, "so I should think you could draw treacle out of a treacle-well . . ." The structure of the two sentences is the same (you can draw b out of a b-well), but the content is different. Carroll's humor is clear and so is his lesson: structure does not guarantee meaning. This is the reason that baby oil does not come from babies, even though corn oil comes from corn.

Emphasis on structure over meaning, so basic to the symbolic approach to truth and knowledge, can lead to nonsense. The meaning-lessness and arbitrariness of Carroll's underground world, the parallels between Carroll's nonsense writings and his study of symbolic logic, are striking. Both stress form or structure over sense (meaning meaning), using words with multiple possible interpretations and failing in most instances to arrive at clear denotation, while definitely arriving at nonsense humor. And the moral of that is: The real world is often more complicated than the world that can be described in sym-bols or logic. On most occasions language, defective though it may be, actually comes closer to the true description than math. For instance, most of us know without much difficulty that there is a difference, a big difference, between a chestnut horse and a horse chestnut. Yet there is no mathematical difference between $h+c$ and $c+h$. Nor is there a dif-ference in symbolic logic between H&C and C&H, as H&C $\equiv$ C&H.

WHY IS TRUTH SO DIFFICULT?

Time out: One of the reasons why the range and depth of subjects dealt with in books is so limited is that authors want, for a variety of reasons, most people to be able to follow what is going on. Technical terms put readers off. So does complexity. Entire classes of trades and professions never make it into books simply because it would be impossible to describe their reality. Truth is often complex, often too complex for little minds or for simple explanations. The descriptions that I have read, for instance, of what it is like to practice medicine are no more than caricatures in response to the delusional expectations of the intended lay readership. Medicine is much more complicated and much more interesting than language or authors (even authors who are also physicians) can truly express.

* * *

"But they were in the well," Alice said to the Dormouse, not choosing this last remark.

Good for Alice. She is not going to get into one of those ridiculous late night dorm arguments about something like a treacle-well, which, after all, does not exist. But isn't it interesting how the mere statement about treacle-well implies that it *does* exist? Our brains are led down the garden path by a trick of language. The fact that we have a name for something doesn't mean that that something exists. The existential (also known as ontological) claims of statements are often questionable. Watch out for them. They are another example of how language sometimes leads us down the garden path.

STATEMENTS AND THEIR EXISTENTIAL CLAIMS

A statement is a sentence that makes a definite claim. In all statements there is the overt claim and there is a covert claim. The covert claim can be an existential claim that the subject or the predicate of the statement actually exists. Whether the existential claim is justified would have to be decided by evaluation of the evidence. Thus, the statement "All unicorns are green" not only asserts that unicorns are green, it implies that unicorns exist and that green exists. About green we have no problem, but about unicorns we do have a problem, as none of them do truly exist. If unicorns don't exist, they can't be green. The statement "God is just" asserts all of God is just and that God exists and that just exists. As that statement is of the same form as the statement about unicorns, the same standards of proof are required.

Me: "My favorite animal is the dragon."

Callie Patten: "Then you don't have a favorite animal."

WHY GOD IS NOT JUST

The scholastic Fathers of the Church had problems with the statement "God is just." Work out on this statement the way Callie worked out on my statement about my favorite animal. See what you come up with. Pay particular attention to the existential claims. Then compare your analysis with mine: "God is just" is a statement because it is a sentence that makes a definite claim. The claim is what it says: God is just. Existential claims, as well, lie implicit in the sentence. They are that God exists and that just exists. Many people would also feel that the person making the claim is thereby asserting that he or she believes in God.

There is another unusual claim attached to this statement, the superdeific claim. That is, the statement "God is just" claims that there is a standard outside of God that God must measure up to, conform to, and obey, and that standard is called just.

GOD IS JUST: THE PROBLEM

If God is just, then there exists a standard outside of God to which God must adhere. If that is so, then God can't be all powerful as she must conform to that standard. Therefore, the statement that God is just cannot be true because God has to be all powerful. If it cannot be true, it must be false. If it is false, then God is not just.

Doctors of the church, like Saint Thomas and Saint Augustine, admit that God is, accordingly, not just. They and the medieval church tried to get around the problem of the theodicy of the superdeific standard by claiming that "God is not just and cannot be just because God is justice."

Here's another statement, a familiar statement from a familiar rogue of history: "We are the master race."

Pause and think for a while and then list all the claims that that statement is making. Compare your list with mine. Dissection of the claims of statements gives us the analytical tools to clearly refute the claims if the claims are not justified by relevant and adequate evidence:

Adolf Hitler's allegation makes the following claims:

1. That we exist.
2. That race exists.
3. That we (the German people) are a race.
4. That there is a master race.
5. That there is only one master race.
6. That the German people are that master race.
7. That the speaker is part of the group included in we.
8. (Subaltern claim) That the speaker is part of the master race as the group is the master race.
9. (Subaltern claim) That because we are the master race, other races must be the slave races.
10. (Subaltern claim) That because we are the master race, we are entitled to enslave the other races, seize their property, punish, or kill them.

Note: Items 3–10 can be easily shown to be not true. Believe it or not, subaltern claim 10 was seriously argued by Hitler as the justification for the invasions of other countries and the enslavement of the defeated peoples.

* * *

"Of course they were," said the Dormouse: "well in."

This answer so confused poor Alice, that she let the Dormouse go on for some time without interrupting it.

"They were learning to draw," the Dormouse went on, yawning and rubbing its eyes, for it was getting very sleepy; "and they drew all manner of things—everything that begins with an M—"

"Why with an M?" said Alice.

"Why not?" said the March Hare.

The confusions of meanings of in the well and well in and drawing pictures and drawing treacle have been covered. We also know that human brains do not usually function at maximum efficiency and that sleepy brains are less likely still to function at maximal efficiency.

Note that it is the March Hare, not the Dormouse, who answers Alice's question. Hare has a vested personal interest in the matter because his name starts with M and he wanted to be part of the story. He wanted to be drawn for the same reason that most wealthy and privileged members of Victorian society in England in the nineteenth century wanted to have their portraits painted by John Singer Sargent. Those aristocrats had a vested interest in seeing themselves well portrayed (PUN intended).

Like most people with vested interests (that need defending), the March Hare's defense is irrelevant. In this case it is an irrelevant appeal to absence of a reason. Failure to know something or (worse) not having a reason to justify a statement (such as March Hare's "Why not?") is not a reason supporting the statement. Absent evidence, ignorance itself, or no reason whatsoever never justifies anything. How could it?

The "Why not?" is one of the classic false arguments that has been given a nice Latin name: *argumentum ad ignorantiam*, the argument as an appeal to ignorance.

Argumentum ad ignorantiam tries to prove a proposition by asserting that it has never been disproved. That something hasn't been disproved is never an argument that it has been proved. How could it be?

Yet, the argument ad ignorantiam has widespread applications among the ignorant: Ghosts must exist because nobody has established that they do not. UFOs exist because no one has proven that they do not.

By the way, I know UFO abductions exist because I am a victim. Years ago I was abducted by twenty Venusians all of whom looked like Marilyn Monroe in her salad days. They took me aboard their space ship and repeatedly subjected me to . . . well, you get the picture. I tell that story each month at the meeting of the Houston support group of UFO abductees. That group believes me of course and gives me globs and globs of sympathy.

Homework 1: Prove that my UFO abduction story is false.

Homework 2: Prove it the same way that you proved that Santa Claus doesn't exist.

* * *

"'Much of a muchness'—did you ever see such a thing as a drawing of a muchness!"

Muchness is a good solid English word. It means a large quantity or greatness. As it is an abstract term, it would be difficult to image a drawing of a muchness. In fact, I doubt that such a drawing exists. Alice probably wants to tell us that she hasn't seen such a drawing, but she is rudely cut off by the Hatter:

"Really, now you ask me," said Alice, very much confused. "I don't think—"
"Then you shouldn't talk," said the Hatter.

This piece of rudeness was more than Alice could bear: she got up in disgust and walked off.

I don't think that the Hatter is nice and I think the Hatter is not nice. Either expression is a valid (though somewhat misleading) figure of speech expressing an opinion about the Hatter. A more direct statement would be: Hatter is not nice. Even better would be backing up the assertion with reasons:

1. Because he interrupted Alice before she finished her sentence, Hatter is not nice.
2. Because he made a personal remark, Hatter is not nice.
3. Because he purposely misconstrued what Alice was saying, Hatter is not nice.

Alice didn't mean she wasn't thinking, although on one level (the concrete level) that is exactly what she said when she said, "I don't think."

But, in general, we get Hatter's point. And in general his point is a good point. People who don't think shouldn't talk. No doubt Lewis Carroll believed that. If people who don't think don't talk, then we will not have to suffer them at the dinner table and at cocktail parties and during election campaigns.

And isn't it true that the key difficulty that students have with logic courses is precisely that these students don't think but should? Therefore, on one level, to any teacher of logic "I don't think" is the cardinal sin. For a teacher of logic and for an author of a book on clear thinking, "I don't think" is not only a BIG DEAL, but is THE BIG DEAL.

"I don't think" is also the negation of the famous statement by René Descartes, "I think," upon which Descartes built a complete philosophic system.

Descartes (1596–1650) focused attention on the problem of how we know things. In his book *Discourse on Method* (1637), he believed he had discovered a single method of reasoning that applied to all sciences, providing a unified body of knowledge. The key was to break down the problem into parts, accepting as true only clear, distinct ideas that could not be doubted. Because Descartes could not doubt the statement "I think, therefore I am," this statement became the first principle of his philosophic system. The Cartesian philosophical system is thus based on doubt and is the direct negation of the philosophical systems based on faith as discussed.

CONDITIONAL SYLLOGISM
(ALSO KNOWN AS IF, THEN)

There are three forms of deductive logic: The categorical syllogism (already discussed), the conditional syllogism, and the disjunctive syllogism. Each of these has valid and invalid forms and each has a long an honorable history. They all have given thousands and thousands of students millions and millions of headaches.

PROPERTIES OF DEDUCTIONS

According to Professor David Zarefsky of Northwestern University,♣ all deductions share two important properties: No new information follows from them and, if the premises are true, the conclusion must follow. Because of these two properties, according to the professor, deductions have limited applications to real world problems. That is why these days formal logic has, in some quarters, such a bad reputation. It's not practical. As the information is already embedded in the premises, nothing new is learned or can be learned.

That is why in modern times informal logic has such a good reputation. It is practical. Informal logic potentially has a direct, important, and real application to the real world. And new things and ideas and new information and insights can follow from it. That is the advantage of informal logic. The disadvantage is that the conclusions that follow from informal logic do not have the absolute certainty of the conclusions that follow from formal logic.

What Professor Zarefsky is calling "informal logic" is really induc-

---

♣ David Zarefsky, *Argumentation: The Study of Effective Reasoning*, 2nd ed., the Great Courses, Teaching Company, 2005.

tive logic: statistics, probability calculus, other scientific methods of reasoning. But, you know, once a conclusion is reached by informal or inductive logic, it is usually tested by the hypothetical-deductive method. This method is the key to testing a proposed explanation (the hypothesis) with experimental observation.

Professor Zarefsky probably is right in his detailed analysis. But from a pseudoscholarly point of view, it seems to me that formal logic has a biting way of helping the user uncover what is implicit in a set of claims. For instance, I can use formal logic to show that the simultaneous existence of evil and of an omnipotent, omniscient, perfectly good god is impossible. To say there is no new information in this deduction is misleading in cases where the deduction discloses something not realized before by the person making or following it. A clue exists at a crime scene just as an implicit truth exists in a set of beliefs; it takes a detective to find the clue and a deduction to make the truth explicit. Hence, I shall continue to use formal logic and deductive logic in this book (and my life as it pleases me) whenever it is useful to uncover what is implicit in Lewis Carroll's book.

ATTENTION! MAIN POINTS!

Conclusions from formal logic are true if the premises are true and the rules have been followed.

Conclusions from formal logic are already embedded in the premises. Therefore, strictly speaking, no new information can be present in the conclusion that is not already present in the premises.

Conclusions from formal logic may or may not relate to the real world. They certainly have an application to the real world in computer systems, as all computer systems are based on forms of formal logic.

Conclusions from informal logic have the endearing feature that they often relate to the real world and help us understand reality better.

Conclusions from informal logic are not 100 percent certain.

THE CONDITIONAL SYLLOGISM
AS AN EXAMPLE OF DEDUCTION

"I think, therefore I am" is a conditional syllogism. It says that if a person thinks, then he or she must exist. It also says that if a person doesn't exist, then he or she is not thinking. It does not say that if people exist, then they must be thinking. It does not say that if people don't think, then they do not exist. The later error (negating the antecedent) is the basis for the following joke:

Descartes was flying Pan Am across the Atlantic Ocean when the stewardess asked, "Would you like a Coke?"

He replied, "I think not" and disappeared in a puff of smoke.

In symbolic logic the form of the conditional syllogism would look like:

If A (and then) B.

Or if A, then B.

The "if" statement is called the antecedent and the "then" statement is the consequent. In more formal logic this might look like:

If A, then B.

A.

Therefore, B.

Another way of symbolizing the relationship is:

A⊃B, which would be read as A entails B, where entails means that the presence of A absolutely requires B.

In practical form an if-then statement might look like this:

If you take cyanide, then you die.

You take cyanide.

Conclusion: You die.

As a logician Carroll knew how important it was to understand that converses are not necessarily true. That is why he gives so many examples to prove the point. In fact, disregard of these ideas leads to some common errors in thinking. For instance:

If you take cyanide, then you die.

You do not take cyanide.

Therefore, you do not die.

or:

If A, then B.

Not A.

Therefore, not B.

The confusion here is that cyanide is a sufficient cause of death by itself. It interferes with the cytochrome respiratory chain so effectively that the transfer of electrons to oxygen is prevented and metabolism stops dead. But that does not mean that because you don't take cyanide you will live forever. There are many other causes of death besides cyanide. Cyanide is just one of a rather large class of poisons that will cause death, and the rather large class of poisons causing death is part of an even larger class of things (eating too much pie, getting run over by a steamroller, choking on a filet mignon, lung cancer, stroke, heart attack, Marchiafava-Bignami disease, Kew fever, etc.) that can cause death. Not taking cyanide will not prevent one of those other causes from eventually taking its toll. In formal logic this error is called "denying the antecedent."

Here's another problem that arises from similarly defective reasoning:

If you take cyanide, then you die.

You die.

Therefore, you took cyanide.

or:

If A, then B.

B.

Therefore A.

"Affirming the consequent" (the name of this fallacy) ignores a nuance. Death doesn't automatically imply that you took cyanide as there are other causes of death besides cyanide. In terms of necessary and sufficient conditions, the error here is the same as the error of denying the antecedent; it is the fallacy of assuming that a sufficient condition is a necessary one. Cyanide is a sufficient condition of dying, not a necessary one.

Thus, in the conditional syllogism there are two and only two valid forms: Affirming the antecedent and negating the consequence. Thus, in the conditional syllogism there are two and only two invalid forms: Negating the antecedent and affirming the consequence.

SUMMARY OF IF, THEN

If, then is a deductive argument. As such it shares the properties of all deductive arguments: If the premises are true, the conclusion must follow and no new knowledge is obtained as all the information is present (implicitly or explicitly) in the premises.

Example: $A \supset B$ means if A, then B.

If you take cyanide, then you die.

You take cyanide, therefore you die. (valid: affirms the antecedent)

You don't take cyanide, therefore you will not die. (invalid: negates the antecedent)

You died, therefore you took cyanide. (invalid: affirms the consequence)

You did not die, therefore you did not take cyanide. (valid: negates the consequence)

Summary of conditional syllogism in symbols:

$A \supset B$

This deductive argument is valid, if and only if, it is not invalid. A deductive argument is valid if it follows the rules:

Valid: Affirm the antecedent: $A / \therefore B$

Valid: Negate the consequence: $\sim B / \therefore \sim A$

Invalid: Affirm the consequence: $B / \therefore A$ (wrong!)

Invalid: Negate the antecedent: $\sim A / \therefore \sim B$ (wrong!)

INTERRUPTING PEOPLE IS RUDE

Alice walks off in a huff because Hatter has interrupted her. Most people have a desire to talk. Some absolutely need to talk. Some can't stop talking. Those souls have what I call motor mouth disease. They just can't stop talking. The ancients, including Cicero and Philo, considered this propensity a vice, and for good reason. The garrulous can be quite irritating. Have you heard this before: God gave us two ears and one mouth so that we can listen twice as much as we talk.

If there is a need to talk, there must be a need to have listeners. Consequently, most people have a need for other people to listen. Has anyone ever said to you, "You're not listening?" Is there a man or woman alive who has not said this or who has not had this said to them? Dear reader out there, I can't see you right now, but I'd bet you're probably smiling. Aren't you?

Not listening is high on the list of causes of argument or relationship strain. In business it causes failure to close the deal, get approval, sell the product, or make the investment. In politics the results can be devastating. On October 15, 1992, during the debate with Bill Clinton, President George H. W. Bush was asked by a nice sincere woman, "How has the national debt affected each of you personally?" The president replied that the debt affects everyone, whereupon the woman interrupted to restate her question. "How has it affected you personally?" Bush then talked about how the high interest rates might affect his grandchildren. "No!" the woman insisted, "you personally." Then the president admitted he didn't understand the question. "Does it imply that the well-to-do are not affected?" he asked. "If you clarify the question, I'll answer it." Political analysts claim that that failure to listen and the failure to make a credible rejoinder to that woman's specific question was one of the material items that sank the first Bush's bid for reelection. He didn't listen.

In my course on mental gymnastics at Rice University I cover the remedy: A skill called active attentive listening. Active attentive listening is especially important when your spouse is doing the talking, as a spouse can usually make your life miserable.

In some cases this need to be heard is dire. When that need is frustrated, people get angry. People get angry and go off in a huff, just as Alice did.

Dale Carnegie in his famous book *How to Win Friends and Influence People* tells us that most people want to talk and most people do not want to listen. So, the way to score high in people's admiration is to fill the *need* of most people by listening—not by talking.

Listen with your whole heart and soul, with rapt attention and without interruption. If you must interrupt, interrupt the smart way by asking a question. The talker will be flattered to know that you are really interested. Also, try to turn off your own head talk. Don't worry about what you are going to say because usually people don't want you to say anything. Just listen. Just listen so attentively that when the talker forgets what he or she was saying (not unusual especially at cocktail parties after a few drinks), you can come back with exactly what was said and the talker can start up again.

"Oh, my God, I lost my train of thought. What was I saying?"

"You hate your mother-in-law."

"Oh, yes. How kind of you to remember."

And while we are on the topic of constructive conversation, it is important to realize what people like to talk about. Is it money? Sex? Politics? Religion?

No way, José.

Their favorite topic: Themselves (of course).

So let them drone on. You will be the life of the party. Many times the hostess of a dinner party, as she was saying good-bye to me, has remarked on what a great conversationalist I was and how so many guests enjoyed talking to me. That often occurred after a full evening in which I hardly said a word, just listened.

Communication science is now taught in colleges across the nation. My daughter-in-law, Michelle Patten, majored in communications. This important subject was not available to my generation. Instead, we had to suffer through Latin and Greek—Laughing and Grief according to Lewis Carroll. There wasn't much laughing in Latin as I recall, but there sure was plenty of grief in Greek.

One of the major areas of application of communication science has been in physician-patient communication.

TELL THE DOCTOR ALL YOUR PROBLEMS, BUT KEEP IT TO LESS THAN A MINUTE

"What brings you to clinic?" the doctor asks. The woman starts to answer. Eighteen seconds later (yes, lady, I said eighteen seconds), the doctor interrupts. Yes, researchers have found that, on average, patients were interrupted eighteen seconds into explaining their problems. Less than 2 percent were able to finish their explanations. Furthermore, researchers have linked this communication style to the same kind of result we saw with Alice. In the case of doctors, however, it is not just a walk-off or a disgruntled walk-out, it may be a malpractice suit. Not only that, poor communication or lack of complete communication in medicine results in puzzled patients (85 percent don't fully understand what the doctor told them; 50 percent leave the doctor's office unclear about what they are supposed to do). In consequence, they fail to follow treatment plans.

In one study, Drs. Wendy Levinson, Nalini Ambady, et al. of Harvard University compared the office manner of surgeons who had been sued multiple times with those who had never been sued.[♥] Doctors with a domineering tone of voice were more likely to have been sued by patients than doctors whose tone expressed more personal warmth. So, advice by experts on how doctors (and, by extrapolation, the rest of us) can most effectively communicate with people reads as if it came straight out of a self-help book:

1. Listen carefully.
2. Ask open-ended questions.

[♥] Nalini Ambady, Debi LaPlante, Thai Nguyen, Robert Rosenthal, Nigel Chaumeton, and Wendy Levinson, "Surgeon's Tone of Voice: A Clue to Malpractice History," *Surgery* 132, no. 1 (July 2002): 5–9.

3. Do not interrupt.
4. Make eye contact.
5. Indicate with body language (open posture, hands at side, leaning forward toward the speaker, smiling, etc.) that you care.

In other words, do the opposite of the Hatter.

Results: Amazingly, listening to the patient has resulted in shorter, not longer appointments. It also tends to eliminate excessive testing. In 1999, a follow-up study was published in the *Journal of the American Medical Association*. Patients were no longer interrupted, on average, at eighteen seconds. Instead, it took twenty-three seconds for the doctor to interrupt. That is progress! But not that much.

* * *

"Once more she found herself in the long hall, and close to the little glass table. "Now, I'll manage better this time," she said to herself, and began by taking the little golden key, and unlocking the door that led into the garden. Then she set to work nibbling at the mushroom (she had kept a piece of it in her pocket) till she was about a foot high: and then—she found herself at last in the beautiful garden, among the bright flower-beds and the cool fountain."

Experience is a great teacher. Alice learned from experience. Notice how Alice has both the correct sequence and the correct method: First she unlocked the door with the golden key. Then she shrank herself to get through the door. She figured it out. How about you? Did you figure out the correct sequence?

Furthermore, Alice shrank neither too much nor too little. She shank herself just right by nibbling to get to the exact right size and fit. Alice was also prepared for the problem. She had saved a piece of mushroom. One of the more important lessons to learn in this life is that you need the material means (the proper tools) to get something done, and you need the savvy to work that means to your advantage. Preparing in advance helps. Be prepared—that's the Boy Scout motto.

And the first thing Alice had to learn to control in Wonderland was her own body. By carefully measuring the amount of mushroom, she gets down to her normal size. Self-control was the major character trait esteemed by the ancients. Volumes have been devoted by them to that subject. If you are interested in what the ancients said, Plutarch's *The Lives of the Noble Grecians and Romans* is a good place to start. If you do get around to reading that book, note how Plutarch's biographies serve as moral instruction, with particular attention to the lives of Alexander and Caesar, Demosthenes and Cicero.

Control of body size is a big current issue in American medicine. You know why, so I won't bother explaining. Type II diabetes is epidemic. Fat people die sooner of all sorts of things.

Kant said it is the task of us humans to understand reality and then manipulate the reality for our own benefit. He was right. He'd be thrilled to know that he was right, except he's dead.

When Alice understands the reality, and when she manipulates it correctly, she gets the result she wants. She gets the right thing: the right procedure, at the right time, in the right place. Follow her example.

Talking about what is right reminds me about the important question raised at the beginning of this chapter: Was it right or wrong for Alice to crash the tea party? Is it right or wrong to discuss that issue? Can it be discussed without boring the reader?

Answer: I don't know. But I'll give it a try.

Those of you who think that they might be bored by a small dip into the ice-cold waters of moral philosophy, north of north, should skip to the next chapter and find out what happens at the Queen's Croquet Ground. Those of you who think that they might be amused and enlightened by a dip into moral philosophy should not skip to the next chapter. Just continue reading. Those of you who don't know what to do, should do what I do when I can't make a decision: flip a coin.

META-UTILITARIANISM: DEMONSTRATION OF THE USEFULNESS OF ECLECTIC MORAL PHILOSOPHY AND SCIENCE COMPARED TO THE USELESSNESS OF LEAVING MORAL DECISIONS TO CHANCE

Friend: This discussion, whose form is based on St. Thomas Aquinas's *Summa Theologiae*, aims to illustrate a practical problem in ethics based on the analysis of one particular human situation taken from *Alice's Adventures in Wonderland*. The discussion proceeds in terms of multiple ethical and moral norms in use today and includes standards of behavior from *The Analects*, *Summa Theologiae*, a real-life standard, English common law, the Boy Scout law, the Ten Commandments, common sense, gut feelings, the categorical imperative, ethical egoism, utilitarianism, social contract, virtue ethics (feminism included), Buddhism, science and the scientific method, and last and probably least, chaos theory (represented here by the flip of a fair coin).

By the end of the discussion, I hope to have demonstrated in a kind of meta-utilitarianism the superior utility of moral philosophy compared to the inferior utility of science and the utter uselessness of leaving moral decisions to chance.

INTRODUCTION

Aristotle, whose importance in the intellectual history of Europe is too well known to need explanation or defense, sincerely insists that the aim of ethical philosophy is practical—to make us better humans. Although the master has a strong interest in human motive, character, behavior, and in the logical problems that cluster around decisions of right and wrong, it is clear that his treatment of questions is by means of a detailed discussion of particular cases. He mentions, for example, the sea captain who jettisons his cargo in order to save his ship and his life. The sea captain performs an action that is in itself unwelcome and in a sense involuntary (as the action is made necessary by and is constrained by circumstances) but that is freely chosen in preference to the disastrous alternative.

Aristotle's point is that we must start at the real-life situation and move toward the moral principle. Just as the doctor treats an individual patient and not disease in general, so must the moralist remember that human actions are particular responses to particular situations and that one must study those actions and treat them in context much as a doctor would examine and treat an individual patient in context. A lot has been written about Aristotle following a medical model in his discussion of ethics. Most of it is probably true. Aristotle's father was court physician to Philip II of Macedon. The medical influence came at least in part from his father.

After detailed study, as in medicine, says Aristotle, we might then reach a conclusion about the general principle involved. In ethics this would be an ethical principle that might be applied. But such a conclusion would never be absolute. Indeed, Aristotle implies that there is only one true universal metaethical judgment—the judgment that all universal ethical judgments are false.

More than once Aristotle compares ethics to science, emphasizing that, just as the sciences cannot all aspire to an equal degree of precision (*akribeia*), moral theories cannot aspire to a degree of precision equal to science. Different subject matters make different demands, and the subject matter of ethics in particular allows only a modest amount of precision.♦ Furthermore, Aristotle says that ethical judgments hold only for the most part. Mathematicians might easily advance a universal categorical affirmative claim such as All S are P; but moralists are restricted by the nature of their subject to generalizations of the Particular Affirmative form: Some F are G or, more likely, Most F are G or "As a rule, F are G." Thus:

- "as a rule, all courageous acts are praiseworthy"
- and not "all courageous acts are praiseworthy"

♦ See *Posterior Analytics* I, 27, and *Metaphysics* II, 3.

- "most promises should be kept"
- and not "every promise should be kept"

The universal affirmative categorical claim that "Every promise should be kept" would sooner or later be refuted by the occurrence of a situation in which, unusually but indisputably, an F failed to be a G: keeping the promise would be a bad idea.

To answer this perpetual possibility of the falsification of his generalization, the moralist falls back, or should fall back, upon such weasel wordings like "as a general rule," "for the most part," or other qualifying language of that ilk.

As for me, I think Aristotle's position on this important issue is reasonable and not extreme, but it does entail a conviction that morals cannot by any means be reduced to a set of universal principles. Thus, any moral principle formulated as such, that is as a universal, and any universal moral judgment (strictly construed) has to be false.

The most we can hope for, then, is a group of roughly accurate generalizations—principles that will meet most ordinary situations but that are always liable to come unstuck. When they become unstuck, we may freely abandon them for more satisfactory principles, if we can find any. Or we may rely on some sort of "moral intuition" (mentioned above and discussed below as "gut feeling"). Or when we really don't know, we may simply confess ignorance and the inability to resolve the moral issue.

An excellent illustration of the problem and Aristotle's position on it appears in *The Ethics* IX, 2, titled, "Of the problems arising from claims of friendship":

Well, it is no easy matter to lay down exact lines in such cases, because they involve a great many differences in every kind in importance and unimportance and in honor and urgency. But it is not difficult to see that no one person is entitled to deference in everything. Then as a general rule it is more important to repay benefits than to make spontaneous presents to one's close friends, just as one should repay a debt rather than give the money to a friend. But presumably there are exceptions to even this.

Even though Aristotle accepts the traditional view that happiness is the highest good for man, he insists that that proposition is too vague to guide us in our detailed moral choices. Accordingly, it should not surprise us to find in *The Ethics* so much descriptive, literary, and novelistic writing—portraits and character sketches, summing up types and traits of human nature (as in the sea captain and doctor analogies above, which, of course, come directly from Aristotle's book).

In effect, these observations of actual specimens of behavior are as essential to ethics, as Aristotle understands the subject, as the examination of plants and animals is to botany and zoology, the study of particular plays to the theory of tragedy, or the study of kingship and the various constitutions of Greek city-states to the concept of polity.

DISCUSSION OF THE PARTICULAR SITUATION TO BE DISCUSSED

With Aristotle's position in mind, the treatment of Alice by the Hatter in chapter 7 of AAW will be appraised using multiple moral systems. Each moral norm will be applied to the situation in Alice, and a conclusion based on that system will be derived. In the end, all the pros and cons from all the moral systems under observation will be considered as a whole and a final conclusion reached based on the predominant weights and strengths of all the arguments in all the mentioned moral systems. The aim of this exercise is to give you an idea where to start and how to proceed when you are confronting a moral issue.

After a general verdict has been thus derived, a coin will be flipped to see what pure chance would dictate as the correct finding. The findings of the coin will then be compared to the finding after the detailed arguments and a final conclusion will be arrived at as to whether, considering time, talent, energy, and other overt and covert costs in reaching the decision, the general utility of flipping a coin is better, worse, or the same as a detailed analysis of reasoned arguments.

ARTICLE THE FIRST: IS IT RIGHT TO USE AN EXAMPLE FROM *ALICE'S ADVENTURES IN WONDERLAND* TO DISTINGUISH A MORAL PERCEPT?

We proceed thus to the First Article:

Objection 1. It would seem that it is wrong to distinguish moral percepts on the basis of analysis of a children's fantasy book. This has to be one of the stupidest things I have ever heard.

Objection 2. It would seem that it is wrong to conclude from the fact that Aristotle considers ethics practical that it is so. What an authority says is of little interest, for an authority can be right or an authority can be wrong. The reasons are what counts, not who says what about what. Aristotle's historic importance does not constitute a reason to apply his ancient writings to a discussion of modern moral philosophy. Multiple authors disagree with Aristotle's extreme position in this matter, but to cite those authors would be to also resort to *argumentum ad verecundiam*, the argument of authority, one of the classic false arguments.

Objection 3. It would seem that it is wrong to use the proposed form of presentation. The proposed form of presentation does not correspond to the form of the book delivered so far. Therefore, it is unlikely that use of a different form (in this case, a bizarre form of discussion as opposed to the right form already accomplished) is likely to result in the aim that has been stated in the first sentence as the end, the "final good" as Aristotle might call it, or the "porpoise" as Lewis Carroll might say, for which the book was created.

Objection 4. It would seem that it is indeed wrong by false analogy to compare the activities of sailors and doctors to moralists. Sailors and doctors by the nature of their professions must deal in particulars. The fact that they must deal in particulars does in no way imply that moral philosophers must also deal in particulars.

Argument to the Contrary

On the contrary, use of literary sources for illustrative purposes is common and helpful in advancing our understanding of human behavior. Literature is one of the few organized systems of knowledge (psychiatry and neuroscience are others), that seeks to fully understand the human psyche.

The Author's Answer

I answer that, although *Alice's Adventures in Wonderland* is based on a profound knowledge of the rules of clear thinking, informal and formal logic, symbolic logic and human nature, I could find no skeleton key to this great work addressed to laymen and pseudoscholars (like myself) that specifically explores whether, in chapter 7, Alice was right or wrong in seating herself at the tea party. I believe that the reason that I could not find such a discussion is that no such discussion exists. I have, therefore, tried to write such an analysis myself. That is my "porpoise." Communal sharing of food and fellowship goes far, far back to the primitive origin of our species. The topic is therefore important in the general scheme of human activity.

Replies to Objections

Reply Objection 1. Serious philosophers such as Martin Gardner, Max Beerhohm, G. K. Chesterton, Walter de la Mare, William Empson, Joseph Wood Krutch, Mark Van Doren, and Bertrand Russell have written detailed discussions of AAW.

Roger W. Holmes examines Alice as a medieval nominalist who ascribes names to objects simply so as not to have to point.♦ Elsewhere, he discusses Alice as a pre-Socratic philosopher—especially when she considers where the candle flame goes when it goes out. Peter Heath

---

♦ Roger W. Holmes, "The Philosopher's *Alice in Wonderland,*" *Antioch Review* 20 (1959).

annotates AAW with explanations of the philosophy he believes Carroll consciously espoused in both books. Winston Churchill (winner of the Nobel Prize in Literature) recommended *Alice's Adventures in Wonderland* to members of his entourage as a means of understanding how government functions.♦

Similar recommendations occur in contemporary America:

In wild, wild Washington, yes means no and up means down. What is right and what is wrong have become so blurred that the distinction is akin to looking for ghosts in a ghost town.

The works of Lewis Carroll continue to be among the most useful guides to contemporary American politics. Forget the towering political theorists of the past and all the great-ism, *Alice's Adventures in Wonderland* and *Through the Looking-Glass* are all that's needed to navigate the madness—that "theater of distraction and misdirection" to use the forlorn Rep. Henry Hyde's words—that the nation's capital has become.♣

This screed from Jamie Dettmer goes on and on and so do others go on and on, proving that AAW has been a subject for serious discussion by many philosophers and historians and journalists. Indeed, Doctor Bernard Michael Patten has stated that the Alice books contain philosophy and logic so deep as to defy complete exegesis. Thus, the use of this children's book for adult philosophic discussion and demonstration is legitimate and right.

♦ All the points in this chapter are more or less well known, but I did think it a good idea to give a reference to the Winston Churchill statement. See Paul Dukas, "Fictory or Faction?" *History Today* 49, no. 11 (1999?): 1. We don't know if Winston was making a joke or if he really believed that you could get a good idea about how government functioned by studying *Alice's Adventures in Wonderland*. Winston possibly meant both.

♣ Jamie Dettmer, "Little Truth and No Consequences," *Insight on the News*, March 8, 1999. As an exercise you might apply the above moral standards to see if torture is justified. Check your answer against the legal standards established by the United States Constitution and the Geneva Conventions. Apply to the torture question the moral systems discussed: To the list you might add the injunctions "Love thy neighbor" and "Turn the other cheek." Your conclusion should be that no moral system justifies torture. In fact, quite the contrary is true. Furthermore, the US Constitution forbids torture under the cruel and unusual punishment rubric and the Geneva Convention forbids torture absolutely.

The Subaltern Utility Claim

If it is right for those people to employ the whole of the book AAW for comment and analysis, then the subaltern claim that it is reasonable to use a part of the book for the same purpose is also right.

Reply Objection 2. Ho ho ho. Is objection 2 some kind of cruel joke? Or is it the display of a vast ignorance and stupidity? Whatever it is, it demonstrates by itself an understanding simple and unschooled. The moral system expounded in *Nicomachean Ethics* stands as one of the most celebrated and influential of moral philosophies. Since its construction in the fourth century BCE, it has had a profound and lasting effect. Multiple philosophers have fervently embraced *Nicomachean Ethics* and others critically rejected it. But never have they ignored it, for, in many crucial aspects, it has helped shape the moral consciousness of the modern world.

Reply Objection 3. As there is no preexisting requirement as to the form of this book, variation in form is permitted. In fact, one could argue that an author has the freedom to choose whatever form the author prefers as a kind of personal preference, the way the Duchess prefers pepper for her little boy. "To every age its art and to every art its freedom," said Jean Paul Sartre. Doctor Patten believes that all great literary works have unity and diversity. Unity to give a sense of familiarity and diversity to give a sense of novelty. Too much of the familiar is boring and too much diversity is disorienting. Too little of the familiar is disorienting. Too little diversity is boring. The magic is in the mix. Not that Doctor Patten considers his humble work in the class of great works, but the idea that great art has the familiar and the unusual is a good idea.

Reply Objection 4. Doctors, sailors, and moralists are similar and different. Insofar as they are similar, the analogy would hold. Insofar as they are different, the analogy would not hold. Now doctors, sailors, and moralists all have twofold tasks: They use their knowledge by applying the knowledge to a particular situation. As doctors, sailors, and moralists are similar in this respect, the analogy is not false.

The objections, answer, and replies to the first article having been noted and taken under advisement, we proceed thus to article two:

ARTICLE TWO: WAS ALICE WRONG TO SEAT HERSELF AT THE TEA PARTY WITHOUT ASKING THE HATTER'S PERMISSION?

The Analects *of Confucius*

The *Analects* are included as a moral norm because they are and have been one of the two moral systems (the other is the Tao) of the Chinese civilization, the oldest continuously surviving cultural system in the world. For moral norms to survive that long (six thousand years) and involve so many people (over one billion), they must have been useful. Discussion of the *Analects* would show that Confucius was keen on rituals. For example, he said to Adept Lu in reference to the ritual slaughter of a sheep to announce to the ancestors the arrival of the full moon, "Lu, you want to stop the sacrifice. That means you love sheep and I love ritual." Confucius was fond of drinking rituals too, especially drinking tea and wine (especially wine). He often spoke of the moral imperative of entertaining travelers and strangers, of seating them at a table and of giving those strangers wine and tea. To a certain extent, this was self-serving as Confucius often inserted himself as a traveler and stranger into the dinner plans of others.

Conclusion from the *Analects* of Confucius: Alice was right to sit down with the Hatter and friends, and the Hatter, March Hare, and the Dormouse were wrong in trying to exclude her.

Summa Theologiae

Summa Theologiae (ST) is included because it is the system of moral norms that has shaped European law and politics for over a thousand years. In 1323, Thomas Aquinas, on the basis of his life and writings, was declared a saint, and in 1879 his philosophy was made the official teaching on matters theological and philosophical in the seminaries of the Catholic Church. Reading of ST shows that Aquinas would have had a definite opinion about Alice's action. He doesn't specifically address a tea party but he does address many similar issues such as "Is it necessary to feed the poor?" Answer: Not in every case. Or "Is an advocate bound to defend the suits of the poor?"

Aquinas's Answer: "*On the contrary*, He that lacks food is no less in need than he that lacks an advocate. Yet he that is able to give food is not always bound to feed the needy. Therefore, neither is an advocate always bound to defend the suits of the poor."♥

The saint goes on to explain that feeding the poor and defending the poor are acts grouped in the general category of works of mercy. As no one is obligated to perform a work of mercy, no one is obliged to feed the poor. On this point Aquinas then quotes St. Augustine: "Since one cannot do good to all, we ought to consider those chiefly who by reason of place, time, or an other circumstance, by a kind of chance, are more closely united to us."

Conclusion from *Summa Theologiae*: The Hatter had no obligation to feed Alice or invite her to sit down at the tea party. Alice was wrong to seat herself uninvited.

Real-Life Standard Child's Tea Party Demonstrated by Callie Patten and Her Real-Life Tea Parties

Callie's tea party experience is included because it represents an actual real-life tea party (actually one of seventeen tea parties that I have attended so far) hosted by my granddaughter Callie Patten when she was two years old.

Callie starts the party by greeting the guests, telling them where to sit, and when and what they should take for (pretend) tea. Her stuffed

---

♥ ST II-II, Q. 71, A. 1, "Duty of Lawyers."

animals also sit at the table, the guests looking much like the March Hare and Dormouse in the tea party in AAW.

Suddenly, without apparent rhyme or reason, Callie will reposition the animals and direct the humans to different seats. After the party, we all run around the living room in a circle to "practice our running." The running in a circle produces no winner or loser and looks suspiciously like a Caucus race in AAW, as discussed above. Callie will brook no interference with format, with how she runs the tea party. She acts and talks as if she were Caesar. With this in mind, it seems reasonable to infer the norms that she uses and expects others to use at her tea party. Stated in words, Callie's tea party norm would probably be: "The host is in charge. Everyone must obey the host. As I (Callie) am the host, everyone must obey me."

Conclusion from Callie's tea party: The host Hatter is in charge and has absolute control over the party. Everyone must obey him. Therefore, Alice is wrong.

English Common Law

English common law is a philosophical, ethical, and logical system used to order society. Since the tea party takes place on English soil, English law applies. The law, I am told, has lots of loopholes, narrow windings, and twistings, but not here. Here the law is quite clear: The law protects possession and ownership of real and personal property. Alice's crashing of the tea party would amount to a tort known as "trespass to land." Alice may also be liable for invasion of privacy. As "invasion of privacy" is considered a lesser tort than trespass to land, suits at common law would suppress it in relation to the trespass.

Torts divide themselves into two main types: intentional and negligent. Since Alice intentionally entered the property of the March Hare (we were told that the party was in front of the March Hare's house), Alice is guilty of intentional trespass. Consequently, the law would conclude that she had violated the legal rights of the Hare and the Hatter, in compensation for which damages (usually money) can be obtained. Furthermore, even if the Hatter or the Hare did not own the property (which is unlikely), the law would consider them "in possession" and therefore still entitled to damages. Furthermore, the law imposes a duty to leave on the request of the owner or the possessor, even if Alice had been originally asked to attend or specifically invited to the tea party. Failure to leave, even after being initially invited, would permit the Hatter or the Hare to exclude Alice by force.

Texas law is different: At night any trespasser may be shot and killed regardless of whether the trespass is intentional or negligent. During the day, a Texan may call the police to have the trespasser arrested or, if injury or damage is being intentionally caused by the trespasser, a Texan may legally shoot the trespasser.

Conclusion based on English common law: *Res ipse loquitur* (the thing speaks for itself); Alice is wrong.

Scout Law

Boy Scouts, a worldwide movement for young people, had about 18 million members in 115 nations in 1995. The scouts and their sister organization, Girl Guides, were founded by Lord Baden-Powell (pronounced Baden-Paul) and patterned by him after the South African Constabulatory (SAC). The slogan "Be Prepared" was also that of the SAC, but the Scout Law was made up by Lord Baden-Powell. Although the Scout Law looks like a divisional definition, it is actually a prescriptive norm. The norm seems strange in view of Baden-Powell's announcement to the scouts of the world that he had discovered that the purpose of life was "to have fun." Here are the specifics of his law:

"A Scout is trustworthy, loyal, helpful, friendly, courteous, kind, obedient, cheerful, thrifty, brave, clean, and reverent." This means the Scout should be those things. Applying the Scout Law to Alice, we find that she failed to be friendly, courteous, kind, and obedient. But the Hatter also failed in those respects and in the same degree.

Conclusion based on Scout Law: Both Alice and the Hatter are wrong.

The Ten Commandments

Although considered a great moral norm, the Ten Commandments, strictly interpreted, do not seem to have any relevant application to the question in article two of this disquisition.

Conclusion: The Ten Commandments give no direct guidance on the issue.

Common Sense

Common sense is probably the quick and dirty moral norm used by most people most of the time, all the people some of the time, and some of the people all the time. What it is and whether or not it is good or bad are topics for another book. Common sense would indicate that (most of the time) one should not crash a party. A tea party is a party. Therefore, we should not crash a tea party.

Conclusion from common sense: Alice is wrong.

Gut Feeling

Gut feelings probably play a major role in the moral judgments made by most people, even in situations that involve important risks or decisions. Juries, confused by the almost equal weight of arguments on both sides, the doubtful balance of rights and wrongs, weary lawyers with endless tongues, in cases, especially, that are complex, tend (according to my father, Bernard M. Patten, the former district attorney of Queens) to make up their minds on the basis of gut feelings. My gut feeling is that Alice is wrong in crashing the tea party. What's yours?

Conclusion from gut feeling: Alice is wrong.

Categorical Imperative

According to Kant, our duty is to follow rules that we could consistently will to be universal laws—that is, rules that we would be willing to have followed by all people in all circumstances. Kant called this prescriptive norm the "categorical imperative." Applied to the tea party situation, we find Alice is obviously wrong as she would not want people crashing her party. The Hatter probably is right as he would probably want a rule that said that hosts had the universal right to exclude unwanted or uninvited guests.

Conclusion from the categorical imperative: Alice is wrong.

Ethical Egoism

Conclusion from ethical egoism: Neutral, as ethical egoism says that each person ought to do whatever will best promote his or her own interests. The ethical egoism of Alice would therefore just about balance that of the Hatter and the Hare. But as there are two of them and only one of Alice, perhaps ethical egoism would come out against Alice.

Utilitarianism

Conclusion from utilitarianism: Alice is wrong as utilitarianism says each person ought to do whatever will promote the greatest happiness for the greatest number. As there are three opposed to Alice seating herself and only herself in favor of being seated, it would appear that the happiness of the Hatter, the March Hare, and the Dormouse is of higher priority and greater weight in this moral situation than is the happiness of Alice.

Ah, but think of the millions of readers of AAW whose amusement was greatly enhanced by Alice's party crashing.

Conclusion from utilitarianism: Alice is wrong unless the readers are considered, in the which case she was right.

Social Contract

Conclusion from social contract theory: Alice is wrong. The right thing to do is to follow the rules that rational, self-interested people can agree to establish for their mutual benefit.

Virtue

Taking a virtue as a trait of character, manifested in habitual action, that it is good for a person to manifest, we would find Alice in the wrong. We would probably find the Hatter in the wrong too, though not as much. Incidentally, virtue as defined this way is the psychiatric definition of personality with a moral value attached. In Aristotle's system of virtue ethics, there would be two evils—excess and deficiency, and one good—the golden mean by which Aristotle indicates (as mentioned) not the exact arithmetic mean but the most excellent way of managing the situation. In that case, virtue ethics would dictate that Alice should have, by habit, learned to ask permission to join the party. If she got permission, then she should join. If she did not get permission, then she should not join.

Conclusion from virtue theory: Alice is wrong.

Conclusion from feminism and care ethics (after I asked forty-seven women in a very random poll): Ditto. Alice is wrong.

Buddhism

Buddhism is included as a moral system because there are (depending on how one counts and the definitions used) 200 to 500 million people who follow the Buddha's teachings today. Buddhism is a great Asian-Oriental religion founded by Gautama Buddha (c. 563–483 BCE). The Buddha led a deep ethical protest against Vedic formalism, rejecting the authority of the Vedas and Brahmin priests and precipitating, out of Hinduism, a new religion.

Here we apply norms of Theravada Buddhism consisting of the four Noble Truths: suffering, its cause (desire), its cessation (loss of desire), and the Eightfold Way—Right View, Right Thought, Right Speech, Right Action, Right Livelihood, Right Effort, Right Mindfulness, and Right Concentration.

Reading over the details, I get the feeling that both Alice and the Hatter might come a cropper over Right Thought and Right Speech. The Buddha suggests, but does not prescribe or command, that we should avoid ill will and cruelty, which are wrong thoughts, and not use harsh language, which is wrong speech.

Interestingly, Right Action doesn't apply to party crashing. In Buddhism Right Action entails only not killing, not stealing, and not engaging in sexual misconduct. That's no accident because the Buddha doesn't concern himself with trivia. If asked about Alice's crashing the tea party, the Buddha would probably consider it neither right nor wrong. He probably would say that the question is not worthy of his attention because the matter at hand is too trivial and too stupid to think about. Or the Buddha would simply pronounce the whole question just Maya (illusion) and therefore not worth our attention, either, as it doesn't really exist.

Conclusion from Buddhism: Neither Alice nor the Hatter is right, nor are they wrong. The question is either a part of Maya (illusion) or too trivial to think about.

Science

It is with unmixed feelings that I presented relevant, reasonable, and adequate evidence that **SCIENCE** does not exist. That is, there is no overarching thing as **SCIENCE** (except as an abstract term). Instead there is only a bunch of sciences, multiple disciplines that have their own methods, knowledge bases, and practitioners. This fact suggests the question, which of the many sciences would then apply to the tea party issue? Is it physics? Of course not! How about chemistry? Are you kidding? Biology? Ho ho ho. Astrophysics? Ocean science? Genetics? Physiologic chemistry? Etc. Etc. No! No! No!

Some might argue that the social sciences apply. If so, how so? And are they really sciences?

Thumbing through my mental index of all the known real sciences (too numerous to recite), I regret to report that not a single one seems to apply to the tea party situation. Therefore, I conclude that there is no currently recognized science worth its salt that would have anything relevant to say on our issue. This result may disappoint many humanists, but their disappointment does not count and is of no importance. What does count, what really matters, is that it is true. In fact, the best we can come up with is a possible and partial application of the scientific method to the issue.

Scientific Method Applied to Alice's Crash of the Tea Party

The sciences have their ethic and that ethic involves the application of a characteristic method to discover truth. The general idea is to define a problem in the clearest possible terms then select the best available methods to study the problem. Usually, the best methods of study involve some measurement or measurements, which are then studied for patterned meaning. Once the meaning is induced, it is (provisionally) stated as a general rule or principle and subjected to analysis for alternative explanations and then retested, and retested, and retested.

To apply the scientific method to the tea party problem would require multiple data gatherings to determine what was normal and natural and characteristic for multiple children's tea parties in mid-nineteenth-century England. In other words, we would have to do some careful dissection of tea parties, just the way Aristotle did careful dissection of cuttlefish, before we could make any intelligent scientific general statement about what was what.

With such data in hand, one might be able to say whether the Hatter's party conformed to the usual standard or did not. If it did, then one might be able to reach a reasonable, though tentative, conclusion about Alice's behavior. In view of the time and money required for such a study, it is unlikely that such an observational experiment would ever be done. But you never know. The government has given grants to study things just as silly. Recently I read in the *New England Journal of Medicine* the report of a six-million-dollar multicenter study to investigate whether or not giving a cane to an unsteady old person prevents falls.

It does.

Another problem: If a tea party study were done, it would be unlikely that the Hatter's tea party would be deemed typical. Therefore, it is unlikely that we would ever be able to reach a reasonable "scientific" conclusion about Alice's behavior as she is not at the normal tea party and certainly not among normal tea party companions. As the AAW tea party is atypical, a scientific study of typical tea parties would not apply.

The fallback position, and probably the best (and admittedly non-scientific) thing that can be done under such constraining circumstances, would be the real-life situation described above with my granddaughter Callie Patten. Beyond that, we can say no more. Certainly science, in the absence of data scientifically collected, should and would say no more.

Conclusion from science and ethics of science: Indeterminate.

Termination and Wrap-Up

Metaethical analysis demonstrates that ethics has much (perhaps too much) to say about the right and wrong of crashing tea parties and that science has little (perhaps too little) to say about the same issue. Some of what systems of ethics have to say is contradictory, but much of it is in agreement.

Applying the standard of the predominant weight of evidence in terms of number, kind, and heft, we might conclude, based on analysis of multiple real-world ethical decisions, multiple ethical norms, and multiple ethical theories, that Alice is wrong. She should not have crashed the tea party.

Application of Chaos Theory to This Ethical Problem

We proceed thus to the trial of chance: I shall now flip a coin to see what the chaos of the universe has to offer us in terms of advice about this situation. Coin flipping to make decisions is unusual in my life, but I have used it on rare occasions when I couldn't reach a consensus with myself on any other basis.

In view of the strength of the above arguments against Alice, I would consider the question well settled and would not, under these circumstances, use the coin for actual decision-making purposes. Therefore, the coin is used here only for heuristic purposes.

COIN TEST

The coin is a United States quarter dollar minted in Denver in 1989. The flip is to take place at 4:08 PM, on American Airlines flight 1203 headed to Houston from Buffalo, New York. If heads comes up, then the coin (we shall say) agrees with the reasoned arguments stated above. If tails, then the opposite.

Ready?

Set.

Flip!

Result: TAILS!

Conclusion: Leaving a moral decision to chance resulted in the wrong conclusion.

At this point in a speech or in a disquisition, the classical orator or writer would give his peroration. In the case of this discussion, it might go like this.

PERORATION

Multiple moral systems were applied to a single particular human situation. In general, the eclectic application allowed us to view the problem from different vantage points and gave us a greater insight into the nature of the moral question and the right way of handling it. Applications of all norms resulted in either agreement or disagreement or a neutral stance or condemnation of both Alice and the Hatter. But clearly, the overwhelming consensus of results indicated Alice was wrong. Coin flip gave a contrary result, showing that, if reason is useful, we should not relegate our moral choices to chance. Science had nothing to add to the ethical arguments and seemed irrelevant to any value analysis. The possible application of the scientific method to the situation was done in theory and not in fact. Therefore, as there is no real data, application of the scientific method to the issue gave only a theoretical answer and not a real-world scientific conclusion.

FINIS ET VALE

Eclectic application of moral norms to a particular human situation led to a conclusion about the indicated behavior that is firmly supported by arguments and reason. Chance led to a conclusion that was wrong. Science was of no help in reaching any conclusion on the issue. Application of the scientific method to the issue would have required massive amounts of time, energy, cash, and skill and still might not have come up with any scientific conclusion.

QUOD ERAT DEMONSTRANDUM

Deployment of multiple standards of morality is useful in reaching moral conclusions.

8

The Queen's Croquet Ground

O f the cards, the one card who spoke first was Two.

Much of the confusion (and the fun in this chapter) is similar to the Abbott and Costello skit in which Who's on first and I Don't Know is on second. That's fun. But embedded in the fun is an important lesson. That lesson is that terminology is important and discussions can proceed intelligently only if all the participants fully understand the meaning of the terms employed in that particular context.

In this chapter of AAW, cards Two, Five, and Seven are doing something wrong: They (like some of our modern politicians and corporate CEOs) are painting over their mistake. This is Enronian action before Enron.

These three gardeners, you see, planted white roses for the Queen of Hearts. They should have planted red roses. Painting over the white roses is liable to kill the plants and make the situation worse. It is an error to conceal their error. It is an error to compound the error by doing something worse to conceal the error.

We see similar actions in politics, business, and even religion. A politician makes a mistake and tries to get out of it with deception. Think about Bill Clinton talking to the joint chiefs while Monica is on all fours. When you think about that, you don't know what to think. But Clinton lost his license to practice law in Arkansas because he tried to cover up by lying under oath. Nixon tried to stonewall Watergate investigators until he was so far into deception that he had to resign the presidency.

The lesson is that what may appear to be an expedient lie eventually may lead to more damage than the initial situation it tries to "deal with" for the simple reason that the expedient is out of line with the reality principle. Martha Stewart went down not for insider trading but for altering records and making false statements to the FBI. In trying to conceal a lesser crime, she committed the greater crime of obstruction of justice. Reality, that twisted jade, has a way of crashing down on those who don't pay attention.

Arthur Andersen went down not for what it did, but for shredding documents in an attempt to conceal what it had done. The result of full disclosure might not have been different, but it could not have been worse. As an accounting firm Arthur Andersen is defunct. The conviction, for obstruction of justice, if it had remained valid, would have prevented the firm from ever again receiving a license to do public accounting.

On May 31, 2005, the Supreme Court of the United States unanimously overturned the Andersen conviction due to flaws in the jury instructions. Despite this ruling, it is unlikely Andersen will return as a viable business. The firm lost nearly all its clients when it was indicted. There remain over one hundred civil suits related to its role in the Enron fraud and accounting fraud in several other companies. From eighty-five thousand employees, the firm is now down to about two hundred, based in Chicago. Most of these people are involved in (you guessed it) handling the lawsuits.

LIES AND THE CATHOLIC CHURCH

Much of the hostility directed against the Catholic Church in Boston not only relates to what the priests did, but also to what Cardinal Law did to conceal their crimes. The archdiocese, forced to sell its many key Boston assets, has moved to the suburbs, where it is involved in (you guessed it) handling the lawsuits.

So the moral of all this is: **Don't paint the roses.**

* * *

"And who are these?" said the Queen, pointing to the three gardeners who were lying round the rose-tree; . . .

"How should I know?" said Alice, surprised at her own courage. "It's no business of mine."

The Queen turned crimson with fury, and, after glaring at her for a moment like a wild beast, began screaming "Off with her head! Off with—"

"Nonsense!" said Alice, very loudly and decidedly, and the Queen was silent.

Good for Alice. She surprised herself and us by opposing the powerful Queen of Hearts. Alice is beginning to question and to react against the inanities of the adult world, the boasts of heraldry, the pomp of power—and with good results.

* * *

"What have you been doing here?"

"May it please your Majesty," said (card) Two, in a very humble voice, going down on one knee as he spoke, "we were trying—"

"I see," said the Queen who had meanwhile been examining the roses. "Off with their heads!"

The Queen is unreasonable. She asked a question and doesn't have the courtesy to listen to the reply. Power corrupts and absolute power corrupts absolutely. This is not just absolute power, it is also stupid, arbitrary, capricious, and illogical power. The Queen of Hearts has only one way of settling all difficulties, great or small, a resort to the argument of force, *argumentum ad baculum*. I know how to handle her: Off with her head! *Sic semper tyrannis!*

* * *

And talking about "off with the head"—one of the big problems posed in this chapter is what to do about the Cheshire-Cat's head that has made a sudden appearance during the croquet game. The Queen and the King have already prefigured their approach to the problem, but the executioner has an objection: *"The executioner's argument was that you couldn't cut off a head unless there was a body to cut it off from: that he had never had to do such a thing before, and he wasn't going to begin at this time of life."*

Matter of fact: You can't cut a head off when it has already been detached. The executioner's argument is reality based, intelligent, valid, and sound. Why didn't he stop there? Why didn't he just stop while he was ahead (pun intended)?

Instead of resting at the point of irrefutability, the executioner continued (by way of supererogation) with the irrelevant continuum argument: Because we never did things that way, we shouldn't start to do it that way now.

Prudence indeed will dictate that things long established should not be changed for light and transient reasons, but all experience hath shown that they must change if the facts require them to change. Otherwise, nothing would change and progress would stop. If progress stopped, then we would still be riding around on horses, using outhouses, and working at night by the light of candles, oil lamps, and gaslights. "If God wanted us to walk," says Willie Wonka in his chocolate factory, "then he wouldn't have invented roller skates."

Yet no mental automatic pilot device, such as tradition or custom, should ever be trusted fully—even when no saboteur has fed bad information into its mechanism, even when the evidence has not been purposely falsified. Such automatic ways of thinking can sometimes go haywire by themselves. We need to check the machine from time to time to be sure that it hasn't worked itself out of sync with other sources of evidence in the situation—the objective facts, our prior experiences, our own judgments, and the changes in situation engendered by a change in time or place.

PAY MORE ATTENTION TO THINKING
THAN TO FOLLOWING RULES

Fortunately, this precaution requires neither much effort nor much time, just a little thought. A quick glance around is all that is needed. Our best defense against the irrational is to recognize it. The best way of recognizing the irrational is knowing when the data are in error and the situation doesn't match with reality. This little precaution is well worth the effort. The consequences of single-minded reliance on tradition or blind obedience to power already in place, for example, can be frightening. So ask not what the rule is. Ask not what you can do for your country or what your country can do for you. Ask what's the best way of managing the situation in that place at that time. Pay more attention to thinking than to following rules. In the long run, thinking serves you better.

* * *

Alice suggests that they consult the Duchess about what to do to the Cheshire-Cat.

> *"It belongs to the Duchess; you'd better ask her about it."*
>
> *"She's in prison," the Queen said to the executioner; "fetch her here." And the executioner went off like an arrow.*
>
> *The Cat's head began fading away the moment he was gone, and, by the time he had come back with the Duchess, it had entirely disappeared; so the King and the executioner ran wildly up and down, looking for the head, while the rest of the party went back to the game.*

And the moral is: Some problems disappear if you leave them alone. In fact, that's the way I solve most of my problems—benign neglect. I call this method the "Little Bo Peep Method" of solving problems: Leave them alone and they'll come home wagging their tails behind them. You can't imagine how many significant illnesses I have guided my patients through by just watching and waiting and keeping my hands in my pockets. How about you? Ever solve a problem by just leaving it alone and seeing if it solves itself?

9

The Mock Turtle's Story

"When I'm a Duchess," she said to herself (not in a very hopeful tone, though)...

Wishful thinking, daydreams, poetry, and fantasy have their places in human life. They give a form of psychological comfort, a surcease of sorrow. The problem is that they often have little to do with the external realities that afflict us from all sides.

Alice is not the only child with fantasies. All children have them, their hopes and dreams. As Alice is a child, she has hers. My granddaughter Callie Patten wants to be a princess. Correction, my granddaughter Callie Patten wanted to be a princess. Now she says she is a princess and has expanded her ambitions into other realms. Now Callie wants to be a bride and a "cat doctor." And a teacher for other little girls of how to be a princess.

As for me, I know I will never amount to anything as I have no ambitions. Hence, I know that I am no longer a child. If I am no longer a child, then I must be an adult. That's the fact. I will never be young again. But I can still be immature. Look at the Queen of Hearts.

* * *

"I won't have any pepper in my kitchen at all. Soup does very well without — Maybe it's always pepper that makes people hot-tempered," she went on, very much pleased at having found out a new kind of rule, "and vinegar that makes them sour—and chamomile that makes them bitter—and—barley-sugar and

such things that make children sweet-tempered. I only wish people knew that:
they wouldn't be so stingy about it, you know—"

A whole book could be written about this paragraph. But I will spare you and myself the trouble. Alice is down on pepper because of the adverse experience she had in the Duchess's kitchen. My mother-in-law is down on pepper because it gives her heartburn. Alice's conclusion against *all* (italics by Lewis Carroll) pepper is an overgeneralization that is simple and simplistic and probably emotionally based. Because too much pepper is bad doesn't mean that the only amount of pepper that is good under all circumstances is no pepper *at all*.

The proper amount of pepper is the amount that satisfies the people using it under the circumstances of its use. This concept of the proper dose—not too much and not too little—is probably the root message of the story about the three bears. Soup can be too hot, too cold, or just right.

Thus, Alice's present position on the pepper issue appears to be a defective continuum argument that we previously labeled *the less the better*. The less the better argument frequently extrapolates to *if less pepper is better, then no pepper is best*. That can't be true for all people at all times. Therefore that argument, when displayed as a general rule, must fail.

Alice's further expedition into rule making devolves around the erroneous belief (based probably on observations in the Duchess's kitchen) that too much pepper makes people hot-tempered. The warrant for that belief is nonexistent and the error in thinking is post hoc propter hoc. This error in thinking is quite common and will be discussed further if I feel like it.

After reaching the conclusion linking pepper with hot tempers, Alice then proceeds to extend her conclusions to vinegar-sour, chamomile-bitter, and last but not least, barley sugar-sweet. Each chain in her four-link thinking would require independent support by evidence that is relevant and adequate. Otherwise, the conclusions of this series of statements (her sorites) don't follow.

As Alice has a particular vested interest in the barley-sugar conclusion, we and she should be even more careful about accepting the judgment that children should be fed abundant amounts of sweets to develop a sweet personality. I wish we could make children sweet that way. But we can't. I wish the training of children were that simple. It isn't.

The rule of the four spices, though, sounds very familiar to a medicine man. Could this be a humorous (pun intended) reference to the ancient Greek concept of the four humors? I say they are.

THE HUMOROUS THEORY OF DISEASE

The Greeks added their contribution to Egyptian and Babylonian medical misinformation by postulating and promulgating the concept of the four humors: blood, black bile, yellow bile, and phlegm. These were believed to be balanced in a healthy person. Any disturbance of these fluids in the body supposedly led to disease. This erroneous doctrine confused medical thinking for centuries. We now know that phlegmatic people are not phlegmatic because they have too much phlegm. Nor are choleric people choleric because they have too much yellow bile. The melancholy are not depressed because they have too much black bile. Bile has as little to do with choleric or melancholy personality as pepper has to do with hot temper or barley-sugar has to do with sweet temper. Alice's theory and the ancient theory as well are just too simple, too pat, and too wrong to be true.

Alice's theories are bunk, like so much of the health food bunk, with one essential difference: with Alice's theories there is no commercial incentive to propagate the bunk.

POST HOC ERRORS: DOES OR DOES NOT PEPPER CAUSE THE DUCHESS TO BE ILL-TEMPERED?

A common error in thinking is the assumption that, because one thing follows another or is associated with it in time, the second thing must relate to the first as a consequence. That is, that the first event caused the second. We have spoken of this earlier. Whether the first event caused the second or not cannot be determined from mere association in time. The cause-and-effect association must, instead, be proven by other evidence.

When two conditions occur side by side, like bad temper and the use of pepper, especially when they occur side by side repeatedly, it is tempting to conclude that the one explains the other.

Don't be too quick to believe it.

There may, of course, be a necessary connection between the two things; but before the relation of cause and effect is established, it must be shown that, if the effect did not follow the cause, some accepted general principle would be violated. A powerful disproof might be to find that the effect occurred independently of the supposed cause.

Bernard Shaw was a vegetarian. He was also a great playwright. Will abstaining from meat make you a great playwright?

No way!

The two things are independent and not codependent variables. Don't believe me? Try eating vegetables for a year. See if it makes any difference in your playwriting ability. After two years as a vegetarian I still can't write plays to save my life.

It rains and the streets get wet. Then it stops raining and the streets get dry. And when the streets are dry, it rains again. Do dry streets cause it to rain? Do wet streets stop the rain? Primitive thinking might conclude that dry streets cause it to rain because, dang it, every time the streets are dry, sooner or later, rain falls.

When Ethel and I were coming back from Delos to the Greek island of Mykonos, our ship ran into a great storm. The Greek sea captain assured us that we would be O.K. He knew we would arrive safe and sound because he had prayed to the Virgin Mary.

"How do we know for sure that she will help us?" I asked.

"Didn't you see all those little churches on Mykonos? Whenever there is a serious storm at sea the captains promise the Virgin that they will build a church to her."

"But where are the churches built by the sea captains who prayed but didn't make it back alive?" I asked.

The captain could not answer. He understood his reasoning was defective. The conjunction A&B does not mean that A caused B.

The captain's reasoning was defective and such defective reasoning could have serious consequences. Why?

Because someone prayed and then survived doesn't mean that they survived because they prayed. The mere fact that one event follows another does not mean the two are connected as cause and effect. To assume that praying and safe arrival are related is to commit the error of post hoc propter hoc. Furthermore, because those who prayed and did not survive wouldn't construct churches, only those who survived would construct churches. Therefore, there would be a partial selection of evidence so that the number of churches on Mykonos would multiply. The number of churches would multiply, proving that people had prayed and survived. But that would not prove they had survived *because* they had prayed.

What we need to know is what would happen if we took a group of similarly endangered sea captains and had one half randomly selected to pray and the other half randomly selected not to pray. If the ones who prayed survived and the ones who did not pray did not survive, then we might be able to conclude that prayer worked.

Until such a study is done, we might be better off and much safer if we followed the standard procedures for safety at sea: Batten down the hatches. Head into the wind and quarter into the waves. Slow to the minimal speed to maintain steering way, put on life jackets, lower the life boats, call for assistance, and so forth. These are reality-based techniques that have been proven effective by numerous studies and are more likely to foster survival than prayer.

A candidate for a sea captain's license or a master's certificate would flunk the required Coast Guard examination if, when asked about what should be done during an emergency at sea, he or she said, "Pray to the Virgin Mary."

Religious mania is associated with post hoc errors.

The ancient Mayans believed that their great god Chaac controlled the rain. The Mayans recognized how dependent on rain the corn crop was. Repeated observations showed that when there was little rain, there was little corn. When there was no rain, there was no corn.

What's the solution?

Get rain. Right? But that begs the question. The real question is how to get water for the crops? The Mayans thought the question was, "How can we get rain when it doesn't rain?" And their elaboration: "How can we make it rain?"

The real solution was to pump water from underground. That effort was beyond Mayan capabilities at the time. They were too busy thinking about something else, a fake solution that didn't work. The Mayan fake solution was called "human sacrifice." Eventually, they did stumble on a solution that worked for them. That solution was to move elsewhere, where it did rain. That is what the Mayans did to finally solve the rain problem. But until they arrived at that solution, the priests experimented with human sacrifice. Whenever a drought took hold, volunteers were drowned in the cenotes♠ at Uxmal and Chichen Itza and elsewhere throughout the Mayan kingdom. Besides humans, many valuable objects were thrown into cenotes. The idea was to appease Chaac and to get Chaac to have his maidens, the maidens of the heavens, pour water down on those beneath using their special water jars.

We know this was the motivation behind the sacrifices because the hieroglyphs written in stone left by the priests as well as the sacred Mayan books tell us it was. The evidence recovered from the cenotes, including human skeletons adorned with gems, confirms the sacrifices.

So what happened?

After some sacrifices, it rained. Conclusion: Sacrifice worked. Action indicated when it doesn't rain, kill people.

According to Professor Willem Frederik Hermans, the Aztecs performed human sacrifices on a nightly basis, to ensure that the sun would rise in the morning. They had done so since time immemorial. Not a

---

♠ Limestone sinkholes.

murmur from anyone, not a soul dared suggest it might be worth finding out what would happen if they skipped the ceremony for once.

All this sounds pretty stupid. But the point is it happened. Whole civilizations went haywire. They went haywire because they assumed that when one event follows another, the two must be related as cause and effect. There was no rain, so they threw people into the cenote. Eventually, it rained. Therefore, the Mayans induced the general principle: For drought, kill people. For the Aztecs it was no human sacrifice and the sun won't rise. For dependable sun, kill a person a night.

Once the erroneous general principle had been accepted, there was no stopping the Mayan theocracy from finding lots of other reasons to sacrifice people for lots of other gods and goddesses, indeed for any special purpose that they could think of. A reasonable theory of the destruction of Mayan civilization is based on the decimation of the population by the need for sacrificial victims. We know that, toward the end of the Mayan classical period, wars were organized mainly to obtain humans for sacrifice. Think about all those young men and women killed for post hoc propter hoc. Think about them and weep.

SALEM WITCH TRIALS— AN EXAMPLE OF THINKING GONE AWRY

In 1692, the Salem witch trials were judicial proceedings and therefore their proceedings were recorded verbatim. Read those over if you have a chance. See how many errors of post hoc propter hoc you can find.

Because a farmer's cart lost a wheel three miles down the road after passing the home of some eccentric old woman, the court assumed the woman was a witch. The court assumed that she had somehow made the cart lose its wheel. Since she was three miles away when she did this, she had to have used witching powers. If she used witching powers, she must be a witch. Therefore, the court sentenced her to death. She, Rebecca Nurse, and eighteen other "witches" were hanged.

The story is fascinating. I didn't make it up. It really happened. It all started in May 1692 with accusations by a few young girls (who said [and may have believed] they were possessed by the devil) against older women in the community. Special court was convened. The trials quickly grew into mass hysteria, and even Governor William Phip's wife was implicated. Fortunately, Increase Mather and his son Cotton were influential in ending the witchcraft trials at Salem in 1692. Both men believed in witches, but they were convinced that the trial evidence was unreliable. Both men disliked the post hoc propter hoc evidence especially when it assumed the form of a specter, an imaginary being resembling the accused. Under the conditions of these trials, the accused was responsible not only for events that happened beyond her control (like the loss of the cart wheel), but also for acts committed by her specter, over which she had no control whatsoever. Modern psychiatry now recognizes the specter as a hallucination of the witness, which, incidentally, it was.

Public opinion first stopped, then condemned the trials. The legislature adopted a resolution for repentance (December 17, 1696), including a fast day on which one of the three judges, Samuel Sewell, admitted his mistakes, mistakes mainly in appraisal of evidence. The jailed ladies remaining were released. Reparations were paid to them and their families. The correction of the errors came too late for the "witches" who were hanged. They were beyond compensation. They were beyond the beyonds. They were dead.

If you can't read the original proceedings of the Salem witch trials, read Arthur Miller's *The Crucible*, which is based on the transcript of the trials.◆ Take a look and weep. Weep for all the innocent people sacrificed to the post hoc propter hoc error in thinking. Weep for all the people killed (once again) by religion-inspired mania.

◆ Arthur Miller's *The Crucible* was first performed in 1953, around the time of Senator Joseph McCarthy's hunt for communists, and is available in many editions from various publishers.

THE PERSONALITY OF THE DUCHESS
IS NOT DUE TO PEPPER

Knowing the pitfalls of post hoc, we can say that it is likely that neither pepper nor yellow bile is the cause of the Duchess's choleric, irascible temperament. If the pepper is not the cause, then stopping the use of pepper will not prevent people from being temperamental. If yellow bile is not the cause, treatments designed to reduce yellow bile will not prevent people from being temperamental. We may not know what *will* work, but there is an advantage in knowing what doesn't work. When Edison was asked what he thought of the 9,990 failed experiments that he had done in an effort to make an effective storage battery, he said, "Those weren't failed experiments, they were 9,990 things we now know don't work."

* * *

"Very true," said the Duchess: "Flamingoes and mustard both bite. And the moral of that is—Birds of a feather flock together."

Note the non sequitur based on a confusion of uses of the word "bite" and the further error of concluding that, since mustard and flamingoes both bite, and since the flamingo is a bird, mustard must be a bird too and therefore must flock with it.

"Only mustard isn't a bird," Alice remarked.

Clever Alice! She defeated the false analogy by stating a fact, a fact that easily trumps the Duchess's crazy argument.

"Right, as usual," said the Duchess, who seemed ready to agree to everything that Alice said.

Oh, my, my, that Duchess! She is something else. The character of the Duchess is one of the most striking features of the book, especially if one reviews what was standard fare for children of that time. When one sees her in action, one gets a strong reaction against didacticism, which so many of the episodes illustrate. Carroll's parodies of the instructive verse that children were made to memorize and recite is a ridicule of solemnity and a criticism of the practice of inflicting it upon the young. Here Carroll is going farther: He is making fun of an authority figure directly.

In the croquet game, the Duchess's motto is "Everything's got a moral, if only you can find it." This of course begs the question, is all-inclusive, is an overgeneralization, and is an assertion that needs support by evidence. From that statement the Duchess goes on to become more and more extravagant and nonsensical in her application of axioms and proverbs to everything. Alice catches on fast and reacts accordingly. And the moral of this is: Adults—UGH! They aren't consistent and they aren't fair. And—this is key—they make things up to intimidate youth.

It's true that everyday language is largely arbitrary and unaccountable, but the Duchess's puzzling use of language is one important manifestation of adult bullying and condescension. This is, I believe, an underlying message of the Alice books, the rejection of adult authority and the vindication of the rights of children, even the right of a child like Alice to self-assertion, clear instruction, and logical thoughts.

The Duchess continues: *"There's a large mustard mine near here. And the moral of that is—'The more there is of mine, the less there is of yours.'"* Another non sequitur as well as a contextual modification of the word "mine." But despite the change in the meaning of the word "mine" in this context, the Duchess is here describing the zero-sum game—a game in which the payoff to the winner exactly equals the losses of the loser—"the more there is of mine, the less there is of yours."

Poker is a many-person zero-sum game because the total amount of money won equals the total amount of money lost. Bets on the outcome of chess and checker games are zero-sum. So are some forms of currency trading.

By contrast, a negative-sum game is one in which the total amount won is less than the total amount that was bet, as in pari-mutuel betting on a horse race. The total amount bet (the handle) is 20 percent more than the total amount paid off because the state extracts 15 percent from the handle and the track takes 5 percent from the handle.

Stocks and bonds can be positive-sum games due to the addition of interest to the betted pool in the case of bonds and the addition of dividends in the case of stocks. But stocks and bonds are mainly negative-sum games because of commissions and trading fees, market manipulations, and withdrawal of money from corporations via fraud.

* * *

The Duchess again continues: *"and the moral of that is—be what you would seem to be—or, if you'd like it put more simply—Never imagine yourself not to be otherwise than what it might appear to others that what you were or might have been was not otherwise than what you had been would have appeared to them to be otherwise."*

Right! And an excellent example of how a clear solid expression of a simple idea (be yourself) in plain English contrasts with the same idea expressed so verbosely that the simple meaning is submerged in abstruse and obtuse verbiage. Lewis Carroll—hats off to your genius!

LAW LINGO

Pretty funny. Has the Duchess had been to law school? It sounds that way. Law school? Why the devil did I think of law school? The reason is, my friends, that what the Duchess says sounds like glorious legalese.

Assignment: translate legalese into plain English.

Legalese: *This agreement and the benefits and advantages herein contained are personal to the Member and shall not be sold, assigned or transferred by the Member to any other party, person, or thing.*

Translation: Membership cannot be transferred.

Legalese: *Title to property in the goods shall remain vested in the Company (notwithstanding the delivery of the same to the Consumer) until the price of the Goods comprised in the contract and all other money due from the Customer to the Company for those aforesaid goods has been paid in full to the aforementioned Company in legal tender received and accepted by the same party to the transaction.*

Translation: Until paid for, you don't own the goods.

Legalese: *No failure or delay on the part of the Bank in exercising, and no failure to file or otherwise enforce the Bank's security interest in or with respect to any Collateral, shall operate as a waiver of any right or remedy hereunder or release any of the undersigned, and the Obligations of the undersigned may be extended or waived by the Bank, and contract or other agreement evidencing or relation to any obligation or any Collateral may be amended and any Collateral exchanged, surrendered or otherwise dealt with in accordance with any agreement relative thereto, all without affecting the liability of any of the undersigned.*

Translation: The bank may delay or change enforcement of its rights under this contract without losing them.

Lesson: Don't be like the Duchess or a lawyer. Make your speech simple, direct, and in plain English.

Laconic speech was also favored by the ancient Spartans. Herodotus tells of the banished Samians who had an audience with the magistrates of Sparta. They made a long speech, as was natural with persons sorely in want of aid. The Spartans answered them saying they had forgotten the first half of their speech, and could make nothing of the remainder. Afterward the Samians had another audience whereat they simply said, showing a bag that they had brought with them, "The bag wants flour." The Spartans answered that they did not need to have said "the bag." However, they resolved to give them aid.

> *"I think I should understand that better," Alice said very politely, "if I had it written down: but I ca'n't quite follow it as you say it."*
>
> *"That's nothing to what I could say if I chose," the Duchess replied, in a pleased tone.*

> *"Pray don't trouble yourself to say it any longer than that," said Alice.*
> *"Oh, don't talk about trouble!" said the Duchess.*

Bravo! Alice is beginning to talk back to an adult. She made her opinions and desires known. The Duchess misses the point, of course, by seizing on and misconstruing Alice's use of the word "*trouble.*" Add to the list of her already manifest faults the fact that the Duchess is a windbag.

* * *

> *"Yes, we went to school in the sea, though you mayn't believe it —"*
> *"I never said I didn't!" interrupted Alice.*
> *"You did," said the Mock Turtle.*

The Mock Turtle is telling Alice that she has just said "I didn't." Never means never and Alice just said "I didn't." Therefore, her statement that she never said what she obviously just did say has to be wrong. That is why the Mock Turtle calls her on it. And let's face it: he seems to be mocking her.

Verbal traps like this are a significant diversion not only for the Mock Turtle, they were also a significant diversion for Lewis Carroll. Humpty, in the next Alice book, catches Alice in a similar verbal trap by referring to something that she didn't say. The Mock Turtle continues:

> *"We had the best of educations—in fact, we went to school every day—"*
> *"I've been to a day-school, too," said Alice. "You needn't be so proud as all that."*

Another confusion: Going to school every day and going to a day school are in fact two different things, though Alice assumes they are the same. The confusion is fun and it is instructive.

Recently, my wife had trouble understanding someone who was talking about ground squirrels. She thought the topic was some exotic kind of burger meat. Looking in the *Oxford English Dictionary*, Ethel learned that a ground squirrel is a terrestrial squirrel-like rodent: a. of the genus *Tamias*, especially the chipmunk (*T. Striatus*); b. of the genus *Spermophilus* (gopher).

THE ONE-UPMANSHIP GAME CONTINUES

"With extras?" asked the Mock Turtle, a little anxiously.
"Yes," said Alice: "we learned French and music."
"And washing?" said the Mock Turtle.
"Certainly not!" said Alice indignantly.
"Ah! Then yours wasn't a really good school," said the Mock Turtle in a tone of great relief. "Now, at ours, they had, at the end of the bill, 'French, music, and washing—extra.'"

Out-of-context quotations are unfair and misleading. They partially select ideas or evidence and frequently lead to erroneous conclusions. The phrase "French, music, and washing—extra" often appeared on boarding school bills. It meant that there was an extra charge for instruction in French and music and for having one's laundry done by the school. It did not mean washing was included in the course of instruction. Notice that the Mock Turtle is playing with Alice, holding her up to ridicule and deluding and befooling her. Thus, he is living up to still another *Oxford English Dictionary* definition of the word "mock": a word prefixed to a noun to form a description for a person that "mocks" or parodies or makes fun of.

Mock can also mean "imitate." Turtle does seem to be trying hard, perhaps too hard, to keep up with Alice on the education front. Mock and mock show up in a famous poem by Percy Bysshe Shelley:

Ozymandias
I met a traveler from an antique land
Who said: Two vast and trunkless legs of stone
Stand in the desert. . . Near them, on the sand,
Half, sunk, a shattered visage lies, whose frown,
And wrinkled lip, and sneer of cold command,

Tell that its sculptor well those passions read
Which yet survive, stamped of these lifeless things,
The hand that mocked them, and the heart that fed:
And on the pedestal these words appear:
"My name is Ozymandias, king of kings:
Look on my works, ye Mighty, and despair!"
Nothing beside remains. Round the decay
Of that colossal wreck, boundless and bare
The lone and level sands stretch far away.

According to John Hollander, a memorized reading of Shelley's poem might very well come up with the two meanings of "mock" in "The hand that mocked them" *imitate* (here, in sculpture) and *ridicule or deride.* Dig? If not, think about it.

Near our house in Texas we have a storefront doctor whose sign reads: "Neurology, Pain, and Headache Control Center." Pain and headache might need control, but one wonders if the good doctor meant to control neurology as well.

The name Mock Turtle is like that too—a confusion. The (incorrect) reasoning here is that if there is a mock turtle soup (that is, a soup that tastes and smells like turtle soup but is made of nonturtle ingredients), then there must be such a creature as a Mock Turtle. There must be a Mock Turtle if there is a mock turtle soup, in the same way as there must be a turtle if there is a turtle soup.

The analogy is false because, although turtle soup and mock turtle soup share a certain property, namely, that they are both hot liquids that you drink from a bowl, they differ in that they are not both derived from a 200-million-year-old reptile species that has protective shells called the carapace and the plastron.

In fact, mock turtle soup was made from veal. Those of you who have an illustrated AAW will find that Sir John Tenniel's original drawing of the Mock Turtle shows the turtle with a calf's head and hooves for feet, reflecting the actual ingredients that went into the Victorian mock turtle soup in question.

REIFICATION AS A DEFECT IN THINKING

On a deeper level, we are dealing here with a fundamental defect in human thinking called "reification," or the propensity to convert an abstract concept into a hard belief. Because we can name something or because we have a name for something does not mean that that thing actually does exist. It might exist and it might not exist. It might merely exist in the realm of imagination and not in the real world. Only in the realm of fantasy does a mock turtle exist. In the real world there is no mock turtle, although in the real world, there is mock turtle soup.

Some people think that Yahweh, the God of the Old Testament, was a social-political idea to help organize the Jews out of Egypt. Thus it is possible that God was an abstract notion that then became reified.

Mock turtles and real turtles. Children in the world of adults often exhibit such confusions. For many years we disciplined our daughter by saying, "Allegra, you're not the only one!" Eventually, she wanted to know who was the only one and how could she get to be the only one.

Other confusions in the Mock Turtle's story are just pure FUN: *"Well, there was Mystery," the Mock Turtle replied counting off the subjects on his flappers,—"Mystery, ancient and modern, with Seaography and then Drawling . . . Drawling, Stretching, and Fainting in Coils."*

Of course, Mystery=History, Seaography=Geography, Drawling, Stretching, and Fainting in Coils=Drawing, Sketching, and Painting in Oils.

"He taught us Laughing and Grief."

It is doubtful, as mentioned, that there was much laughing in Latin. But the Grief sounds pretty real for Greek as taught in that era.

Note that just a slight modification of the sounds of a word may change the meaning entirely. A subtle alteration of the usual spelling or pronunciation suggests images and meanings and shades of meanings that might if correctly handled expand the (rather limited) expressive power of language. James Joyce mastered this technique. By many allusions he credits the Alice books. In *Finnegans Wake*, for instance, Joyce writes, "Alicious, twinstreams twinestraines, through alluring glass or alas in jumboland?" And again: "Though Wonderland's lost us for ever.

Alis, alas, she broke the glass! Liddell lokker through the leafery, ours is mistery of pain."♣

Ours is mistery of pain! Wow! What power! Mistery expresses the ideas of mystery and misery in one easy-to-assimilate new word.

* * *

Alice thought to herself "I don't see how he can ever finish, if he doesn't begin."

Novels that are never started are never finished. There is a certain vector that controls the direction of time in the universe. That time vector (with minor subatomic exceptions) moves forward only. Hence, Alice's conclusion is firmly based.

* * *

"Why did you call him Tortoise, if he wasn't one?" Alice asked.

"We called him Tortoise because he taught us," said the Mock Turtle angrily. "Really you are very dull!"

"You ought to be ashamed of yourself for asking such a simple question," added the Gryphon.

No, she shouldn't be ashamed of herself! Simple questions are often the best questions. They get right to the heart of the matter. Simple questions can expose ignorance in its pristine essence, as is the case here. Other than the similarities of the sounds, there is no real or sensible relationship between a *tortoise* and the verbal phrase *taught us*.

Therefore, Alice's question was pertinent. It is not unusual for someone who asks a pertinent question to be attacked personally with an ad hominem argument. Gryphon is a great offender in this respect: a name-caller. He finally ends up calling Alice a simpleton (which she is not). After that, Alice gets discouraged and stops asking the Gryphon

♣ For the hundreds of references to Carroll and the Alice books in *Finnegans Wake*, see Ann McGarrity Buki, "Lewis Carroll in *Finnegans Wake*," in *Lewis Carroll: A Celebration* (New York: Clarkson N. Potter, 1982).

278 THE LOGIC OF ALICE: CLEAR THINKING IN WONDERLAND

questions. Intimidation, that old jade, did finally work its spell on Alice and her curiosity. It wrought havoc, but not that much. Alice got through her "mock," which is also a British term for the examinations that public schools use to test students prior to the real examinations for the GCE (General Certificate of Education).

We will soon see that Alice recovers her courage and her audacity in the trial chapters that follow.

10

The Lobster Quadrille

The quadrille is a square dance in five figures and was one of the most difficult of the ballroom dances fashionable at the time Carroll wrote AAW. The orders that are barked out by the Mock Turtle and the Gryphon will sound familiar to those who have (like the Liddell girls) endured dance lessons: advance twice, set to partners, change lobsters, and retire in same order.

* * *

"Will you walk a little faster said a whiting to a snail,
   "There's a porpoise close behind us, and he's treading on my tail."

The Mock Turtle's song parodies the first line and adopts the meter of Mary Howitt's death poem (in turn based on an older song) "The Spider and the Fly":

"Will you walk into my parlour?" said the spider to the fly.
   "'Tis the prettiest little parlour that ever you did spy.
   The way into my parlour is up a winding stair,
   And I've got many curious things to show when you are there."
"Oh, no, no," said the little fly, "to ask me is in vain,
   For who goes up your winding stair can ne'er come down again."

Another poem, recited by Alice with a trembling voice, also ends in apparent violence:

"I passed by his garden, and marked, with one eye,
How the Owl and the Panther were sharing a pie:
The Panther took pie-crust, and gravy, and meat,
While the Owl had the dish as its share of the treat,
When the pie was all finished, the Owl, as a boon,
Was kindly permitted to pocket the spoon;
While the Panther received knife and fork with a growl,
And concluded the banquet by —"

Carrollians have occupied themselves by replacing "eating the owl," which I believe is the correct (and most amusing) ending of this poem with various alternatives.

By the way, suffering death is the most appropriate punishment for a bird foolish enough to eat with a panther. Old Chinese maxim: "Who serve powerful sleep with tiger."

Among other phrases reported from time to time in the Lewis Carroll Society's newsletter, here are some endings: "taking a prowl," "wiping his jowl," "giving a howl," "taking a trowel," "donning a cowl," and (to conclude on a more hopeful note) "kissing the fowl." Indeed, come to think on it, this whole chapter has more verse than usual and is perhaps more suited to *The Nursery Alice* (launched in 1889), a retelling of AAW in shortened and simplified form for children below the age of five. By any standard, it is a virtuoso display of Carroll's knowledge of children's verse and his ability to exploit well-known poems, adapting them to his own uses. Carroll was both a poet and a logician—and, also a show-off. Quite a combo. Rare one too. He demonstrates a pretty good understanding of children's interests here, as so often, also by highlighting (their obsessions with) eating and drinking and animals and fun. My granddaughters always squeal with delight when I quote Carroll's version of "Twinkle, Twinkle":

Twinkle, twinkle, little bat
How I wonder where you're at
Up above the sky so high
Like a tea tray in the sky.

* * *

Mock Turtle said, "No wise fish would go anywhere without a porpoise."

"Wouldn't it, really?" said Alice, in a tone of great surprise.

"Of course not," said the Mock Turtle. "Why, if a fish came to me, and told me he was going on a journey, I should say 'With what porpoise?'"

"Don't you mean 'purpose'?" said Alice.

"I mean what I say," the Mock Turtle replied, in an offended tone.

Sometimes the porpoise of this writing is just plain nonsense. Sometimes the purpose of the writing is to show how touchy people get when they are shown to be wrong.

So let's pass on to the next item.

* * *

"How the creatures order one about, and make one repeat lessons!" thought Alice. "I might just as well be at school at once."

Quite true and a good hint that the creatures in AAW are in fact Oxford dons or schoolteachers known to Alice.

* * *

"Oh, as to the whiting," said the Mock Turtle, "They—you've seen them, of course?"

"Yes, said Alice, "I've often seen them at dinn—" she checked herself hastily.

"I don't know where Dinn may be," said the Mock Turtle, "but, if you've seen them so often, of course you know what they're like?"

"I believe so," Alice replied thoughtfully. "They have their tails in their mouths—and they're all over crumbs."

Here we see a flash of psychological maturity. Alice is more sensitive now to the emotional needs of others than she was with the mouse in chapter 2 and with the pigeon in chapter 5. No more talk about her cat Dinah's ability to eat mice and birds. Alice now recognizes the possibility that she might offend these creatures by mentioning that she eats fish.

In Victorian days whitings were served by presenting them on bread-crumbs with their tails inserted in the gill arch. Alice mistakenly thinks the tails are in their mouths, which they are, but only because the gill is the backdoor to the fish mouth. Other authorities say the whiting tails were inserted in an eye. This is hard to imagine as the eye of a fish is much, much smaller than its tail. The whiting business is another proof that Carroll is a humorist oppressed by a sense of gravity and death.

Like Alice, my granddaughter Callie has a social conscience that is animal friendly. Callie refuses to eat lamb. But Callie has no qualms about eating the same lamb when it is served to her as *meat*. Callie is not very old, but a whole barnyard of animals has already been bloodsoaked and sacrificed to maintain her existence, a reminder of the harsh fundamental realities and the primitive mayhem and terror that exists on this planet. Whew! What a place!

Notice Alice doesn't utter the last syllable of "dinner." Consequently, dinn becomes a place called Dinn. The Mock Turtle doesn't know where Dinn is. And for good reason, as Dinn doesn't exist.

Turtle also misses the significance of the crumbs. Alice associates crumbs with whitings because that is the way she eats whitings for dinner. Once two items are associated in the consciousness, they tend to recall each other. Hence, whiting (for Alice) recalls crumbs and vice versa, crumbs recall whiting. Aristotle noted that the order in which original learning took place does also influence the facility of recall. Hence, if Alice first associated whitings with crumbs, then whitings would be more likely to recall crumbs and crumbs would be less likely to recall whitings than whitings would be likely to recall crumbs. In the same way, it is easier to recall XY than it is to recall YX because we usually learn the alphabet forward and not backward. Aristotle offered the proof that it is much easier to recite the alphabet forward than it is to recite it backward. Furthermore, he added that if a person can recite the alphabet backward, he would be able to recite it forward, for as a general rule, if you can do the harder thing, you can do the easier thing also.

11

Who Stole the Tarts?

WARNING!

ere in the last two chapters please pay attention to the Queen of Hearts, a character who probably represents the embodiment of ungovernable passion in a person of power—a blind and aimless Fury, a Hitler or Stalin type. Her husband, the King, is just a bungler. She is the real thing: the primeval ancient führer, a kind of demiurge, the Gnostic Archon. Her constant orders for beheading are shocking to those modern critics of children's books who feel that juvenile fiction should be free of all violence.

As far as I know, there have been no empirical studies of how children react to such scenes in AAW and what harm if any is done to their psyche. Absence of evidence, however, is not evidence of absence. So the question must remain open.

My guess is that the normal child finds it all very amusing and that it is not damaged in the least. However, I do feel that this stuff is not entirely suitable for adults. It especially should not be permitted to circulate indiscriminately among adults who are undergoing psychoanalysis.

The depiction of royalty here set forth contains an enormous amount of the paraded dignity, arbitrariness, and pseudoprestige necessary to bolster the absurd pretensions of incompetent leaders. Here is a matter with contemporary resonances, something that has modern implications, something we should think about when we hear "Hail to the Chief" or read about the shenanigans of the royals of England, or pay 3 million dollars for the elaborate state funeral of a former president like Gerald Ford who was never even elected.

The reason that the Queen of Hearts and the subsequent trial of the Knave of hearts can be so terrifying to adults is that most adults realize that they live in a slapstick modern world, under an inexplicable sentence of death. When they try to find out what the castle authorities want them to do, they are shifted from one bumbling bureaucrat to another, receiving no reasonable answers.

Kafka's *The Castle* (which I believe was inspired by AAW) represents the stratified, organized, controlled, completely bureaucratized society, a comic and dystopian *Avalon* (the movie) or Ingsoc (the government of Oceania in the novel *1984*) in which the individual is a number and has lost the essence of specific and distinct individual dignity, integrity, freedom, and all appearance of such. Such a society is not only terrible, it is also terrifying and sucked dry of any semblance of humanity as we currently know it.

Yes, Kafka is true, but often we don't recognize Kafka as true because, at the time we are going through the Kafkaesque experience, we are kicking, biting, fighting, trying to survive, doing lots of things but not reading Kafka.

Added to the horror of it all is the ready perception that the arbitrary, bloody Queen of Hearts is an ineffective, abysmally stupid person. Yet she has the power. Her pointlessness is the point. Her gibberish conveys unmistakable meanings to those of us who read hidden messages. But sometimes, I admit, there is nothing but nonsense in nonsense. And sometimes the nonsense is just ridicule of stuffed shirts.

Perhaps, adults should take consolation in the underlying joyful certainty that they (the leaders) who are trying day and night with unstinted effort to control us are, after all (as Alice tells us), only a pack of cards.

More than one critic has commented on the similarities between another of Kafka's books, *The Trial*, and the trial of the Knave of Hearts; between Kafka's *Castle* and the chess game in *Looking-Glass* in which living pieces are ignorant of the game's plan and cannot tell if they move of their own will or are being controlled by invisible strings moved by invisible fingers. This vision of the monstrous mindlessness of the powers-that-be can be grim and disturbing, especially to those who know history. As Winston Churchill did know history, he recommended AAW to those who need to learn how governments work.

ITEM: THIS CHAPTER IS A CRITICISM OF PLATO'S *REPUBLIC*

The ideal of the philosopher king was classically expressed by Plato in his *Republic* V, 18, and VII, and *Laws* IV, and is demonstrated dramatically by the example of Marcus Aurelius. The concept remained alive in the "Kingship Discourses" of Dio Chrysostom (Orations 1–4). As we wade through this chapter of AAW and the chapter that follows, let's keep in mind the possibility that Carroll is trying to show us by a rather negative counterexample exactly what a king should not be, and that this chapter will be a severe criticism of kingship in general.

Counterexamples are major tools in the teaching of logic. Their use by Lewis Carroll comes as no surprise.

* * *

"Off with her head!" said the Queen.

All attempts to divert attention from real issues are irrelevant. All violence and all threats of violence are irrelevant. A chopped-off head is not a substitute for a logical argument. Nor is a chopped-off head a substitute for a trial on the issues.

OFFICIAL VIOLENCE IS MORE DANGEROUS THAN NORMAL VIOLENCE

Please never forget this important point: Official violence and oppression can be much more dangerous and difficult to control than individual private violence. Major checks are therefore required to prevent the major dangers of too much governmental power. That is why we in America have a constitution. That is why the Constitution must be followed exactly. Eternal vigilance, said Thomas Jefferson, is the price of freedom. Eternal vigilance is also the price of everything else that we hold dear.♥

* * *

"I wish they would get the trial done," she thought, "and hand out the refreshments."

That sounds familiar. Lewis Carroll must have heard that from some kid. I know I have: At a recent piano recital, the kid next to me, Paul Advincula, whispered, "I wish this were over so we can get to the refreshments."

Although predictable, this rush to refreshments can be a bad idea especially when it entails a rush to judgment.

RUSH TO JUDGMENT IS WRONG

Rush to judgment, in the absence of a compelling reason, is wrong as it tends to disregard evidence. It substitutes expediency for reasoned analysis. The results of a disputed presidential election, for example, are too important to rush to a conclusion without adequate study and reflection. Otherwise (for the bogus reason of avoiding some kind of

---

♥ The quote of this ilk I like best: "Eternal vigilance is the price of good navigation." This proverb appears on the wall of Luce Hall, the seamanship and navigation building of the US Naval Academy. Second best: "...is the price of celibacy."

vaguely defined national angst), the wrong person might get into office. And getting the wrong person in office could lead to national disaster. The wrong person in office can in a short amount of time do enormous damage. Don't believe me? Look around you. It is there.

Due diligence and due process are more important than speed in deciding the true result of an election or of anything else important.

Speeding up a trial so as to speed up the arrival of refreshments is *clearly* wrong. But I am sympathetic to Alice. She knows what she wants and is not afraid to say so. But sometimes blunt honesty may not be the best policy. I once told a patient to speed up her questions because I was hungry and I wanted to go eat dinner. The patient's reaction was not nice. Under current conventions, what she said to me is not printable.

* * *

"The twelve jurors were all writing very busily on slates. "What are they doing?" Alice whispered to the Gryphon. "They ca'n't have anything to put down yet, before the trial's begun."

"They're putting down their names," the Gryphon whispered in reply, "for fear they should forget them before the end of the trial."

This slur on the competence of English jurors is supported by the evidence immediately offered that their memories were so bad that they feared they would forget their own names. Further evidence comes in the next paragraph, where Alice calls the jurors "Stupid things!" and the jurors write that on their slates—just as so many modern students take notes on things they don't understand. Alice could even make out that one of the jurors didn't know how to spell "stupid" and had to ask his neighbor to tell him!

Here Carroll is also playing with the double meaning of the phrase "writing stupid things": You can write the actual words "stupid things" and you can also write things that are stupid and would therefore be considered "stupid things." The jurors here are probably doing both those two things at the same time. Again Carroll is making fun of slippery meanings. And he is again making some sort of comment on the jury system. Its true import escapes me. Got any ideas?

* * *

> "Herald, read the accusation!" said the King. The White Rabbit blew three blasts on the trumpet, and then unrolled the parchment-scroll . . .
>   After the reading, the King says to the jury, "Consider your verdict."
>   "Not yet, not yet!" the Rabbit hastily interrupted. "There's a great deal to come before that!"

The rabbit knows whereof he speaks. The King is out of sequence. First we hear the evidence, then we consider the verdict. The procedure is called "due process." The King is putting due process on the back burner in favor of rush to judgment.

Watch out for impetuous leaders like the King of Hearts. They are dangerous. They think they know what is right. They think they know what is just without the need for a fair and open trial based on analysis of evidence or, what is worse, without any need to consult with others.

Just as official violence can be much more dangerous than unofficial violence, official stupidity can be much more dangerous than individual stupidity. Therefore, we should erect greater safeguards against official stupidity than we have against individual stupidity. We need to do this just as much as we need to have great safeguards against official violence.

* * *

Later on, the King again shows his impatience during the examination of the Hatter. This is a good illustration of the kind of bad court that the King is running: *"Give your evidence," said the King: "and don't be nervous, or I'll have you executed on the spot."*

Evidence given under duress or torture is no evidence at all. According to Charles Mackey, LLD, in his book *Extraordinary Popular*

Delusion and the Madness of Crowds, hundreds of thousands of women confessed to being witches and were burned at the stake during the Inquisition. Their confessions said that they could fly about, that they had had sexual intercourse with the devil, that they could change into black cats and other familiars, and so on. All the things the torturers wished them to say, these women did say in writing under oath.

Now we know those things are not possible. As versatile as some women are, none of them can change into a black cat or fly on a broom. As for having sex with the devil, that would be possible, if and only if, the devil existed.

Darkness at Noon by Arthur Koestler discusses how, during the Stalin era in Russia, this problem led to confessions of guilt from perfectly innocent communist party members. *The Rise and Fall of the Third Reich* by William L. Shirer handles the same subject in great detail during the Nazi era in Germany. Orwell's novel *1984* depicts a totalitarian society gone further awry by being able to extract any confession from anyone about anything, often for no real reason except to exert power and control or to maintain power and control. Or both.

* * *

> *"I'm a poor man," the Hatter went on, "and most things twinkled after that—only the March Hare said—"*
> *"I didn't!" the March Hare interrupted in a great hurry.*
> *"You did!" said the Hatter.*
> *"I deny it!" said the March Hare.*
> *"He denies it," said the King: "leave out that part."*

Whether the Hatter is poor or not is irrelevant to the evidence he is giving. Also, the word "poor" here is exploited for its several meanings: The Hatter says he's a poor man as an appeal to pity, but the King says the Hatter is a poor speaker. Again we don't know if poor speaker is a speaker who has no money, a speaker who speaks poorly, or both. Either appeal to pity is emotionally based and irrelevant, as all emotional appeals are irrelevant.

And what the devil does "and most things twinkled after that" have anything to do with anything, much less this trial? Hatter is confused and nervously speaking nonsense. In this case the nonsense takes the form of a non sequitur.

Notice the March Hare is so eager to deny things that we never get to know what the matter is that he is denying. The King doesn't care, however, and tells the jury to leave that part out, an impossible task since they don't know what that part was. But it is also a possible task since they have to leave it out. Dig? This is another demonstration of the peculiar property of the null set. You can leave it in or take it out and make no difference as it is nothing anyway. Nothing added to or subtracted from something gives the same result. Zero plus one is one and one minus zero is also one.

MISSING EVIDENCE IS NEVER ADEQUATE
TO PROVE ANYTHING

Respect for all the evidence must be the cornerstone of trials at law. We don't see that respect here. Denying counterevidence and ignoring evidence produces inadequate evaluations, leads away from truth and toward error. Missing evidence is never adequate. The King of Hearts, as a judge, is clearly derisory, a complete and utter failure.

With the above in mind, work out on the following evidence from Senator Joseph McCarthy, who in 1954 had the gall to include President Dwight D. Eisenhower on his list of communist traitors: "I do not have much information on this except the general statement of the agency [FBI] that there is nothing in the files to disprove his Communist connection." This is McCarthy in response to a question for evidence to back up his accusation that a certain person was a communist.♠

* * *

♠ Cited in Anthony Wesson, *A Rulebook for Argument*, 3rd ed. (Cambridge: Hackett Publishing, 2000), p. 74.

Here one of the guinea pigs cheered, and was immediately suppressed by the officers of the court. They had a rather large canvas bag, which tied up at the mouth with strings; into this they slipped the guinea pig, head first, and then sat upon it.

Why they picked on this guinea pig and not the others in the courtroom who were also out of order is not clear. This may have been another example of the arbitrary exercise of power, or it could have been the manifestation of a prejudice against the guinea pig, or it could have been both those things, or neither. Who knows? Alice did have a thought about the matter but it wasn't particularly sympathetic or nice:

"I'm glad I've seen that done," thought Alice. "I've so often read in the newspapers, at the end of trials, . . ."

Suppressed evidence and sealing of files is common at the end of trials, especially civil suits. But what Alice is referring to probably is quash, meaning to set aside or annul as in "the court quashed the indictment." Some supposedly educated attorneys say squashed instead of quashed and that, I suppose, is the origin of what happened to the guinea pig. Pretty funny, if you know what's up. Not funny, if you don't know what's up.

* * *

"What are tarts made of?"
   "Pepper, mostly," said the cook.
   "Treacle," said the sleepy voice behind her.
   "Collar that Dormouse!" the Queen shrieked out. "Behead that Dormouse!"

Ignoring counterevidence, denying counterevidence, and suppressing counterevidence result in biased appraisals that are likely to be wrong. Here the cook is giving testimony that is obviously false. The Dormouse tells the court so. Yet it is the Dormouse, not the cook, who is punished. The Dormouse is like Socrates. Socrates tells the truth and, for his trouble, gets to drink the hemlock. Power corrupts and absolute power corrupts absolutely, said Lord Acton. Authorities can be wrong. Kings can be tyrannical. Queens, ditto. Carroll is not telling us that that happens, he is *showing* it happening. And he is giving us insights into the root causes of the abuse of power. And, more important, he is showing us that once this kind of abuse gets started, it is a nightmare.

12

Alice's Evidence

At this moment the King, who had been for some time busily writing in his note-book, called out "Silence!" and read out from his book, "Rule Forty-two. All persons more than a mile high to leave the court."

Everybody looked at Alice.

Alice is now growing on her own. Previously, a food or drink had caused her to grow physically. This time she is in some sense growing emotionally, intellectually, and independently of external things. She is growing naturally. With this increase has come an increase in boldness. That boldness threatens the King. So the King wants her out.

* * *

"I'm not a mile high," said Alice.

"You are," said the King.

Ah! Here we have a dispute about fact. Is Alice a mile high or is she not? For if she is not a mile high, she is not in the category of persons to whom the rule applies.

Thrice armed is he that hath his quarrel just. But how is Alice to prove that she is not a mile high?

Actually, it should be easy to settle this issue by objective measurement. "Measurement began our might," wrote the Irish poet William Butler Yeats in his *Last Poems*. And Yeats was right: Measurement began our might.

Numbers are nice. I like them too. Numbers (if correct) often lead to truth. "I have always believed in numbers," said John Nash, who won the 1994 Nobel Prize for Economics.

In the case of the King vs. Alice, why not get some numbers? Numbers that would prove things one way or another. To prove Alice's height we need only measure her and report the result in a number and a unit of extent. In this case the unit of extent will probably be feet and the number will probably be 3 and 1/2. That height (3 1/2 feet) would be considerably smaller than 5,280 feet, the number of feet in a mile. Thus the measurement would prove that the King is wrong.

DIRECT MEASUREMENT
IS A FORM OF VERIFICATION

Verification leads to truth because it is a procedure designed to confirm or deny a stated view of reality. As such, verification is at the heart of scientific inquiry and the very reason for experiments. Verification was at the heart of the dispute between Iraq and the United Nations. Iraq said it had no nuclear or biological weapons of mass destruction. But Iraq did not fully submit to inspections to prove it. The failure to fully submit led to suspicion that Iraq was hiding something. The suspicion led to war. No "massive stockpiles of weapons of mass destruction" were found. In fact, no weapons of mass destruction were found.

CERTAINTY IS BEST, PROBABILITY NEXT BEST

If the King of Hearts permitted measurement of Alice, he would be proved a liar. Without measurement to know the reality situation for sure, we have to rely on probabilities. The probabilities are that the King of Hearts is wrong. It would be unheard of to have anyone a mile high, much less a seven-and-one-half-year-old girl. The King knows that. So does Alice. But getting official recognition of the fact is another question.

For years suffragettes claimed that the Declaration of Independence indicated that women must have the vote; otherwise they were taxed without representation. The suffragettes claimed that the Declaration of Independence clearly states that government must derive its powers from the consent of the governed. Since women were governed without having a voice in the government, the government was proven wrong by its own admission. It took many years and many long battles, frequent imprisonments of women in Saint Elizabeth's Hospital for the insane, and so forth before that simple fact was recognized by the 19th Amendment to the United States Constitution.

BEWARE THE RULE 42S OF THIS WORLD

This misstatement of fact, the problem of Alice's height, was of course caused by the King himself. He had just written Rule 42 and made it so excessive that he thereby gave himself away. In the secret workings of his unconscious mind, he wrote a rule that is so blatantly absurd its irrational origin became obvious. Just as the habit does not make a good monk, the scepter does not make a good king. This is a fact we should never forget. It is now obvious that the royal scepter is held by a royal moron. Nothing unusual. Recall that there was once a king who wanted to exchange his kingdom for a horse. Recall that the sage of Baltimore, H. L. Mencken, predicted that the American people would elect a moron president. Behold! They elected George W. Bush.

The King's actions have led to Alice's further defense that Rule 42 is not a regular rule but just invented, hence not binding.

"Nearly two miles high,' added the Queen." Denying the obvious, stonewalling, as in the Watergate fiasco, does no good because the truth will out. If a person a mile high is absurd, then a person two miles high is twice as absurd. The Queen is wrong, twice wrong. She is wrong to

support someone who is obviously wrong and she is wrong about the fact under discussion.

"'Well, I sha'n't go, at any rate,' said Alice." Good for Alice! This last argument is extremely powerful. It is the ultimate refusal to participate in something unreasonable or unlawful. In effect, Alice is saying that even if Rule 42 were coherent and consistent, which it isn't, she doesn't have to follow it unless she chooses, which she doesn't. Sometimes brave men and women have to take a stand and oppose the powers that be:

> ...that whenever any Form of Government becomes destructive of these Ends, it is the Right of the People to alter or to abolish it, and to institute new Government, laying its Foundation on such Principles, and organizing its Powers in such Form, as to them shall seem most likely to effect their Safety and Happiness.
>   —Declaration of Independence, July 4, 1776

Alice has sensed what most of us need to understand about power—that it derives from the consent of the governed—that the foundation of any political system is pure will.

The unilateral proclamations of the Dodo in the caucus race, the outrageous answerless riddle of the Hatter, the shifting terms and rules of capital punishment–risk croquet that renders the Queen of Hearts sure to win, and now a court that invents laws on the spot as it goes—all these things and more—convince our heroine that the terms, rules, laws, games, and what-have-you in the adult world are founded upon fiat. If that is true, then why not hers as well as theirs?

Is it possible that, in some way or other, Alice has been "improved" by her adventures? Is it possible that the Queen of Hearts, the Cheshire-Cat, the Hatter, and the rest of them have been working out her redemption? She seems moral, honest, and, at this point, just—especially by contrast with those around her who appear to be so markedly immoral, dishonest, and unjust.

Not only has Alice become moral, honest, and just, she has also become fiercely logical, subversive and revolutionary, destructive and terrible, merciless to privilege, established institutions, and comfortable habits. She is now indifferent to authority, careless of the well-tried wisdom of the ages. She fearlessly contradicts the King! A child contradicts the King! Recall it was a child who told the emperor about his new clothes. And it was a little girl at that, a little girl like Alice.

Alice looks into the pit of hell and is not afraid. She sees herself as a child, a little girl, a feeble speck, surrounded by unfathomable emblems of power and control; yet she bears herself proudly, as unmoved as if she were lord of the universe and as unmovable as if she were the immovable object of classical logistics.

My young granddaughter Callie often behaves the same way. "(I don't care what you say) The moon is following us." "(I don't care what you say) It looks like steam and it is steam." "No nap! I don't want to get out of the pool. I want to play more." "I am angry at Mommy and Daddy because they put me in time-out."

Good for Callie. And good for Alice. Callie and Alice are thinking as individuals and are thinking well. They know what they want. They dare to tell people what they want. That has to happen. Else, how would they get what they want?

Although all that is true about Alice (and Callie), various internal evidences still make me suspect Alice of having a "past"—of having been naughty, of being naughty the way Callie is sometimes naughty. With Alice and Callie, as with us all, there is room for improvement. Later on we see in the *Looking-Glass* book that Alice improves and has even developed a kind of (primitive) social conscience:

> *"Alice declared that she likes the Carpenter better than the Walrus because he was just a bit sorry for the poor oysters."* . . .
> *"Yes, but he ate more of them," said someone.*

Wow! That's a reply that is a more delicious indictment of sentimentalism than any other ever made.

* * *

[The King replies to Alice's cutting remark]: *"It's the oldest rule in the book," said the King.*
"Then it ought to be Number One," said Alice.

The King turned pale.

As well he should. Alice caught the King in a lie. And the moral of that is: People in power do make up rules to support themselves and friends. And people in power do lie. In the literature of the Western world, Rule 42 (like a catch-22) has become an emblem of arbitrary barriers and regulations. As a kind of inside joke, Isaac Asimov considered 42 the secret of the universe. If you understood 42, according to him, you understood life.

TIME OUT FOR MORE ON 42

Among the basic tenets of Pythagoras was the belief that reality, at its deepest level, is mathematical in nature and that certain numbers have a special mystical significance.

In the Pythagorean system, 7, written as H aspirate, was the numeral of Light and 6, written as Digamma F (W in Hebrew), was that of Life. But 6 also stood for Glory, and 7 for Peace. So 6 times 7, namely 42, expressed Life and Glory multiplied by Light and Peace.

Was Carroll familiar with the Pythagorean system? You bet. Did Carroll understand the significance of 42 in Pythagorean philosophy? You bet. So what can we make of the King's statement about Rule 42? Is it an over-the-top joke about Pythagoras and his philosophy? You bet. The quasi-sacred number enshrined as the number of Light, Peace, Life, and Glory is arbitrarily used by the King for the aggressive abuse of Alice. The King is using a sacred number as part of his profane, arbitrary, and immoral attack.

More about 42: Carroll knew that the number 42 had been assigned many other significances just as irrational and arbitrary as the significance imposed by the King of Hearts. 42 is the number of:

- Children devoured by Elisha's she-bear
- Days from the beginning of the H month, which is the preparation for the midsummer marriage-and-death orgy in European paganism
- Infernal jurymen who judged Osiris, and 42 is the number of days between his midsummer death and the end of the T month, when Osiris reached Calypso's isle as mentioned in the priestly *Book of the Dead*
- Books of Hermetic mysteries, according to Clement of Alexandria

And so on.

As a mathematician Carroll knew 42 does not exist in nature. It is a construct of the human mind designed to count (I almost wrote enumerate) 42 things. Other than that exclusive meaning, 42 means nothing. To pretend that it does mean something else is silly.

Although arbitrary action and behavior are common enough, they are not reasonable and they are not right. At this point you should be able to explain why arbitrary action and arbitrary behavior are not reasonable and (hence) not right. If you need to, use the ethical analysis from the tea party chapter to justify your answer.

The King, the poor fellow, like so many of our present leaders is in over his head. The King like some of our past presidents (Clinton and Nixon) has lied in public to the public and therefore has lost face.

THE IMPORTANCE OF EVIDENCE

Next we have the discussion of the written evidence against the Knave. Follow along. Identify the errors in the King's thinking as they occur:

> "What's in it?" said the Queen.
>
> "I haven't opened it yet," said the White Rabbit; "but it seems to be a letter, written by the prisoner to—somebody."
>
> "It must have been that," said the King, "unless it was written to nobody, which isn't usual, you know."

This is the null class (a set with no members) problem again. From medieval times to the present, philosophers have debated the existence or nonexistence of nobody, nowhere, nothing, and the like. Does nothing exist or is it nothing? Treating a "null class" as though it were an existing thing is a rich source of Carrollian logical nonsense, as we should know by now. We saw the March Hare offer nonexistent wine. The King of Hearts thinks it unusual to write letters to nobody. Alice wants to know where the candle flame goes when it "goes" out— Tweedledum has the same concern about the flame in chapter 4 of the second Alice book. The Gryphon tells Alice "they never executes [*sic*] nobody" and we subsequently encounter the unexecuted Nobody walking along the road, and so forth.

The confusions engendered about nothing have a long and honorable history in literature. Recall that Ulysses deceived the one-eyed Polyphemus by calling himself Noman. When Polyphemus cried out, "Noman is killing me!" no one took this to mean that someone was actually attacking him.

So what is Lewis Carroll's position on the null set problem?

LET'S REVIEW ONE LAST TIME

Carroll is a nominalist. Nominalists think that some terms exist as mere necessities of thought or convenience of language. Nominalists think such terms do not have an external real existence. There is a name, that's true, but more important there is the thing itself. Sometimes the name is just there to fill in the blank, to indicate the absence of a real thing and to denote that absence. The most elementary principle of semantics is that agreement about the use of signs rather than the signs themselves enables us to communicate. Thus Nobody exists in name only. The no thing itself is no person and is not real. Nobody has a general reality that corresponds to it. Nobody is only a way, a shortcut, for saying no person. Nobody is just a shorthand way of saying there is no real person under discussion. The White King from *Looking-Glass* (in the statements below) admits the nonexistence of Nobody when he contrasts Nobody whom he can't see, but whom he thinks Alice sees, to a real person whom he can't see either.

By the same token, nothing means no thing and nowhere means no where. Therefore, nothing has no existence. Nothing merely designates nonexistence. Nowhere designates no existence in any place including all those places that do exist. An understanding of this concept would have prevented the White King's confusion, a confusion that is caused by his confounding what a thing is called with what a thing is:

> *"I see nobody on the road," said Alice.*
>
> *"I only wish I had such eyes," the King remarked in a fretful tone. "To be able to see Nobody. And at that distance too! Why, it's as much as I can do to see real people by this light."*

Notice Nobody's reification is confirmed by the capital "N" when the king refers to him. When Alice does the talking, nobody is a nobody with a small "n." Later (or is it earlier, for time is reversed in the looking-glass?) the King asks the messenger:

> *"Who did you pass on the road?"*
>
> *"Nobody," said the messenger.*

(Here we don't know if the messenger is reifying nobody or not. The capital "N" might be there simply because the sentence needs to start with a capital.)

> *"Quite right," said the King. "This young lady saw him too. So of course Nobody walks slower than you."*
>
> *"I do my best," the messenger said in a sullen tone. "I'm sure nobody walks much faster than I do!"*
>
> *"He can't do that," said the King, "or else he'd have been here first."*

(Note the apparent contradiction: Can nobody walk slower and faster than the messenger? Also note the contextual change: This is the property previously referred to as characteristic of the null set. If you don't get it by now, I am afraid you are hopeless. You are never going to make it. You are a nobody, a zero. Close this book. Go watch TV.)

The king is talking about Nobody as if he were a real person, and the messenger is talking about nobody as if he were the absence of a real person. Hence, the confusion and the fun. The difficulty is partly the result of one of Lewis Carroll's favorite devices in entertaining children, the play on words and exposition of the failings and difficulties of language.

By the way, nobody should conclude that the honorable author of this book is denigrating the concept of the null class or insulting readers. Quite the contrary. The author has an inordinate respect for nobody since he knows that he is a nobody.

NOTHING IS IMPORTANT

The concept of nothing has applications: The Hindu discovery of nothing, symbolized by the zero (0), enables any grade school child to make calculations that our ancient Greek and Latin ancestors could only do on an abacus. Don't believe me? Try doing long division in Roman numerals. Hint: You can't.

The null class, 0, is defined by negating any defining form of the class one (1). So it follows that the universe class and the null class are each other's complements. Every element that is not included in "everything" is "nothing." Nothing includes all the interesting characters in AAW as well as square circles, secular churches, married bachelors, elephants that fly, dragons and unicorns, and anything else that doesn't exist. The class of female presidents of the United States, for instance, is a genuine class, but as a simple matter of empirical fact as of 2009 it is a class without members.

* * *

"Who is it directed [addressed] to?" said one of the jurymen.

"It isn't directed at," said the White Rabbit; "in fact, there's nothing written on the outside." He unfolded the paper as he spoke.

"Are they in the prisoner's handwriting?" asked another of the jurymen.

Note that the two jurymen have decided to have a go at getting some real evidence. They want to know who the letter is addressed to and they want to know if the Knave wrote it. Both those two things might bear an important relationship to the significance and weight that should be attached to the letter. It turns out the letter is not a letter at all but a poem that only by contorted analysis can possibly relate to the theft of the tarts, much less to the prisoner, the Knave of Hearts.

"No, they're not," said the White Rabbit, "and that's the queerest thing about it." (The jury all looked puzzled.)

"He must have imitated somebody else's hand," said the King. (The jury all brightened up again.)

Here the King assumes a fact not in evidence. Whether the Knave forged the handwriting of another would have to be proven by evidence that is relevant and adequate. So far that assertion is not proven; it is merely an assertion, the King's assertion, the assertion of a proven liar. The other fault, which is common enough, and what we have seen in him before, is that the King is too quick to arrive at unwarranted conclusions. Beware hasty decisions and rushes to judgment. And the moral of that is: Think first, then act.

* * *

"Please your Majesty," said the Knave, "I didn't write it, and they ca'n't prove that I did: there's no name signed at the end."

Ho, ho, ho. That's funny. It reminds me of the fairy tale about Reynard the fox. When it was announced that a chicken had been stolen, Reynard screamed, "Don't look at me. I didn't eat the chicken!"

Who said the chicken had been eaten? Who's pointing at him? If no one is accusing him, why is he being defensive? And how does he know that the chicken had been eaten? The only thing that had been announced was that the chicken had been stolen.

In a recent court case, the judge announced that he had received a threat about the case and that he was not going to let the threat influence his decisions. Whereupon the opposing lawyer jumped up and said, "Don't look at me, your honor, I didn't make that call." Then the judge did look at the guy, rather disdainfully, and said, "I didn't say you did. Nor did I say it was a call. But as a matter of fact it was a call." After that, all the decisions went against the opposition and in my favor.

SOME PEOPLE NEED TO LEARN TO KEEP THEIR MOUTH SHUT

If the opposing lawyer didn't know there was a call, how come he called it right? If the Knave didn't write the note, how did he know it wasn't signed? Furthermore, the absence of a signature is neither here nor there. It certainly doesn't prove the Knave didn't write it. And it doesn't prove he did write it either. The Knave sounds defensive, as defensive as Reynard. As defensive as the opposing lawyer in my case. The Knave would have to explain how he knew the poem was not signed. If his explanation was not relevant and adequate, the jury would be correct to assume the Knave did write the poem.

Moral: When people sound defensive, it is usually because they *are* defensive. Freud observed that the amount of defense is usually directly related to the amount one needs to conceal. *"If you didn't sign it,' said the King, 'that only makes the matter worse. You must have meant some mischief, or else you'd have signed your name like an honest man.'"*

There was a general clapping of hands at this: it was the first really clever thing the King had said that day.

Here the King's argument is reasonable but off the point. The question is, did the Knave write the poem or not? And if the Knave did write the poem, so what? How does it relate to the case at hand? The King would have done well to question the Knave on how the Knave knew the poem was not signed. Instead, the King launches a general discussion about anonymous notes, which in general do mean mischief and in general do reflect adversely on the character of their writer. Whether this anonymous note, the one in question during this trial, also means mischief and also reflects adversely on the character of the writer must be determined by an evaluation of the particulars of the note itself.

What's your analysis?

My analysis indicates that the poem in this note like the Lobster Quadrille of chapter 10 and the Hatter's rendition of "Twinkle, Twinkle, little bat!/ How I wonder what you're at" as well as the Jabberwocky of Looking-Glass House is pure unmitigated nonsense. It is pure unmitigated nonsense placed here at our disposal for pure unmitigated fun.

> "*That proves his guilt, of course,*" *said the Queen:* "*so, off with—*"
> "*It doesn't prove anything of the sort!*" *said Alice.* "*Why, you don't even know what they're about!*"
> . . . "*No, no! said the Queen.* "*Sentence first—verdict afterwards.*"

That last statement by the Queen epitomizes the major problem in this final chapter of *Alice's Adventures in Wonderland*. As I see it, that problem is that both the King and Queen are obsessed with their power and position. They do not know how to evaluate evidence for relevance or adequacy. As a result, none of the evidence presented has anything whatsoever to do with the crime of stealing the tarts. Even if it did, it would have been inadequate to convict the Knave. None of the evidence implicates the Knave in any direct way. Even Alice, a seven-and-a-half-year-old girl, has figured that out.

Another view, and one I believe is correct, is that it is now time, at age seven and a half, for a little girl like Alice to begin questioning the adult world's organization, thinking, customs, ethics, and procedures.

Each generation does that. Each generation has to. For each generation must work out its own salvation.

Alice is growing up, maturing. And, as a maturing human, she is beginning to assume the set of thinking so necessary for the forward progress of our race: critical inquiry.

Alice has reached the end of her hero's journey, from innocence to experience, from preconscious acceptance to conscious questioning. In telling the King and Queen off, Alice becomes child-as-judge. And as judge, in the fierceness of her now-independent thought, she dismisses them all as a meaningless pack of cards.

Alice—child heroine—asserts in the face of a primitive, threatening universe the reasonableness of her own (and the Knave of Hearts') right to exist, and actively to rebel against a social order that sentences to death ("off with her head") all those who demur from its mad decrees.

In fine, Alice concludes that grown-up stupidity is imposing itself illegitimately. That grown-up culture is nothing but ridiculous bombast. And that grown-up culture is, to quote her directly, "stuff and nonsense."

This raises the same question raised in Kafka's *Castle*: Why do we adults accept all those useless rules with so much conviction? Why do we, with such acquiescence, follow moronic governments and politicians? Why do we obey the Rule 42s of our time? Why do we tolerate contradictions like in *Catch-22*? Why is there so little serious protest?

But notice, Alice's fury was ignited by the King's attempt to exclude her from the court (that is, from the company of adults). Children don't like that (especially when it means going to bed early or not being privy to family secrets).

Here is where children draw the line and react accordingly, often with a temper tantrum like Alice's.

But on a higher plane, let's not forget that the creatures she has met, the whole dream, are Alice's. Those things reflect her psychology, for she is the dreamer. They are Alice's personality, transmuted but reflecting the words and attitudes of her teachers, family, and pets as they appear to her, a little girl.

The verisimilitude comes from Lewis Carroll's full understanding of the reactions of a child's mind to academic training, particularly to instruction in logic and mathematics, where often the work was too hard and the books (unlike this one, I hope, that you have in your hands) too difficult to understand. In that context, Alice's reactions seem right because they are based on reality. They are based on reality because Carroll drew upon the comedies and tragedies of the schoolroom for his fun. Like all good writers, Lewis Carroll wrote what he knew. Like all good teachers, he knew and loved his students.

Vale (Farewell)

Although Lewis Carroll was quick to point out that unlike the fairy tales (à la Grimm Brothers or Hans Christian Andersen), his stories have no moral, I think he might have been hinting in a moral direction when he showed the general pandemonium of *Alice's Adventures in Wonderland* at the end of the trial at the end of his book.

That bedlam is the result we can expect when thinking stops and emotions ride fierce and unrestrained. Such mayhem and anarchy are the opposite of what Carroll loved so dearly—clear rational thinking and right behavior. His moral, if there were one, might have been that bad thinking results in chaos. Whether that was his moral or not is not particularly important.

What is important, what really counts, is that it is the truth.

Selected Bibliography

Note: The list contains only those books that Dr. Patten recommends as general reading for the interested general reader. More extensive reviews of indicated works are on Dr. Patten's review site on Amazon.com.

LEWIS CARROLL AND THE ALICE BOOKS

Carroll, Lewis, and illustrated by John Tenniel. *The Annotated Alice—The Definitive Edition*, edited by Martin Gardner. New York: Norton, 1999. Alice was written for a British audience of another century. To fully capture its wit and wisdom, we need to know a great many things that are not part of the text. This book supplies that need. Read it after you have read the book about the life and times of Alice and her creator by Stephanie Lovett Stoffel referenced below.

———. *The Hunting of the Snark*. London: Chatto & Windus, 1953, 1969. "The bowspirit got mixed with the rudder sometimes." Want to read real Carrollian nonsense? Read this.

———. *Mathematical Recreations of Lewis Carroll: Symbolic Logic and the Game of Logic*. New York: Dover, 1958. Two books in one. Both books are great. His solutions to the syllogisms by using visual methods and his profound knowledge of category theory deserve to be better known. Symbolic logic to Carroll isn't what we moderns understand by that term. Carroll's symbolic logic is a way of expressing logic in unique diagrams of propositions and conclusions.

———. *The Political Pamphlets and Letters of Charles Lutwidge Dodgson and Related Pieces*. New York: Morton N. Cohen Publishing Trust for the Lewis Carroll Society of North America/Charlottesville: Distributed by University Press of Virginia, 2001. These are the political pamphlets and letters of Charles Lutwidge Dodgson (Lewis Carroll), compiled and annotated by

Francine F. Abeles. In his letters and pamphlets, we see Carroll's inventive mind at work. Particularly interesting is the discussion of how to make horse racing bets and win every time and his plea for a more intelligent system of voting and election.

Cohen, Morton N. *Lewis Carroll: A Biography.* New York: Vintage, 1995. Cohen, formerly a professor at City University of New York, is the world's foremost authority on the life and times of Lewis Carroll. His views, as discussed above, differ from those of Leach, but both are probably correct as they both explore different facets of a complex person. In every respect, his book is an entertaining and convincing work with power and pathos. Don't consider yourself a Carrollinian unless you have read it.

Fisher, John. *The Magic of Lewis Carroll.* New York: Simon & Schuster, 1973. A mass of logic and mathematical games lies behind the scenes in the Alice books. Some of these come out here in the full light of brilliant illustrations.

Leach, Karoline. *In the Shadow of the Dreamchild: A New Understanding of Lewis Carroll.* London: Peter Owen, 1999. This important and detailed study of the new data about Charles Dodgson and his alterego, Lewis Carroll, shows that much that has been assumed about the man and his private life is as clearly fantasy as the Alice books themselves. Relevant and adequate evidence from the letters, diary, and contemporary writings now shows that Lewis Carroll was pretty much a normal, healthy adult person with a normal, healthy social and private life. True, Dodgson did have an affection for little girls, especially a little girl named Alice Pleasance Liddell (rhymes with little), but he also liked boys and men and photographed many of them. And in his later years he loved women, many, many adult women, perhaps, as Leach pointed out, too many. Although Karoline Leach, a much-loved and well-known British actress, appears to contradict the view of Carroll expressed by Cohen in Cohen's book, which has now become the (gold) standard biography of Carroll (see below), both are probably correct. At Oxford and in his early years, Carroll concerned himself more with children and later in London and at the shore he concerned himself with adult women. At both times in his life, Mrs. Grundy objected. Yet, Carroll was clear in his own conscience and nowhere is there the slightest piece of evidence that he did anything wrong by modern cultural standards. Oh, yes, one of the main things I enjoyed about Leach's book is the clear presentation of what it was like at Oxford during the time that Carroll was a student there. The boys with noble titles wore gold tassels and dined at the high table. Commoners worn black tassels and dined in the commons. No one could matriculate at Oxford unless he signed off on the thirty-nine principles of the Church of England and therefore only those who were adherent to the state religion had a go at an Oxford degree. Also interesting is the amount of wealth controlled by the clergy and the penchant they had for distributing two-thirds of the income from the vast estates held by the church to (whom else?) themselves. The nepotism within the church is too appalling to discuss. For good reasons, America's founders decided on strict separation of church and state.

Rackin, Donald. *Alice's Adventures in Wonderland* and *Through the Looking-Glass.* Woodbridge, CT: Twayne, 1991. Sophisticated discussions of sense, nonsense, and meaning in the Alice books. Some of the discussion is itself nonsense, but it is an interesting demonstration of how far one can get carried away.

Stoffel, Stephanie Lovett. *Lewis Carroll in Wonderland. The Life and Times of Alice and Her Creator.* New York: Harry N. Abrams, 1997. Beautifully illustrated handbook about Carroll and friends by a scholar and collector who works for the Lewis Carroll Society of North America. Start here if you want a bird's-eye view of Lewis Carroll's life and times.

CLEAR THINKING

Browne, M. Neil, and Stuart Keeley. *Asking the Right Questions.* Upper Saddle River, NJ: Prentice Hall, 2001. This guide to critical thinking uses abundant examples and a cross-cultural approach to teach important skills on how and when to ask crucial questions. The focus on evidence-based decision making is in direct line with the reality principle.

Cannavo, S. *Think to Win.* Amherst, NY: Prometheus Books, 1998. Lesser-sense reasoning is that reasoning used to boost one's own argument and support one's own beliefs. Greater-sense reasoning is that reasoning used to discover truth. Although the title of this book suggests that it is concerned with lesser-sense arguments, its actual mission is to help people think better and, therefore, this is a greater-sense logic book. Consult the more extensive review on Bernard M. Patten's review section at Amazon.com.

Capaldi, Nicholas. *The Art of Deception.* Rev. ed. Amherst, NY: Prometheus

Books, 2007. The work is uneven and lacks focus. It is definitely misnamed. Had I not had a background in logic, I think some of the author's points would have passed me by and probably other points would have been just downright confusing. One wonders about a book on the art of deception that deceives people into believing that that is what it is about when it is really about clear thinking and logic. Consult the more extensive review on Bernard M. Patten's review section at Amazon.com.

Crusius, Timothy, and Carolyn E. Channell. *The Aims of Argument.* Mountain View, CA: Mayfield Publishing Company, 2000. This is a brief and effective rhetoric designed to help people plan and deliver their arguments. Most texts on the subject are too formalistic and prescriptive—not this. Particularly important is the analysis of pictures and the deconstruction of visual arguments.

Damer, T. Edward. *Attacking Faulty Reasoning.* Belmont, CA: Wadsworth/Thomson Learning, 2001. Wow! One of the best on the subject. Over sixty fallacies are attacked according to general principles of clear thinking. Particularly interesting is the discussion of the answers to the exercises.

Flew, Anthony. *How to Think Straight.* Amherst, NY: Prometheus Books, 1998. A good introduction to critical thinking by an expert in the field.

Russo, J. Edward, and Paul J. H. Schoemaker. *Decision Traps.* New York: Doubleday/Currency, 1989. Light reading and a little simple and simplistic, but worth a look for those interested in direct applications of clear thinking to practical problems and business decisions.

Skyrms, Brian. *Choice and Chance: An Introduction to Inductive Logic.* Belmont, CA: Wadsworth/Thomson Learning, 2000. This is a good introduction to logic, inductive and, to a lesser extent, deductive. It probably serves better as a textbook than as an aid to individual learning, but under the proper conditions and with the proper reader, it could serve both purposes. I like it best when it is explaining the truth tables (chapter 1) and the rules of the calculus of probability (chapter 6). Particularly interesting are the practical applications in the exercises, especially in cards and dice playing and, to a lesser extent, horse racing. The concepts of utility and belief need amplification because they come off too briefly in relation to their importance. Consult the more extensive review on Bernard M. Patten's review section at Amazon.com

St. Aubyn, Giles. *The Art of Argument.* New York: Emerson Books, 1976. This is a little book, but, boy! does it pack a wallop. Especially interesting is the appendix on the good old days and how a political speech may be taken to task for its errors in thinking.

GROUPTHINK

Janis, Irving L. *Groupthink*. Boston: Houghton Mifflin, 1982. Get the revised and expanded second edition of this classic. If you need to refresh your memory about that perfect failure, the Bay of Pigs fiasco, chapter 2 is the place to go. This classic of social psychology is based on the idea that people in groups might think differently (and by implication) less well than they would have thought as individuals on the same issue. That is probably true for some groups at some times just as it is also probably true that some groups at some times actually think better than any individual member of the group could or would have thought alone about the given issue at that time. In fact, most of the evidence in this book supports the idea that group thinking, like thinking in general, goes awry when there is a failure to evaluate all the available evidence for relevance and adequacy. Most individual thinking also goes awry when there is a failure to evaluate all the available evidence for relevance and adequacy. Consult the more extensive review on Bernard M. Patten's review section at Amazon.com.

Lewis, James R. *Doomsday Prophecies*. Amherst, NY: Prometheus Books, 2000. Wonderful documentation of the outer reaches of sanity in some of the most nefarious doomsday cults, including Happy Hookers for Jesus, Heaven's Gate, Aum Shinrikyo, Millerites (Adventists).

LOGIC AND REASON BOOKS NOT FOR THE FAINTHEARTED

Aquinas, St. Thomas. *On Laws, Morality, and Politics*. Edited by William P. Baumgarth and Richard J. Regan, SJ. Indianapolis: Hackett, 1988. Absolutely brilliant in form and content; this work clearly shows St. Thomas as a master of logic and reasoned argument.

Aristotle. *Ethics*. New York: Penguin Classics, 1976. This little book has had an enormous impact on moral philosophy, particularly in the West. It may surprise you to know that Aristotle regarded ethics as a practical, not a theoretical, science.

Langer, Susanne K. *An Introduction to Symbolic Logic*. Symbolic logic is an instru- ment of exact thought, both analytic and constructive; its mission is not only to validate scientific methods but also to clarify the semantic confusions that daily beset the human mind. This book is (probably) the clearest book ever written on symbolic logic and no special knowledge is needed to understand it. Read the chapter on the assumptions of *Principia Mathematica* before you attack the *Principia* itself.

Smullyan, Raymond M. *First-Order Logic.* New York: Dover, 1968. The work is self-contained and serves as an introduction to both quantification theory and analytic methods. The material on trees is difficult but necessary for an understanding of the tableau method. Here are the fundamentals of propositional logic in their pristine pure native state.

Whitehead, Alfred North, and Bertrand Russell. *Principia Mathematica.* 1910; Cambridge: Mathematical Library, 1997. This great three-volume work is deservedly the most famous ever written on the foundations of mathematics. It aims to deduce all the fundamental propositions of logic and math from a small number of logical premises and primitive ideas, and so to prove that mathematics is a development of logic.

WORTH A LOOK FOR THOSE
WHO HAVE INQUIRING MINDS

Crews, Frederick. *Postmodern Pooh.* New York: North Point Press, 2001. Should be required reading for anybody who wants to understand the absurdity of some recently potent culture theory ideas and the damage they are inflicting on us. The logic is brilliant and fun.

Frankfurt, Harry G. *On Bullshit.* Princeton, NJ: Princeton University Press, 2005. A good exposition of the problem, but no solution offered. Truth is what is as opposed to what is not. Knowledge is a justified belief that what is true is true. And *bullshit* is a statement made for effect without regard to whether it is true or not.

Howard, Philip K. *The Death of Common Sense.* New York: Random House, 1994. How law and its applications often result in misadventure and irrational action. Multiple examples prove that government often acts like some extraterrestrial power, not an institution that exists to serve us. It (the government) almost never deals with real-life problems in a way that reflects an understanding of the reality at hand.

Kelly, Fred C. *Why You Win or Lose.* 1930; Flint Hill, VA: Fraser Publishing Company, 1998. The logic and psychology of stock market speculation in a 177-page nutshell. As you might have expected after reading Dr. Patten's investment book, vanity, greed, wishful thinking, neglect of reality, and the will to believe are the major reasons that you lose.

Mackay, Charles. *Extraordinary Popular Delusions & the Madness of Crowds.* 1841; New York: Three Rivers Press, 1990. Over and over again the public is duped. This book explains how and why. Want to know why the Dow in October of 1929 went from 381 to 41? The principles discussed in this book are applicable and explain what happened. Want to know what happened in the Tulip Mania and the South Sea Bubble? Human nature never changes. Here are the details. Read and weep.

Paulos, John Allen. *Innumeracy, Mathematical Illiteracy and Its Consequences.* New York: Vintage, 1990. In this entertaining book, it is argued that our inability to deal rationally with numbers, or with probabilities, results in misinformed government policies, confused personal decisions, and an increased susceptibility to pseudosciences of all kinds. Innumeracy is the mathematical counterpart of illiteracy, another disease that is also ravaging our technological society.

Quinn, Daniel, and Tom Whalen. *A Newcomer's Guide to the Afterlife.* New York: Bantam Books, 1997. I see this interesting book as a discussion of, and in many cases a refutation of, the religious logic of an afterlife. Many of the implications of living forever are addressed with wry wit and intelligent thinking, leaving a pretty dim view of the concept of life after death as it is traditionally presented to us.

Salk, Jonas. *Anatomy of Reality.* New York: Columbia University Press, 1983. A better title would have been "The General Field Theory of Everything Including Evolution." The book is a part of the Convergence series that looks at the deep philosophical and scientific issues of our time. Salk has come up with a general idea of how nature works; from what I can see from his multiple examples, he is on the right track.

Santoro, Victor. *The Rip-Off Book.* Port Townsend, WA: Loompanic Unlimited, 1984. This book outlines the basic principles of fraud and gives a good picture of how fraud artists bilk the public. It should be required reading in every high school economics course.

Schiffman, Nathaniel. *Abracadabra!* Amherst, NY: Prometheus Books, 1997.

Excellent in telling how the human mind is so easily deceived by spatial and time misdirections.

Schulte, Fred. *Fleeced!* Amerhst, NY: Prometheus Books, 1995. This is an excellent account of telemarketing rip-offs and how to avoid them. Too bad this book has not had a much wider readership: It might have prevented some of the great frauds of our time.

Sommerville, C. John. *How the News Makes Us Dumb.* Downer's Grove, IL: Intervarsity Press, 1999. Beautiful discussion of the topic. He proves his point by showing an array of the contradictions in the daily flow of so-called news.

Biographical Notes— Opinions expressed are those of Dr. Patten

Aristotle (384–322 BCE). Born in Stagira in northern Greece, the son of Nicomachus, a physician in the Macedonian court. Aristotle studied with Plato in Athens between 367 and 347 BCE. From 342 to 339, he tutored the heir to the Macedonian throne, later known as Alexander the Great. Aristotle later returned to Athens, where in 355, he opened his own school, the Lyceum. His intellectual pursuits include rhetoric, art, physics, metaphysics, logic, ethics, biology, and politics.

Cicero (106–43 BCE). Roman orator, philosopher, and politician. He suffered exile, served in the Roman Senate, and was a bitter opponent of Caesar and Anthony. Anthony had him killed and his head hung on the city wall, his hands nailed to the podium of the forum. His personal letters, essays, handbooks, and famous orations show an enormous amount about ancient Roman life.

Epicurus (341–270 BCE). Philosopher in the Greek Stoic tradition who thought that the chief good of life is pleasure but that the true pleasure comes from virtue—defined as the habit of doing the right thing at the right time in the right place for the right reason.

Kant, Immanuel (1724–1804). Kant ranks with Aristotle and Plato as a philosopher. He is most famous for creating a link between idealists—those who thought that all reality was in the mind—and the materialists—those who thought that the only reality lay in the things of the material world. According to Kant, there are two realities—that of the mind and that of the material world. But the reality of the world is more important because it does not depend on the other reality for its existence.

Peirce, Charles Sanders (1839–1914). As a logician and philosopher, he was America's most original and versatile thinker. Peirce originated pragmatism, cofounded semiotics, designed an electric computer, and created an algebra of logic that now empowers the computers of the world.

Plato (428–348 BCE). Born of aristocratic parents in Athens. At age eighteen, he became closely attached to Socrates, and for the next decade, until Socrates' execution, accepted him as teacher and friend. Plato's youth was spent under the shadow of the civil war between Athens and Sparta that ended in 404 BCE with the total defeat of Athens. This defeat may have suggested to him that democracies were weak. The defeat might be the event that triggered the production of the *Republic* and the evolution of Plato's politics away from democracy toward dictatorship.

Plutarch (46?–120? CE). He was born in Chaeronea in Boeotia, educated in philosophy at Athens and Rome. No historian of ancient times is more widely read. Shakespeare drew plots for several of his plays from Plutarch's stories.

Pythagoras (born c. 507 BCE). Founder of a religious society in Crotona. The main tenets of this group were primitive tabu-conceptions. Some examples: 1. To abstain from beans (main prohibition of the religion). 11. Not to walk on highways. 13. When the pot is taken off the fire, not to leave the mark of it in the ashes, but to stir them together. Dikaiarchos says that Pythagoras taught "that the soul is an immortal thing, and that it is transformed into other kinds of living things." Like St. Francis he preached to animals, but unlike St. Francis he claimed that he was a god. Pythagoras, as everyone knows, said that "all things are numbers." This statement, interpreted in a modern way, is logically nonsense, but what he meant was not exactly nonsense. He believed that numbers were behind the reality of the material world and that knowledge of numbers could describe that reality. He discovered the importance of numbers in music and in the movements of the heavens. His greatest discovery was in geometry: Starting from axioms, which are (or are deemed to be) self-evident, and proceeding by deductive reasoning, he arrived at theorems that are far from self-evident. Thus it was possible to discover things about the actual world by first noticing what is self-evident and then using deduction.

Socrates (469–399 BCE). Athenian philosopher and teacher of Plato. In his youth as a stone mason, Socrates fought as a hoplite for Athens during the Peloponnesian War. Famous for his view that the unexamined life is not worth living, Socrates was found guilty of not believing in the gods of the city of Athens and executed for that crime.

Thales of Miletus (fl. 585 BCE). The first person in the West, as far as we know, to do some serious thinking about the nature of discovering truth. His method (observation + thought) is still used today. Using the empirical method Thales cornered the olive oil market and became rich thereby. He measured the height of the pyramid in Egypt by waiting until the shadow of a vertically positioned stick equaled its own length and then paced off the length of the pyramid's shadow.

Index